CONDOS

TOWNHOMES and HOME OWNER ASSOCIATIONS

How to make your investment safer

Necessary Financial Reserves

E   F

Financially, is your Association running o

First published in the United States of America by:
Patrick Hohman Services, LLC
3044 Bardstown Road, No. 196
Louisville, KY 40205-3020

ISBN 978-0-9822345-0-1
First Edition 2010

Limit of Liability/Disclaimer Warranty

This publication is designed to provide accurate and authoritative information with regard to the subject matter covered. It is sold with the understanding that the publisher is not engaged in rendering legal, accounting, or other professional advice. **If legal advice or other expert assistance is required, the services of a competent professional person should be sought.**

> —From a Declaration of Principles jointly adopted by
> a Committee of the American Bar Association and
> a Committee of Publishers and Associations

About the Author

Patrick Hohman, from Louisville, Kentucky, has been the volunteer president of his condo association for more than 20 years.

In 1982, without fully understanding what he was getting himself into, he bought as a "starter home" a low-cost condominium unit in what had been an older apartment building. Now, 28 arduous years later, he still lives there.

The intervening years have presented the author and a succession of fellow co-owners with ongoing challenges in co-owner housing education, planning, renovation, financial reporting, vendor oversight and consensus-building in order to protect property values.

He has a B.A. in journalism, is a former corporate advertising manager, and has been a self-employed writer and advertising project manager for 12 years.

The idea for the book and web site originated in the fall of 2005 when Hohman wrote and organized a non-credit university class in Louisville called "Condominium and Home Owner Association Best Practices." He expected 4 or 5 students to sign up but got 231 students.

Now, teaching about this form of housing—and the urgency for its financial soundness—has become a personal mission for him.

In This Book
Icons with Notes to Speed and Deepen Your Understanding

 **Best Scenario**

While dangers lurk from missteps, the Best Scenario shows examples that indicate good outcomes.

 **Warning!**

Yikes! Watch out here. This note highlights where possible dangers arise.

 **Insight**

The Insight notes help provide you with quick-reference background information.

 **Ideas**

These are practical, useful ideas for you to use.

The 'Snowflake' Disclaimer Icons

Like the unique composition of a snowflake, each property is unique.

These snowflake icons are placed near our sample budgets, reserve studies, preventive maintenance lists and renovation costs. These snowflake icons are to underscore that, for planning accuracy of your own property, you need your own custom analysis and financial review.

Sample Disclaimer:

DISCLAIMER—Life expectancy of component parts will vary based on many factors, such as:
• Quality level of original components
• Local climate conditions
• Interim preventive maintenance if applicable

Dedication

With gratitude, to my mother and father, to Henry Heuser, Jr., and to my aunt, Sister Margaret Hohman, SCN.

Acknowledgments

Thanks to the hundreds of volunteer board members and vendors I have talked with at local educational meetings throughout the United States.

Current and Former Association Board Members

Mary Coblentz
Lawrence J. Eul
Michael J. Gartzke
Stuart Goldberg
Michael M. Hoskins
Susanne C. Jones
David Kaman
Leon LaJeunesse
Marleen Levi
James F. MacDonald
Cleve Parkins
Theodore J. Salgado
Louise Shawkat
Tony Stottmann
Barbara Vetter
Mike Wilcher

Reserve Specialists

Peter Miller, RS
Miller-Dodson Associates, Inc.
Annapolis, Maryland

John Poehlmann, RS
Theodore J. Salgado, P.E.
John C. Decker, P.E.
Reserve Advisors, Inc.
Milwaukee, Wisconsin

Scott Clements, CPI
Les Weinberg, RS MBA
Reserve Studies Incorporated
Chatsworth, California

Interior Design & Renovation of Association Public Spaces

Michael M. Hoskins, KYCID
Hubbuch and Company
Architecture and Interior Design
Louisville, Kentucky

Construction Management Engineers and Consultants

Frank Arms
F.L. Arms & Associates, Inc.
Oakland, California

Leon LaJeunesse
Custom Contracting, Ltd.
Lake Zurich, Illinois

William B. Early RRC, CCS
K2N Crest
Oak Brook, Illinois

Stephen Varone, AIA
Peter Scallion
Dave Brijlall
Rand Engineering &
    Architecture, PC
New York, New York

Homa Ghaemi, S.E., P.E.
Peter J. Power, R.A.
Katie Collier
Klein and Hoffman, Inc.
Chicago, Illinois

Acknowledgments (continued)

Community Association Managers

(all from Louisville, KY)

Kim Brice
Owl Creek Community Association

George Lasley (retired)
On-Site Association Manager

Robert Massey, Jr., CPM
The Robert Massey Company

Daphne Walls
Mulloy Properties

Glenda Winchell, CMCA
Lake Forest Community Association

John Payne, CPA, MBA
Paragon Management Group

Julia Smith, PCAM, ARM
Ann Tidwell
Prudential Parks and
    Weisberg Realtors
Property Management Division

Lawn Care & Snow Removal

Wayne Volz
Wayne's Lawn Service, Inc.
Louisville, Kentucky

Pest Control

Donnie Blake
OPC Pest Control, Inc.
Louisville, Kentucky

Community Association Attorneys

Tyler P. Berding, Esq.
Berding-Weil, LLP
Alamo, California

David W. Kaman, Esq.
Kaman & Cusimano, PC
Cleveland, Ohio

Insurance Specialists

Joseph P. Waldron, AMS,
    PCAM, CIRMS
Robins Insurance Agency, Inc.
Nashville, Tennessee

Banking and Financial Services

Kathy R. Beaulne, PCAM
Alliance Association
Financial Services
Las Vegas, Nevada

Thomas C. Engblom, PCAM, CPM
Community Association Banc
Oak Lawn, Illinois

Certified Public Accountants

Michael J. Gartzke, CPA
Goleta, California

John E. Payne, CPA, MBA
Paragon Management Group
Louisville, Kentucky

Other Professionals

Jacquie Berry
HOA Document Review, Inc.
San Jose, California

Tony Campisi
Gold Star Community®
    Recognition Program,
    administered by the
    Pennsylvania & Delaware
    Valley Chapter of Community
    Associations Institute
King of Prussia, Pennsylvania

Peter Grech
Superintendent's and Resident
    Manager's Technical
    Association
New York, New York
www.nycsta.org

PART ONE: Problems and Ideas for Solutions

PART TWO: Samples and Appendices

In-Depth Maintenance & Financial Planning Documentation

FIVE Unique Property Examples

Sample financial and maintenance planning data for the five property examples

- Property Overview
- Annual Budget
- Monthly Income Statement
- Monthly Balance Sheet
- Monthly Accounts Receivable Report
- Reserve Study (condensed version)
- Preventive Maintenance Check List
- List of Major Structural Renovation Expenses for a "Same Neighborhood" Single-Family Home
- Who Does What? (Thumbnail List of Job Titles)

Major Repair and Renovation Project Summaries

Cost estimate ranges and photos

> *Don't forget the importance of maintaining "curb appeal" and beautifully designed and maintained common areas*
>

Appendices

> *Talking Points for Frequently Asked Questions*
>
> - What percentage of the budget do we set aside for reserves to be safe?
> - I'll be dead by then anyway. Why should I help pay for a new roof?
> - If we raise the monthly fees, how can I ever sell my unit?

> A Businesslike Request for Proposal (RFP) for an Association Can Be Detailed and Often Technically Complex.
>
> Sample RFP for Lawn Care and
> Snow Management Services

 **Warning!** ━━━━━━━━━━━━━━━━━━━━━━━━━━━

Potential liability for home owner "do-it-yourselfers" regarding Reserve Studies and other professional services at your association

1. Real Estate Professionals and Community Managers will tell you, correctly, that each property is unique, just like a human fingerprint or a snowflake.

2. **The adequate reserve fund amount and adequate monthly maintenance fee for a property will vary from property to property**, based on factors such as:

   - Year the property was built
   - Quality of original construction
   - Maintenance level since construction
   - Number of units in the association
   - Local climate conditions
   - And other factors

   - Type of property (for example, a condominium usually has more shared infrastructure and expense than a detached single-family home within a Home Owner Association, but all types will need reserves)
   - Maintenance responsibilities of the Association as defined by governing documents or state law

3. **Therefore, there is no "standard percentage" for how much to charge each month, or how much to reserve.**

4. The best mechanical and financially sound way to know how much your association needs to charge each month, and how much to reserve, is for your association to hire an accredited professional Reserve Study firm, which performs services in your area. A professional Reserve Study most often is performed by a cross-disciplinary team of accredited professionals in both engineering and finance. A professional reserve study is required by law in some states. In California, the Reserve Study must now be reviewed and updated annually, as property conditions continually evolve.

5. While there is apathy among some home owners about providing voluntary assistance to their own association, other well-meaning home owners are eager to voluntarily perform professional services, for which those volunteer home owners may or may not be trained or qualified.

6. **Home owner volunteers are placing themselves at considerable liability risk, especially if their complex technical and mechanical evaluation or the financial analysis and modeling in their Reserve Study proves to be incorrect or is not updated in a timely way.**

7. **Therefore, do not use the custom example reserve studies shown in this publication, as a basis for your own monthly fees or reserve fund needs. The purpose of these custom-created samples is to give you a simplified, sample Reserve Study, in order to educate yourself and your neighbor co-owners about what a Reserve Study is, and why a Reserve Study is an important element for the long-term financial soundness of your community association.**

8. If you do not agree with the statements above, you may return this book to the publisher for a full refund.

9. Also, based on laws in some states, there is a legal concept known as the **"Business Judgment Rule," which helps to shield the volunteer board of directors from liability, barring any other board malfeasance**. One aspect of the Business Judgment Rule is that for controversial decisions, such as levying special assessments, the board relies on the advice and counsel of paid, outside, third-party professionals, such as licensed or accredited Engineers, Accountants, Attorneys, Community Managers and Reserve Specialists.

Part One
Problems and Ideas for Solutions

Key Financial Questions for You and Your Neighbors

1 What expenses will you have as an association?

2 How much money do you need to set aside every month to be prepared for these expenses?

Answer key questions

3 If you live in an association now, how was your monthly assessment fee originally determined a at the start of the development?

Four Key Ideas in This Book

1 Unrealistically low monthly maintenance fees are as dangerous to consumers as an **underfunded pension plan**.

2 If you remember only two words from this book, remember the words **"RESERVE STUDY,"** which can help provide the community of co-owners with a detailed road map for the financial future. Otherwise, without a detailed financial plan, you are just keeping your fingers crossed or ignoring the funding issue, and that approach carries great risk.

Is this your Association's plan?

3

Please be realistic: **Can you afford your current housing arrangement?**

If someone cannot afford both their mortgage and the monthly maintenance fee or special assessments, as indicated by the Reserve Study, then unfortunately, that person cannot afford their current housing arrangement. That person needs to find a housing arrangement that they *can* afford.

Not too many generations ago in the United States, to save money, multiple generations lived together under one roof. Few people could afford the luxury of living alone. More people may return to a multiple-person household living arrangement.

For people to live together successfully, whether in one home or a community association, it takes some basic (written) ground rules and ongoing, respectful communication.

4

The **fundamental difference** in two housing types:

The scale and magnitude of Community Association housing repair and replacement costs make planning essential.

Detached, single-family home

Future Repair and Replacement Costs:

Generally not planned

Example Repair Costs (single-family home):

Roof replacement: **$10,921**

Siding replacement (aluminum): **$17,033**

Townhome / patio home association

Future Repair and Replacement Costs:

MUST be forecast and planned in order to be successful

Example Repair Costs (240 units):

Roof replacement: **$2.4 million**

Siding replacement (wood): **$3.1 million**

What Is a Community Association?

To start, we will define two key terms:
- Community Association
- Reserve Study

Community Association

A Community Association is the broad term describing a form of housing where
- Units are individually owned
- But the "common elements" of the property are jointly owned by all the owners

Different forms of Community Association housing include:
- Condominiums
- Townhomes
- Patio homes
- Cooperatives
- Home owner associations
- Planned unit developments
- And more

Insight

**"Shared expenses" housing …
Do you already have experience with this?**

Have you ever lived with roommates?

With a spouse or significant other?

If so, you may have already experienced a form of "shared expenses" living. There are benefits, and there are also some tensions. It is what it is.

If you reached a mutual understanding, congratulations. That was quite an achievement.

Community Association living is also a form of shared expenses living.

There will be benefits. There will be some tensions. Try to minimize the tensions with careful planning and respectful communication.

Different Degrees of "Shared Expenses Housing"

Within the Community Association, the degree of "shared expenses" can vary greatly. At the low end of shared expenses is a single family home, within a home owner association.

At the higher end of shared expenses are condominiums, with much shared infrastructure.

MINIMAL Shared Expenses

Single Family Home in a Home Owner Association
- Recreational building
- Administrative expenses

MAJOR Shared Expenses

Condominium or Townhome
- Roofing
- Siding
- Exterior painting
- Landscaping and paving
- Wood fencing
- Recreational building and pool
- Administrative expenses
- And more

Reserve Studies: Frequently Asked Questions

What is a Reserve Study?

A Reserve Study is an estimate of an Association's major repair and replacement expenses for each year for the next 20 to 30 years, plus a review of various funding plan options to pay for those repairs.

A Reserve Study is a non-invasive building component report and financial forecast. It is different from a consulting engineer's report.

The term "non-invasive" means the Reserve Specialist will not, for example, open walls to inspect the condition of plumbing pipes or electrical wiring. He will not do "destructive" testing, such as tearing off a roof shingle to analyze its age.

What are the two major parts of the annual budget of the Association?

1. Operating expenses
2. Reserve expenses

What are examples of
• Operating expenses?
• Reserve expenses?

Operating Expenses are:
Ongoing annual expenses, which often arrive as predictable monthly invoices, such as:

- Lawn care services
- Property management and bookkeeping services
- Ordinary, minor repairs
- Insurance

Reserve Expenses are:
Higher-cost, major repairs and replacements such as:

- Roof replacement
- Foundation repairs
- Siding replacement
- Parking area resurfacing
- Street repaving

Sample Annual Budget

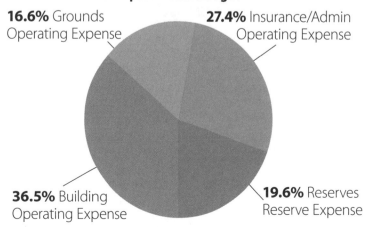

16.6% Grounds Operating Expense

27.4% Insurance/Admin Operating Expense

36.5% Building Operating Expense

19.6% Reserves Reserve Expense

Reserve Studies: Frequently Asked Questions

Why is a professional Reserve Study becoming more important?

Many financial institutions, such as mortgage lending firms and insurance firms, and some state laws require that this forecast of Association expenses be created by a professional Reserve Study provider.

Can an owner at the Association volunteer to create a reserve study for his or her association?

Check your current state and local laws to be sure for your area.

When some well-intentioned owners first learn of the concept of a Reserve Study, they sometimes begin compiling bids for major repairs and replacements, then attempt the sophisticated financial modeling for projecting upcoming year-by-year expenses in a variety of areas.

For the untrained or quasi-trained volunteer, there can be great personal risk in volunteering to create this Reserve Study for the Association:

1. If your forecast of expenses is incorrect, especially if it's too low, your neighbors will be less than thrilled with you if they are suddenly hit with a large, unexpected special assessments for repair expenses.

2. Also, the volunteer owner is assuming considerable legal and therefore financial liability in attempting this Reserve Study physical analysis and financial forecast.

3. A professional report may gain the confidence of other owners in the Association, as well as help to gain the confidence of mortgage bankers and insurance companies, who may want to see your Reserve Study report before they are willing to provide mortgages or insurance to the association.

I've never heard of a Reserve Study. How long has this profession existed? What training do these individuals have?

In the United States, many Reserve Study firms trace their origins to the early to mid-1980s.

Compared with other professions that provide services to associations — like lawyers and accountants — the Reserve Study profession is the new kid on the block.

The engineering assessment tasks of the Reserve Study firms are often handled by engineers, architects or those with experience in construction management.

The financial modeling tasks of the Reserve Study firm are helped with the specialized software programs that the firms use on a regular basis.

Are reserve study providers licensed or accredited in some way?

Check with your current state and local laws to be sure for your area.

There are two primary non-profit organizations within the United States that have a designation program for Reserve Study professionals, which are listed below.

Organization name	Community Associations Institute (CAI)
Web site	www.caionline.org
Designation	RS — Reserve Specialist

Organization name	Association of Professional Reserve Analysts (APRA)
Web site	www.apra-usa.com
Designation	PRA — Professional Reserve Analyst

How closely does the Association adhere to the year-by-year repair priorities listed in the Reserve Study report?

Like an annual budget, the reserve study is a GUIDE to future spending, not an iron-clad list. The priorities for spending in the Reserve Study are subject to review and revision as time passes.

Why would we need an update to the Reserve Study, and how often would we need an update?

A Reserve Study can quickly become outdated. In California, the reserve study must now, by law, be updated each year.

Some Reserve Study firms recommend an update at least every three to five years.

What causes a reserve study to become outdated?

- Some components may wear out sooner than expected. Other components may last longer than expected, especially with proper, regular preventive maintenance procedures.
- A change in local laws or building codes in your area.
- Repairs or replacements that may be required by banks, insurance companies or other financial institutions.
- A change in spending priorities by a new board of directors at the Association.
- Current worldwide demand for raw materials impacts the costs and affordability of the forecasted repairs.
- Local availability of skilled labor.

How much does a Reserve Study cost?

Costs vary by size and type of the Association, and to a lesser degree by region of the country.

Like other major purchases at your Association, It is wise to develop a Request for Proposal (RFP) and obtain competitive bids before you award your Reserve Study report business.

To give you an idea of costs, we look at the five sample reserve studies in this book.

From Example A: Two-or Three-Story Stacked Flats

Number of buildings in the complex — 6
Total number of housing units — 24
Year(s) built — 1962 to 1964

Cost range for reserve study	$2,000 to $3,000+
Cost range for reserve study update	$1,500 to $2,500+

From Example B: Townhome / Patio Home

Number of buildings in the complex — 45
Total number of housing units — 240
Year(s) built — 1976 to 1980

Cost range for reserve study	$1,850 to $2,750
Cost range for reserve study update with site visit	$1,500 to $2,000
Cost range for reserve study update without site visit	$600 to $1,000

From Example C: Mid-Rise

Number of buildings in the complex — 1
Total number of housing units — 78
Year(s) built — 2000 to 2002

Cost range for reserve study	$3,000 to $6,000+
Cost range for reserve study update	$2,250 to $4,500+

How much does a Reserve Study cost? (continued)

From Example D: High-Rise

Number of buildings in the complex — 1
Total number of housing units — 128
Year(s) built — 1988 to 1990

Cost range for reserve study	**$4,500 to $7,500+**
Cost range for reserve study update	**$3,400 to $5,000+**

From Example E: Home Owner Association of Detached Single-Family Homes

Total number of housing units — 400
Year(s) built — 1970 to 1974

Cost range for reserve study	**$2,500 to $4,000**
Cost range for reserve study update with site visit	**$1,250 to $2,500**
Cost range for reserve study update without site visit	**$600 to $1,200**

Where do I find a Reserve Study firm in my area?

If your Association has a property management firm, the Community Manager at the firm will likely have already worked with some local or regional providers of Reserve Studies.

You could also check with other nearby local Associations for their recommendations of which Reserve Study firm to get a proposal from.

An online search will probably quickly yield some leads on Reserve Study firms for you to review and contact.

Most major urban areas in the United States are serviced by Reserve Study firms, even if the firm personnel have to travel within your region to reach you.

If we have a Reserve Study created, do we have to fund the reserves according to the various funding plans?

The short answer is a qualified NO.

The primary purpose of the Reserve Study is to create a road map for the financial future, if the owners chose to follow it.

Check your current state and local laws to be sure for your area.

What is a Transition Study?

A Transition Study is very similar to a Reserve Study.

The difference is that the Transition Study is for Associations that have not been turned over from developer control to owner control.

Both the developer and the owners may hire their own specialist to create the Transition Study. The same firm would not work for both the developer and the owners because their interests are different.

The Transition Study creates a punch list of work yet to be done by the developer in order to prepare the property for turn over to the owners.

What are common component parts of a Reserve Study?

In the five sample Reserve Studies in this book, we show seven common elements of Reserve Studies.

Part A - Physical Analysis
1. Condition assessment
2. Major component parts and estimated remaining useful life of those components
3. Components that are excluded from the Reserve Study calculations

Part B - Financial Analysis
4. Estimated reserve fund expenditures by year
5. Estimated reserve fund expenditures by category
6. Alternative funding plans for needed reserves
7. Cash-flow analysis

More detailed explanations are on the next two pages.

Vertically displaced concrete flatwork can likely be a trip hazard causing legal exposure to the association.

Cracked brick siding could be indicative of structural problems. It will also allow for moisture intrusion and potential damage to the structure. Water intrusion can also open the possibility of mold problems.

Part A — Physical Analysis

1. Condition Assessment

A qualified, insured inspector makes an in-person site visit to the property.

Usually the inspector is trained as an engineer or architect or has long experience in the construction industry.

Sometimes, the condition assessment digital photos are part of the final report.

2. Major Component Parts

Frequently this list contains:

- Major component parts at the property
- Approximate quantities of those parts
- Useful life & remaining useful life of component

Regarding cost presentations, Reserve Study firms use various reporting methods including:

- Current average replacement cost
- Current and future estimated replacement costs, based on estimated inflation rate

It is important to regularly revisit these cost estimates in the future, due to many unpredictable factors that could affect the accuracy of the cost forecast, including material shortages, inflation, changes in local laws, worldwide demand for construction materials, and other factors.

3. Components that may be *excluded* from the reserve study calculations

Types of excluded components include:

- Unit owner responsibility components
- Long-life components
- Utility components
- Maintenance and repair components
- Below-threshold cost components
- Government-funded components

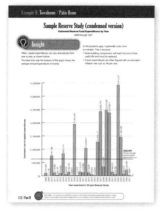

Part B — Financial Analysis

4. Estimated Reserve Fund Expenditures by Year

- Often there is a written list of expected costs for major repairs and replacements for each of the next 20 to 30 years.
- Sometimes there is also a visual chart that graphically depicts these same expenditures.

5. Estimated Reserve Fund Expenditures by Category

Sometimes there is a list or chart that summarizes, by category, the anticipated major repair and renovation expenses for each of the next 20 to 30 years.

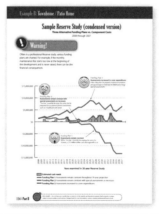

6. Alternative Funding Plans

Often, a chart is included that projects the Association's ability to pay for anticipated repairs and replacements, based on the Association's projected income levels.

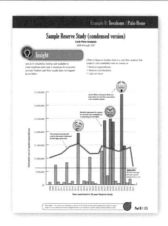

7. Cash-Flow Analysis

Often in Reserve Studies, there is a cash-flow analysis that projects cash availability with an overlay of:

- Reserve expenditures
- Reserve contributions
- Cash on hand

Why Some Community Associations Are Not Financially Strong

Annual Budget Underfunding: How Does It Happen?

REVIEW:

Earlier you were introduced to the two major parts of the annual Association budget:

1. Operating expenses — Day-to-day expenses

2. Reserve expenses — Major repair and replacement expenses

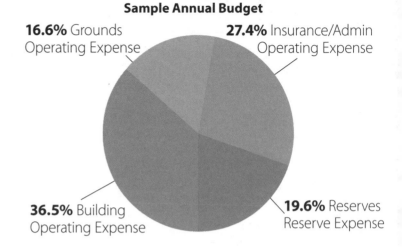

Sample Annual Budget

16.6% Grounds Operating Expense

27.4% Insurance/Admin Operating Expense

36.5% Building Operating Expense

19.6% Reserves Reserve Expense

Insight

How was your monthly assessment fee originally determined at the start of development?

Often, new developments have lower monthly assessments, as set by the developer.

The original monthly assessment fee may have been set without the analysis and data provided by a Reserve Study.

It is true that repair and replacement expenses are lower when a development is new.

Also, a developer may be subsidizing the operating budget in order to hold monthly assessment fees to a lower amount during the build out and selling phase of the development.

If the beginning annual Association budget is low and is comprised of low monthly assessment fees, there may not be an adequate accumulation of reserves in order to pay for needed repairs later in the life of the development.

Adding to this problem is the reluctance of board members to raise the monthly assessment fee to a level suggested by the Reserve Study.

Over time, these funding issues will lead to significant budget shortfalls.

Why do operating expenses tend to get paid *first*, before a contribution toward Reserve Expenses?

Operating expenses are day-to-day expenses with invoices coming to the Association that are payable monthly, or on a regular basis.

Examples of everyday operating expenses:
- You need to pay for lawn care services.
- You need to pay for insurance.
- You need to pay for utility expenses for the common areas.
- You need to pay the Property Management firm for their administrative and bookkeeping services.
- You need to pay for the steady stream of small, everyday repairs and maintenance work that have to be taken care of.

Like the squeaky wheel getting the grease, operating expenses are day-to-day expenses that "cry out" to be paid right away, and these invoices generally get paid promptly.

Why does the annual amount intended to fund upcoming reserve expenses, often *not* get put into a savings account each year as planned?

Because operating expenses tend to get paid *first*, often there is not enough money left over for that year's full contribution to reserve expenses, as called for in the Reserve Study.

This problem is an indication that the monthly assessment fee is not high enough to cover *both* operating expenses, and this year's contribution for upcoming reserve expenses.

Reserve underfunding is a very common Association problem.

In the graph below, you can see the underfunding problem illustrated graphically with the white unfunded portion of the annual budget. This amount will become an accumulating deficit each year.

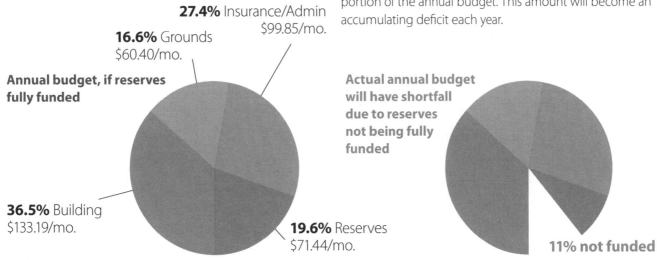

27.4% Insurance/Admin $99.85/mo.

16.6% Grounds $60.40/mo.

Annual budget, if reserves fully funded

Actual annual budget will have shortfall due to reserves not being fully funded

36.5% Building $133.19/mo.

19.6% Reserves $71.44/mo.

11% not funded

The Even Nature of Operating Expenses Spending

Operating expenses remain somewhat even from year to year.

Notice that the year-by-year projections of spending for operating expenses are somewhat even.

The stair-step effect you see is because the budget is projected to increase about 3% each year for inflation, taking into account the increased costs of goods and services that the Association must buy each year.

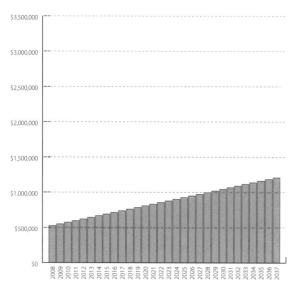

Example A:
Stacked Flats Operating Spending Projection

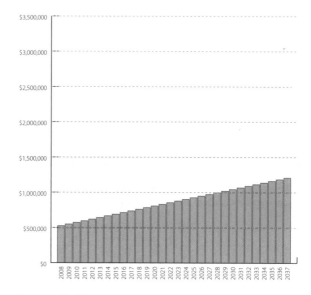

Example B:
Townhome Operating Spending Projection

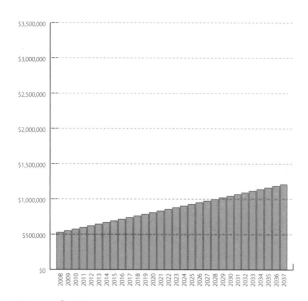

Example C:
Mid-Rise Operating Spending Projection

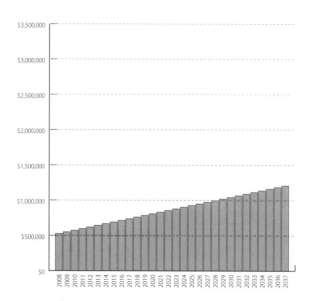

Example D:
High-Rise Operating Spending Projection

The UNEVEN Nature of Reserve Expenses Spending

Insight

Reserve fund expenses spending is usually very *uneven* from year to year.

The Reserve Study charts projected spending for major repairs and replacements for each year for the next 20 to 30 years.

Spending for these expenses is almost nothing in some years, then hits hard in another year.

The unevenness of this type of spending is why you need to be prepared, and have money set aside for these expenses, and other unexpected expenses that will occur, particularly as the building ages.

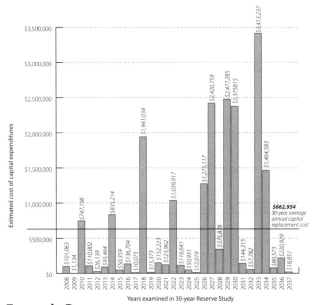

Example A:
Stacked Flats Reserve Spending Projection

Example B:
Townhome Reserve Spending Projection

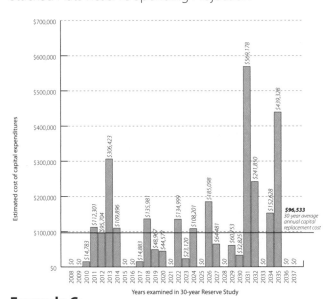

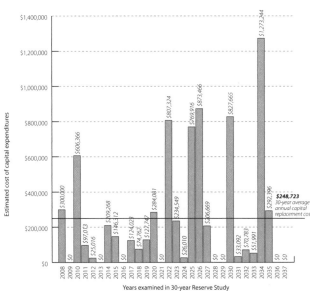

Example C:
Mid-Rise Reserve Spending Projection

Example D:
High-Rise Reserve Spending Projection

How Owners Are Hurt by Association Financial Weakness

What causes a property to age in a not-so-graceful way?

Some unsettling realities can happen if your association property ages in a not-so-graceful way.

This "perfect storm" can result from any of several factors, which may include:

- A lack of accurate advance planning, or a history of resistance from the board of directors or a majority of owners regarding planning for the future or funding the reserves.
- Expensive component parts of the buildings that wear out sooner than expected.
- A lack of owner awareness or action to solve problems before the problems get even worse.
- The plain bad luck of a location that is no longer commercially insurable.
- A neighborhood that is in decline.

Let's look at examples of what owners have to live through, when these Association financial shortfalls have happened to them.

Like living with end-stage cancer: When buildings are *condemned*

Like the final stages of a fatal human illness, this city-condemnation scenario is currently a small minority of advanced cases of property decline, for both suburban and urban properties. Often these properties are 30 years old and older.

When condemnation finally occurs, residents are often stunned because they have been given as little as 24 hours to gather what they can and leave their property.

In these situations, the owners within in the association — often lower-income owners and renters by the time the property reaches this point — have to suffer day-to-day with declining living conditions and sometimes the loss of whatever they have invested. Their association and property experience a slow, painful death.

If a team of committed and competent owner/leaders can emerge and gain consensus for a plan of action among the owners, sometimes these troubled properties can rebound.

Other times, provided the owners can obtain the super majority vote often required by the Association governing documents, the building and land might be sold "as is" to a developer. Then, the remaining owners and renters can move away and start a new chapter of their lives.

Another form of the day of reckoning: Large Special Assessments

A special assessment is an amount of money, in addition to the regular monthly assessments, that is payable from owners within the Association.

Most often, the special assessment money is raised for large repair and replacement expenses. Sometimes a special assessment is used to build up the reserve funds again after major repair and replacement expenditures have depleted the reserves.

Unanticipated repair and replacement expenses happen at Association properties, just as they do at single-family homes. This is one of the financial risks of home ownership.

A professional Reserve Study, with its physical component analysis and financial forecast, will help to lower this risk of unanticipated expenses for major repairs and replacements. The caveat for potential new buyers, is that often, an Association may choose to only partially fund the reserves, so the Association can still be financially vulnerable to a special assessment.

Amount of the Special Assessment can vary widely

The amount of the special assessment will vary, depending on a variety of factors, including how much money is needed immediately for repairs, and what size special assessment is allowed by both Association governing documents and local laws.

A special assessment may be as low as a few hundred dollars, but can also be tens of thousands of dollars.

For owners with greater financial assets, while they are often irked at having to pay a special assessment, they have the resources to pay the special assessment and life goes on.

But at the middle and lower income levels, coming up with the special assessment money is difficult, if not impossible. If an owner has home equity, sometimes the owner obtains a home equity loan in order the pay the special assessment.

Some state laws allow the Association board of directors to impose a special assessment in an emergency, when the building conditions could constitute a danger to resident health or safety. In non-emergency cases, sometimes there is a requirement for a super majority vote of the owners to pass a special assessment.

How Owners Are Hurt by Association Financial Weakness

Obtaining a bank loan by the Association for repairs and replacements may or *may not* be an option

Another avenue for obtaining money for building repairs and replacements is an Association bank loan.

But there are several hurdles for this option to become a reality, including:

- Monthly assessment fees may have to be raised to cover the loan repayment and interest expense.
- Only a small number of banks in the country specialize in lending money to Community Associations for repairs and replacements. (For a list of some leading national and regional Community Association banks, see page 31.)
- A common lender requirement is that no more than 5% of the owners be more than 30 days late in paying their monthly assessment fee. Other lender requirements apply as well.
- Governing documents of the Association, and local laws, may require a majority vote of the owners to obtain a loan. Check your governing documents and local laws to be sure.

Lower property values, and more difficulty selling property

A decline in maintaining "curb appeal" elements at the property – like landscaping, exterior painting, seal coating and repaving, lobbies and hallways, and entryways and signage – can translate into fewer potential buyers who develop an initial interest in the property.

In areas of the country where private-sector business exists that investigates Association financial strength for new buyers, the Association reserve shortfalls represent dollars deducted from the sales price of the individual unit … provided that the buyer still has an interest in buying a unit within that Association.

At some Homer Owner Associations there are fewer shared expenses

In associations with fewer shared infrastructure expenses – like some Home Owner Associations of detached, single-family homes – the Association can sometimes more easily catch up on funding reserves, because their total reserve requirements are often lower than at other types of Associations.

If the Home Owner Association has major expenses though, like repaving the roads within the association, playing financial catch-up will remain difficult.

Associations with many high-net-worth owners can more easily come up with cash for a special assessment

In Associations where a greater percentage of owners have a high net worth, a large special assessment can be irksome, and some owners will grumble, but most owners are in a position to pay the special assessment, make the needed repairs and move on.

Even in an association that primarily has owners with a high-net-worth, almost always there will be owners who are stretched thin financially and may have to resort to a home equity loan, or other method to come up with the money for a special assessment.

Older properties, with many low-income owners, often have the most difficulty in achieving a financial turn-around

Associations with mostly poor and marginalized owners have the toughest time achieving a financial turnaround. These associations are sometimes located in properties that have already experienced many years of declining property values.

Often, these associations are located in older apartment buildings that were legally converted to condominium status by a developer, but without the benefit of a gut renovation of the property at the time of the conversion. Therefore, many of the component parts of the buildings are near the end of their useful life.

Already overwhelmed with increasing day-to-day maintenance problems, these poorest association owners may not have among their ranks a group of owners who can step forward and become effective leaders. These owners may lack business and organizational experience, communication and persuasion skills in order to turn around a large, troubled Association.

There more marginalized owners may also not have personal and professional local networks of trusted business peers and associates who could help provide guidance to the board of directors for key technical decisions in the areas of engineering, accounting, law, management and construction.

Thoughts on Association Financial Survival During this Prolonged Economic Crisis

To invest means to risk total loss.

A sobering truth is that when you make an investment, you are taking the chance that your investment will lose all value.

© iStockphoto.com / 3DStock

Economic crisis lesson:
It is wise for Associations to
1. Consistently maintain property every year
2. Reserve for major repairs every year

If a property is continuously and consistently maintained, and reserves are continuously funded during good economic times, when the inevitable bad economic times happen, the Association will be better prepared to ride out the storm.

Lower-cost "curb appeal" projects can help signal to owners and new buyers that the Association is alive and well.

Always maintaining curb appeal – whatever the age of your property – may help attract new buyers, plus helps the current owners to have faith that the Association will make it through the current hard economic times.

How is your Association faring with:
- Lawn care and grounds maintenance?
- Paving and seal coating?
- Exterior surfaces and painting?
- Hallways, lobbies and common elements?
- Entryways and signage?

A consistently applied preventive maintenance program can help maintain your building's curb appeal like this …

… before curb appeal fades to a look like this.

© iStockphoto.com / Tim McClean

Consider hiring a professional engineer to inspect and make a priority list of repairs for the buildings, ranked by urgency.

Especially for aging buildings or neglected newer buildings, an engineer's priority list of repairs can be a useful road map for Association budgeting and expenditures.

Usually, eliminating and minimizing forms of water intrusion are at the top of the engineer's priority list. The many forms of water intrusion can damage the structural elements of buildings and can often cause expensive hidden damage as well.

Examples of common water intrusion problems include:
- Cracked or chipped concrete exteriors and deteriorating mortar in masonry walls, which allow water intrusion.
- All roofing and especially areas of roof flashing.
- Sealing at lintel joints and around window flashing.
- Water that pools at foundations after a rainstorm. Regrading so the water flows away from the foundation is a start to fix this problem.
- And many other items that the engineer will list.

For these purposes, the engineer's report will likely be more comprehensive than the standard Reserve Study forecast for major repairs. That's because a Reserve Study is a non-invasive building component report and financial forecast.

The term "non-invasive" means the Reserve Specialist will not, for example, open walls to inspect the condition of plumbing pipes or electrical wiring. The Reserve Specialist does not do "destructive" testing, such as tearing off a roof shingle to analyze its age and condition.

During bad economic times, sometimes Associations benefit from lower construction and renovation costs.

Associations lucky enough to have cash on hand during the economic crisis, may find lower-than-expected renovation costs from some of the construction firms bidding for Association major renovation projects.

When bidding major renovation projects, it is always useful to hire an appropriately sized engineering firm to create a Request for Proposal (RFP), then have the engineering firm oversee the process of several qualified, insured contractors bidding on the project.

It also benefits the Association to retain the engineering firm to perform site visits during the course of the work to ensure construction company compliance with the project specifications.

If Associations can meet the lending requirements, some Associations borrow money when reserves are too low to pay for urgently needed repairs.

Only a small number of banks in the country specialize in lending money to Community Associations for repairs and replacements.

Association monthly assessment fees may still need to rise to cover loan and interest expense. A common lender requirement is that no more than 7 to 8% of the owners be more than 60 days late in paying their monthly assessment fee. Other lender requirements apply as well.

Some of the larger national and regional banking and lending institutions in the United States that seek Community Association business include:
- Alliance Association Financial Services
- Community Association Banc
- First Associations Bank
- First Bank
- Harris Bank
- NCB Banking & Financial Services
- Popular Association Banking
- Smart Street, a division of RBC Bank
- Union Bank

What Is the Expected Useful Life of Your Building?

Ideas

QUESTIONS:
What is the expected useful life of your building?

Is a home often misclassified as an "investment," with an incorrect assumption of automatic profitable returns in the form of annual appreciation?

Is buying a home really more like buying a car, which might be classified as a "durable good" that will inevitably age over time, that we pay to maintain, and then we dispose of it at the end of its useful life and start the cycle again?

If a home is a "durable good," how can we make it last as long as possible?

Best Scenario

If you have not already done so, now is a good time to establish written plans of action for good stewardship of the property within your Association.

Preventive Maintenance Check Lists to guide proactive seasonal, monthly, weekly, and sometimes even daily maintenance procedures within your Association.

Reserve Study with its priority list for major repairs and funding plans for those repairs.

Engineer's priority list of infrastructure repair projects for properties with severe problems. This priority list helps the board to know which actions to take first, to secure the building from further damage, especially water intrusion.

Shorter life versus longer life

© iStockphoto.com / PhotObvious

A short useful life?
Obsolete 1960s tower being torn down

Is the property – even if it was built just 40 years ago – already at the end of its useful life?

Or can that useful life be extended almost indefinitely?

© iStockphoto.com / Tony Tremblay

A long useful life?
1790s colonial homes still going strong

When can the useful life of a building go on for almost as long as a civilization endures?

In North America, especially in some neighborhoods on the east coast, homes built in the Colonial era during the 1790s and earlier are still going strong.

Each succeeding century or era required significant investments in new technologies, like plumbing, wiring, then the complete replacement of those systems after the end of their useful life.

Why Some Community Associations
Are Financially Strong

1

Plan of Action	What is the short-range and long-range plan of action for your Association?
1. Reserve Study	The year-by-year projection of major repair and replacement costs for *each year* of the next 20 to 30 years
2. Preventive Maintenance Check List	The detailed list of seasonal, monthly, weekly or even daily activities that guides day-to-day maintenance activities
3. Annual Budget	The Operating and Reserve Expense projections for the upcoming year

2

Action Steps	What regular activities take place to communicate, monitor and manage the plan of action as it unfolds?
1. Monthly Board Meetings	Well-organized, well-run monthly meetings of the board of directors, with prompt followup action on all board decisions. The ideal board makes decisions that are • Prudent • Fair • and sometimes courageous
2. Ongoing Communications with All Owners	Ongoing, two-way, respectful communications with all owners • Letters, newsletters and e-mails, plus updates to the Association web site • An informed, well-organized person who can answer owners' questions via phone call and e-mail on a day-to-day basis • Annual or semi-annual owners meetings

Are You Lucky Enough to Have a Prudent, Action-Oriented, Sometimes Courageous Board of Directors?

When you buy, there is an element of "Condo Roulette" based on board skillfulness.

Board leadership is practically invisible, but is of prime importance to the safety of your investment.

Curb appeal is easy to see and helps us decide to buy.

But at the heart of a property that stays financially strong is the pure luck of having committed and competent neighbors (or you) stepping forward to provide prudent, and sometimes courageous service on the Association Board of Directors.

Why is the leadership of the volunteer Board of Directors so important?

Because the actions of the Board of Directors are the *engine* that drives the Association forward.

What factors contribute to turning a random group of neighbors into a unified, effective Board of Directors?

1. Respectful, team approach to problem solving
Learn to approach problems together, with a sense of flexibility, then be open to compromise on the solutions generated by the "wisdom of the group."

2. Well-organized meetings and prompt follow-up
Well-organized, well-run monthly board meetings will bring out the best in the board members (we hope). Also important is prompt and efficient follow-up on all monthly board decisions.

Can board consensus for an action plan happen quickly?

Usually not, unless it is an emergency repair situation. Gaining consensus for solution to a major problem is not going to happen in one board meeting.

Studying issues, brainstorming solutions, maybe hiring an outside consultant who is a technical expert for advice, then deciding on a course of action can be a multi-meeting process.

With a minority of issues, you need to add another time-consuming step to the action process. That step is education and outreach to all of your fellow owners about an issue of major importance … and that's an even longer process because it involves so many more people.

How does a board reach consensus for an action?

It helps if board members can develop two traits among themselves:

- Trust
- The ability to compromise
  (Being flexible in solutions)

Why is TRUST so important?

If you build trust, you are more likely to succeed together.

Why is COURAGE so important?

Some board actions are going to require courage, and courageous action is what moves your Association toward greater financial strength.

The best way to get board members ready for an action, and then the remaining owners ready for this needed action, is through ongoing education and communication of the issues.

Sell the benefits of the plan. Then act.

From Random Neighbors to a Unified Board of Directors

Board member interpersonal relationships: A philosophy of behavior

1. Try to respect some trait or ability in each fellow board member.

We all have strengths and weaknesses. Try to see and value the strengths that each individual board member can bring to the table.

If you are lucky, maybe in turn, a fellow board member will be able to see your strengths and be forgiving of your weaknesses.

2. Strive for open, honest, but respectful communication with other board members.

Our discerning minds may quickly reach a decision about what we think of someone on our team. We already know the wisdom of not saying every hurtful thing that happens to cross our mind.

3. Anger rarely makes a good decision

At work, we know that ill-chosen words or a flash of anger could get us fired. But in our own homes, many people are less inclined to censor their words or emotions. The angry person will often pay a price for this outburst, whether they realize it or not.

Sometimes with displays of anger, you get 10 seconds of satisfaction, but must invest a much longer time trying to repair the damage, if it can be repaired at all.

**Board member goals and actions:
A philosophy of behavior**

1. Put the common good above your own interests every time.

You will immediately destroy trust among the larger pool of owners when it even *appears* that a board member is giving themselves some kind of preferential treatment.

2. Be open to modifying your plan of action, based on feedback from others.

A comforting reality in working with your fellow board members is that, especially in a real-time brainstorming meeting, different people will think of entirely different ideas to solve problems, some of which you may not have even considered. Incorporate those good ideas into one plan of action.

3. Be open to incremental change.

You'll get there, but maybe a little at a time. So be it.

4. Strive for excellence.

Build it to last. Quality endures.

5. Follow through.

Do what you say you are going to do.

Association president to maintenance and lawn care workers:

"Work on my building *last*."

The president of an association noticed a pattern with vendors, from lawn care providers to painters to the maintenance staff.

In the vendors' apparent desire to please her, in working on Association-wide projects, they started the project around her building first, and sometimes even lavished more time on the project when it was right outside her windows.

She learned an important lesson. To avoid even the *appearance* of conflict of interest among all of her fellow co-owners, vendors got instructions to work on the president's building *last* for any Association project.

Who Makes a Good Board Member?

Who is likely to become a good board member?

Personal traits

- An honest person
- A friendly person with good communication skills
- A reasonable and prudent person
- A person who has an understanding about the common good
- A person who is inclined to put others first instead of their own self-interest
- A person who follows through on their commitments

Work and life experience

- Has somehow in their life experience learned the value of teamwork and understands give and take in reaching compromises
- Previous business or organizational experience is helpful

Why do board members quit or not serve another term?

Common reasons for volunteer board members to quit	Additional explanation
Burn out.	Board members can get tired of fielding complaints, especially from those who are frequent complainers, who also show little interest or ability in helping to solve the problems.
Spouse demands that they quit volunteering so much time to the Association.	This is a common reason that an effective board member may end their service.
Overwhelmed in their new board role.	Especially for a new board president in a troubled, self-managed association, the demands can be overwhelming. Within a few months, or even a few weeks, they resign.
One angry confrontation becomes the tipping point.	Anger often has destructive and unfortunate consequences. A long stretch of board service can end for good with one especially nasty (and unnecessary) confrontation.
A new job, a changed family situation, or new priorities for community service.	Sometimes there is just no more free time to offer in volunteer service at the Association.

Insight

Thoughts about addressing problem behaviors in:

- **Board members**
- **Owners**
- **Property management firms**

We all have rights.

But we also have responsibilities.

There will be troubling behaviors from neighbors who take on the role of board members.

There will be troubling behaviors from neighbors who are owners.

There will be troubling behaviors from vendors and suppliers of services to the Association.

It helps when there are rules, and everybody understands the rules. It helps when there is respectful communication.

What is a crime? And what is merely an irritating personality quirk?

There is a major difference between criminal behavior and irritating but mere personality quirks.

The criminal behavior rarely happens in most Associations, but you can count on the personality quirks happening all the time.

It can be a comfort, when it comes to personality quirks, that over time, you will start to see a pattern of behavior from certain neighbors. At least you will no longer be surprised by some of their behaviors, because apparently, that's just the way they are, short of a miracle in personal growth and the ability to change.

A Few Common Behavior Problems in Some Board Members

Problem	Possible corrective action
A board member who is consistently rude and abrupt with owners and other board members…or doesn't communicate at all.	This person needs to be off the board. The only good result of this person's behavior is that it may motivate other owners to step forward to serve on the board.
A board member who takes care of their own needs first.	If this behavior persists, this person needs to be off the board. An example "educational" conversation: BOARD MEMBER: "Some rainwater from clogged roof gutters, spilled rain water into my unit windows. Have the leaves cleared out of *my* roof gutters so this doesn't happen to *me* again. BOARD PRESIDENT: "Good idea. But we need to have the handyman check *all* the problem drainage areas. We have to be fair to *all* the owners."
A board president who lacks: • People skills • Business or organizational experience	Usually, this person needs to be removed form the role of board president because the job is not a good match for whatever skills this person may possess. Often, this person may have had work experience in a purely technical area, without much experience in seeing the "big picture," managing an organization or even dealing with people.
A board president who sees no urgency to fix pressing problems.	It is healthy to have a diversity of opinions on the board about when to act. However, if the president consistently sees no need to act to fix problems, this person needs to be out of the president's role.
Disorganized board members, who rarely follow up on what they say they will do.	QUESTION: Is this disorganized person an honest and insightful person? If so, they may continue to be useful in real-time brainstorming sessions at the monthly Board of Directors meeting. You may want to unburden them from project management if they show no skills in this area.
A board member who is no longer paying their monthly assessment fees.	Most governing documents state that this person is no longer a member "in good standing" and therefore is ineligible for board service.
A board member is taking kickbacks from vendors or embezzling money.	Have zero tolerance for this behavior. Be careful not to make accusations without a shred of evidence. Other board members need to immediately consult with the Community Association manager, the Association attorney and possibly the association accountant for advice. For the sake of a check and balance, and credibility with those who can help you with this investigation, it is best if at least two board members pursue this investigation together. If proven guilty, the offending board member faces stiff personal criminal penalties.

A Few Common Behavior Problems in Some Owners

Problem	Possible corrective action
Selfish and inconsiderate people who seem oblivious to the harm and disruptions that they cause to others.	If someone is breaking the law, any owner can report this immediately to the local police. If there are noise issues for example, often, there are local noise ordinances that are enforceable by local police. While some owners may want to address these perceived infractions in person with their neighbor, there can clearly be a danger in doing so, especially if you do not already know that neighbor, or have a history of difficult relations with that neighbor. The hired Community Association manager, as an outside third party, is a good choice as the messenger of the enforcement message.
Anger, as the first reaction to almost any request for a change in behavior.	Almost invariably, the first reaction of many people, when asked to stop some behavior, is to react with indignation and anger. A skilled Community Association manager, as an outside third party, is the better messenger of the enforcement message.
Owners, especially in infrastructure-intensive condominium associations, who insist that repairs be delayed or skipped entirely.	Ongoing education of owners is always useful. A minority of owners are going to remain in denial about the costs of operations and repairs. Decisions about common area repairs within a condominium association are fundamentally different than an individual's options for delaying repairs within a single-family home for as long as the owner chooses.
An owner who is a very troubled individual.	A very troubled individual is not always rational and can present many challenges to other residents within a community. The Community Association manager, as an outside third party, is the better messenger of the enforcement message.
Owner with views shaped without the benefit of feedback from other owners.	In their own mind, without benefit of airing their ideas with someone who might not fully agree with them, some owners can get increasingly self-righteous about their own ideas. Sometimes what is a real eye opener for such a person is when this person happens to speak at a community meeting, they see that their idea is not as universally accepted as they imagined it would be. The most potent ideas for an Association are usually not created in a vacuum.
Owner apathy regarding serving as a board member or committee member in order to solve problems.	You have to do this gently and with a smile, but the classic invitation to a chronic complainer is to suggest, "You have a very good point. We would like for you to be in charge of this committee to solve the difficult problem that you describe." Owners have different demands on their time at different points in their lives. Therefore, community service may temporarily or always be a low priority for them. Unfortunately, especially in smaller Associations, if everyone feels the same way about not serving others, the property will eventually be in distress.

A Few Common Problems with Property Management Firms

Problem	Possible corrective action
The property management company lacks follow through in solving problems.	Someone needs to "manage the managers," and that task falls to the Board of Directors of the Association. Monthly board meetings, with careful review of monthly financial statements, all pending projects and monthly maintenance reports, help the board to keep important projects on a follow-up list until those projects are completed.
The property management company is reactive, rather than proactive about building preventive maintenance.	A detailed, custom created Preventive Maintenance check list for the Association property is a great start to staying on top of these complex tasks. Sample Preventive Maintenance lists are included in this book.
The property manager doesn't return my phone calls or answer my emails	This can be a frequent problem, especially for a single part-time, off-site property manager who may be trying to manage up to 15 to 25 different Association properties with a total of hundreds or even thousands of owners and residents. Without adequate office staff support, one property manager can quickly be stretched thin. A few ideas for options: • Especially if a part-time manager is well organized and has good people skills, it may be worth renegotiating the property management company agreement, so there is payment to the property management firm for an increased number of hours of service to the Association. • If the manager still doesn't return phone calls or emails, ask for another property manager at the firm. • If the second option doesn't work, consider developing a Request for Proposal for management services, and solicit bids from other property management firms.
Some of our vendor invoices were not paid. The monthly financial statement is always late.	Being consistently late paying invoices or consistently late in compiling monthly financial statements is often a violation of the written management agreement and therefore just cause to begin the search for a new property management firm.

Why a Well-Planned Monthly Board Meeting Is So Vital

Why is a well-planned monthly meeting of the Board of Directors so vital?

- A high-functioning Board of Directors is the *engine* that drives the Association forward.
- A meeting is an opportunity for brainstorming and generating the wisdom of the group.
- Some Associations start each monthly meeting by reviewing the latest monthly financial reports, thereby helping to ensure monthly review of the financials by board members.
- If there is information, vendor bids or other data for the board to absorb, provide this, as well as at least a skeleton outline of the meeting agenda, a few days *before* the meeting, so board members can prepare.
- In as many meetings as possible, have the board decide on issues from vendor bid selection, to the best approach to solving some owner problem. By making *decisions* at every meeting, you keep the meeting *vital*.

Ideas

An idea to save time in planning and organizing the monthly board meeting agenda

Label a manila folder "Next Monthly Meeting."

During the month, add to the folder:

- Random ideas that occur to you
- A printout of any e-mail requests that you may need your followup
- Vendor bids
- Data you did not have time to discuss at last month's meeting

Then, a few days to a week before the next monthly meeting, sort through your folder of notes and arrange them into a one-page meeting agenda. Along with copies of bids and other data, forward the meeting agenda to the board members to both remind them of the upcoming meeting and prepare in advance for what will be discussed.

What other key points to remember for monthly board meeting planning and organizing?

- Try to limit the board meeting to 90 minutes maximum.
- Start the meeting on time. End the meeting on time.
- Whatever doesn't get discussed is carried over to the next monthly meeting.
- Consider creating meeting agendas that list the most financially important topics *first*. That way, the "big picture" items are discussed at each meeting.
- A good compact reference book is *Robert's Rules of Order Newly Revised In Brief* by Robert, Evans, Honemann and Balch from DaCapo Press.

Who creates the monthly meeting agenda and how much time does it take?

Sometimes this meeting preparation and organization task is handled by the board president, sometimes by the Community Association manager, especially if the manager is a full-time employee of the Association.

The preparatory notes during the month, plus creating the meeting agenda, can easily take 8 hours of preparation time.

If multiple vendor bids have to be obtained, and meeting contractors to get those bids, the preparation time for one meeting can easily zoom above 40 hours.

How much time is invested in follow up activities *after* each monthly board meeting?

Expect at least another 8 hours in follow up activities *after* the monthly meeting, including letters to owners, contacting the winning bidder for a work project and creating the meeting minutes.

Ideas

Keep an action list or to-do list as a part of the monthly meeting minutes.

A useful writing style in the meeting minutes is to end each topic within the minutes with an action list of who is going to do what, and when, to implement the latest board decisions.

Who do you call or e-mail when there are day-to-day problems to solve?

- Does a volunteer fill this role?
- Does a part-time, off-site manager fill this role?
- Does a full-time manager fill this role?
- Does no one fill this role?

You get what you pay for, folks. Unfortunately, problems don't solve themselves. Buildings and grounds do not plan their own future and maintain themselves.

When you think about it, the sales phrase, "Carefree, no-maintenance living" is a myth, or an illusion.

You may not have to do physical labor in external home repairs within a condominium association, but at least a few owners will always need to step forward to plan, to communicate, to manage the managers, or Association financial distress will be inevitable.

But take heart; there are ideas for solutions. And everyone has a strong incentive to make it work for the long haul, because most of us need a safe, affordable place to live.

A good experience

A neighbor, volunteering on the Board of Directors, answering a question from another neighbor.

© iStockphoto.com / Rebecca Ellis

A bad experience

A neighbor, volunteering on the Board of Directors, taking a complaint call from another neighbor.

© iStockphoto.com / Andy Dean

A bad experience

Maybe the neighbors who used to volunteer to help have quit, and no one else has stepped forward to serve.

© iStockphoto.com / Paul W. Brian

A Comparison of Communication Styles

A landlord to the tenants	Association board members to their fellow co-owners
Top-down orders from the landlord to tenants might work.	1. Someone needs to be available to all owners to answer questions via phone calls and e-mails. 2. Frequent, well-written information about Association problems and solutions. "Persuasive" communications are in order if you are trying to get Association members to adopt, for example, better business practices.

What is a definition of "persuasive" communications?

A short answer is that with persuasive communications, you sell the *benefits* of a plan of action, in addition to explaining the technical details.

Example:

Goal: To raise the monthly assessment fees in order to make needed major repairs and replacements.

The *benefits* of this plan include:

- Protecting property values
- May help protect owner health and safety, if it is a major infrastructure repair, like roofing, plumbing or wiring
- May help the Association maintain its ability to obtain insurance policies for coverage of the property
- Improving "curb appeal" which may help with sales of units
- Improving "curb appeal," which creates a more pleasant place to live, day-to-day

Do you care about the well-being of the people of the Association?

If you care about the well-being of the people of the Association, it likely will be noticed by many owners.

When they understand that you care, your message will be better received.

Effective, Regular Communications with All Owners

Ideas

A few suggestions for Association-wide communications:

- Brief and to the point
- Well-written
- Visuals in communication will help owners to understand:
  - Digital photos are especially useful to show the need for repairs and replacements.
  - Pie charts help explain budgets
  - Tables and graphs are useful for comparison data

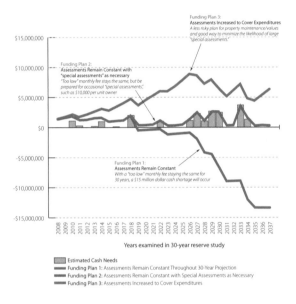

▲ In 7 years, without monthly fee increases, we start operating in the red.

▲ We've delayed repainting long enough. (Maybe too long.)

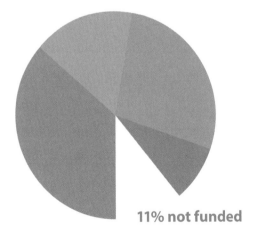

11% not funded

▲ The reserves are underfunded again this year.

◄ Luckily, the engineer's report says the building has settled as much as it is going to settle ... but we still need to repair the foundations so water intrusion does not cause further damage.

© iStockphoto.com / DIGIcal

▲ In addition to technical skills, successful, long-term employees at associations often have patience and well-developed "people skills" due to the "people intensive" nature of providing service work within an Association.

© iStockphoto.com / Edward Bock

▲ While boards of directors will often change from year to year, the trusted, skilled, long-time service providers to the Association offer useful continuity to owners, and help to educate the new boards about past board practices.

✔ Best Scenario

Maintaining mutually beneficial long-term business relationships with trusted, skilled service providers to the Association

Just as in any business or organization, employees of the Association – especially key, long-term employees – can be vital to the success of the organization.

The Community Association manager is usually a skilled generalist who understands people, Association budget planning and the coordination of most of the service providers at the Association.

As time goes by, the Community Association manager learns more about the personalities of owners on the board of directors and also owners in the Association.

The skilled trades workers who fix problems year in and year out at the Association get to know the many physical nuances in each building. This accumulated property knowledge helps the service providers to work more efficiently.

Continuity of Association staff can be reassuring to owners, especially when their good work has resulted in earning a position of trust.

If there is an egregious vendor error, the board is justified in reviewing services from competitive service providers, and making a change.

However, minor mistakes and some wrong choices are going to happen. It is wise to stick with good employees when you find them.

Reviewing the Basics: Reserves, Collections

Annual budgeting for reserves

Throughout this book we discuss the wisdom of knowing how much you need for reserve expenses and funding the reserves each year. This is basic for an Association to create financial strength.

Annual budget, if reserves fully funded

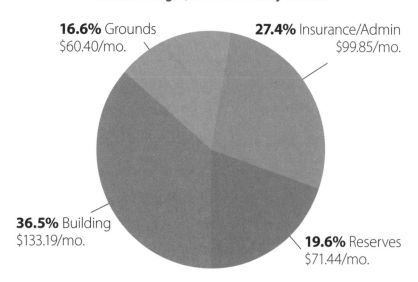

16.6% Grounds
$60.40/mo.

27.4% Insurance/Admin
$99.85/mo.

36.5% Building
$133.19/mo.

19.6% Reserves
$71.44/mo.

Actual annual budget will have shortfall due to reserves not being fully funded.

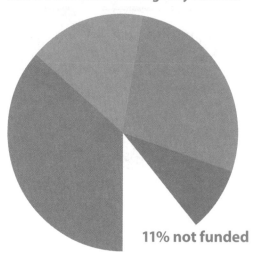

11% not funded

Best Scenario

Have a payment and collections policy.

Sample collection policy
- Monthly payments due by first of month
- 10 days late - Late letter (or late charge, if permitted by governing documents and local state law)
- 30 days late - More urgently worded late letter
- 60 days late - Account turned over to a collections attorney, with attorney fees to be paid by the late-paying owner. At the county courthouse, a lien is filed against the property

Collection letters are best handled by the Community Association lawyer
- Collections are best handled by a hired outside third party. Often, this is the Community Association Lawyer, who will comply with the Federal Fair Debt Collections Act.

Collections: Financial lifeblood of the Association

Monthly fee collections are the *lifeblood* for the financial health of your association and therefore for your property values.

The collections policy of your association must be clear to owners, along with other information when new owners move in.

Some owners, while pressed hard for credit card debt and mortgage payments, especially during economic recessions, think the monthly association dues might not be as urgent to pay. But that is an incorrect assumption.

Review the accounts receivable at least monthly. When collections spiral out of control, the maintenance of the Association can suffer.

Ideas to Improve the Financial Soundness
of Community Associations

Ideas

The benefits to society from privately owned, multifamily housing

From ancient Rome to the present, where many people live in crowded cities with a limited amount of land and other resources, privately owned, dense, multifamily housing has emerged as a way to house the population.

"Assisted living lite"

Also, for an aging population, this form of housing can be a form of "assisted living lite" – a convenient, labor-intensive, sometimes costly set of services are provided to plan and maintain the property, so many individual home owners are freed from these responsibilities in home ownership.

"Carefree, maintenance-free living"?

Despite an appealing but naive sales claim of "carefree, maintenance-free" living, properties do not plan and run themselves.

Association financial failures hurt real people.

When financial failures occur in Associations, real people are hurt.

The benefits of well-run Associations

- Financial security
- Peace of mind

Here are some key ideas that can help solve some fundamental problems with this form of "shared expenses" housing.

IDEA #1

Reserve Studies, required by law in every state

If you only remember two words from this book, remember the words *Reserve Study*.

As of this printing, only a small number of states require a professional Reserve Study: California, Hawaii, Nevada, Virginia and Washington state.

Some other states have laws with wording that says in effect, "maintain adequate reserves," but how can you translate that phrase into a plan of action at an Association without the hard data in a Reserve Study?

Reserve study requirement does not mean the reserves actually have to be funded.

Ironically, state laws rarely require that the reserves be funded. Usually, owners are given the option of not funding the reserves, which is all the more reason that a potential new buyer at an Association should check the needed reserves versus reserves on hand, before buying.

BENEFITS:

- A Reserve Study serves as a financial road map for the Association's near-term and longer-term financial future.

- It lowers the likelihood of large, unexpected special assessments.

- Owners contribute to that part of the useful life of a component that is "used up" or "extracted" during their time of ownership.

- With full disclosure of reserve recommendations versus actual reserves, new buyers, mortgage lenders and insurance companies get a better picture of the financial health of the Association.

IDEA #2

Laws that give the Board of Directors the ability to have cash to make needed repairs

Sometimes at the beginning of a development, the original monthly assessment fee may not be based on a Reserve Study and is not high enough to sustain the property once repairs and replacements are needed.

Plus, as the property ages, the cost of repairs and replacements will rise.

Some states have enacted laws that give the elected Board of Directors some financial flexibility to act to fix these cash shortages.

These state laws include:

- Board has the power to annually increase regular monthly assessment fees within a certain percentage if needed.

  For example, in Illinois, the board can raise the monthly assessment fee by as much as 15% per year. In California, the board can raise the monthly assessment fee by as much 20% per year.

- Board has the power for an emergency special assessment for conditions that could affect the health and safety of owners.

- Board has the power to borrow money for repairs, provided the Association can meet the lender's financial requirements.

BENEFITS:

Having enough cash for needed repairs and replacements can help curb appeal, help protect property values and in some cases, help protect the health and safety of residents.

IDEA #3

Private sector businesses that investigate Association financial strength for new buyers, lenders

You've heard of a traditional physical home inspection before buying a home.

This business concept operates on much the same principle as a physical home inspection, except this firm has experience sorting through sometimes complex financial documents to report to their customer the current difference between the recommended reserve amount and the actual amount that the Association has in its reserves.

If the Association is underfunded, this amount could soon turn into a large special assessment. The firm reports the amount of the association underfunding, divided by the ownership percentages, and this translates into a deficit per unit.

If the potential buyer is still interested in buying at the property, the deficit per unit is the starting point for negotiating a lower sales price for the unit.

This private-sector business model was developed in 1998 in California, which is one of the few states that requires the Association to obtain a professional Reserve Study.

BENEFITS:

- New buyers are less likely to be surprised by a large, unreported Association deficit, which could mean a large special assessment.

- Lenders and other financial institutions can decide if they want to make a loan or insure a property with low reserves.

- Current owners and board members at an Association have a strong market-driven incentive to maintain the financial health of their Association, because potential new buyers may prefer to buy in only more financially sound Associations.

IDEA #4

Better pay for off-site, part-time property managers

For a $10 to $15 per month "door fee" (or monthly management fee per unit), the level of management and administrative services may not be at the service level that some owners would like it to be.

Especially for smaller Associations, the Association may not generate enough in monthly fees to make the property inviting to a talented manager and his or her office support staff.

With only a meager number of manager hours available, the manager may only be able to be reactive rather than proactive when it comes to serving the Association.

In the last 25+ years, this is one area of pay to Association vendors that, due to many competitive pressures, has not been raised for decades.

Property management is a service business with few barriers to entry. Even if one Board is satisfied with their property management firm, the new Board may be approached by a new, "hungry" property management firm, with cut-rate fees, and the downward pricing cycle for property management services (and maybe a corresponding lack of service) starts all over again.

Home owners, please note, you often get what you pay for.

BENEFITS:
- At many Associations, there are shortages of trained, committed and competent volunteers to handle key tasks within the Association.

- For some Associations, hiring the skills you need to operate the Association may be the best guarantee of a steady supply of those needed services. This will also lighten the load for Association volunteers, which may help the Association to retain the volunteers.

IDEA #5

Boards that follow the Business Judgment Rule

Board members carry the responsibility to act prudently and thoughtfully. When deciding Association issues of complexity, Board members are advised to consult with appropriate technical experts, who are credentialed (and insured) specialists in their respective fields. Board members need to listen to all sides of an issue and weigh those options before deciding an issue.

This deliberate, consultative approach, on the part of the Board should be documented in the meeting minutes. This planful approach helps to guard against Board decisions that are arbitrary or nonsensical.

In the United States, when a non-profit Board of Directors is acting in good faith, looking out for the best interests of the association, and following this careful, deliberate approach, there is a legal shield which *may* apply to the board decision, called the Business Judgment Rule.

Consult with your Community Association manager and/or Association legal counsel for the details. This concept is reviewed here, just so you know this exists as a possible extra protection for difficult board actions.

Also, all Boards of Directors should carry Director's and Officer's (D & O) liability insurance. Your insurance agent, or your Community Association manager can provide details.

BENEFITS:
Board member liability risk is lower when the board relies on insured, outside third parties for key financial and technical advice, such as what you would receive from a certified public accountant, engineer, reserve specialist or attorney.

IDEA #6

Experimental idea: The condo ownership/infrastructure rental hybrid

A long-time California real estate attorney has outlined this idea as a possible way to reduce the perpetual problem of Association underfunding for infrastructure repairs, particularly in infrastructure intensive condominium properties.

Briefly, the idea is that a condominium owner would still buy their "box of air," which is their condominium unit.

But, with this idea, ownership and maintenance of the common elements would be the responsibility of a landlord, not the group of condominium owners.

For example, the infrastructure of the building (wiring, plumbing pipes, steel girders, hallways, lobbies, grounds) would be owned by a landlord.

A portion of the monthly assessment fees would be paid to the landlord for the upkeep of the common elements. This way, one business entity, the landlord, would have responsibility for maintaining the infrastructure.

BENEFITS:

- Especially for aging condominium properties, the expensive upkeep of infrastructure elements can be made more difficult by the fact that there are so many owners.

- At least theoretically, having one owner of the common elements may make business decisions easier to reach and implement.

IDEA #7

Experimental idea: An outside, paid Board of Directors

Experienced property managers sometimes speak longingly for the day when — just maybe — a professional, paid, outside Board of Directors takes over the decision making at an Association.

The reason for the property manager consternation is that too frequently, the property manager must deal with a volunteer board member who puts their own needs ahead of the Association as a whole or a Board of Directors that, as a group, seems to lack focus and business sense.

Adding to the problem is that in some associations, few owners are willing to volunteer to serve on the Board of Directors.

While paid board members are still almost unheard of, conditions may arise in the future where a paid, outside Board of Directors may be needed. There would be legal and financial details to be worked out before this could happen.

BENEFITS:

- Following the model of some for-profit business corporations, a non-profit Association could conceivably have at least some outside, paid board members in Associations where no owners are willing to volunteer.

- A benefit would be to lower the possible conflicts of interest among owner board members and to field a board whose members possess the training and technical and management experience that could help the Association.

IDEA #8

Annual, data-driven, local recognition of well-managed, financially sound Community Associations

The Community Association Institutes (CAI) chapter for Pennsylvania and Delaware Valley created an annual recognition program in 2000 for well-managed local Associations, according to Tony Campisi, Chapter Executive Director.

The recognition program is called the Gold Star Community© Program.

To apply, Associations fill out a detailed four-page check list that details the financial and administrative planning of the Association and submit a fee of from $75 to $150 depending on the size of the Association. (Associations do not have to be members of CAI to apply for the recognition status.)

The applications are reviewed by a local, independent review panel consisting of an attorney, insurance specialist, an Association volunteer home owner board member, a certified public accountant, and a Community Association manager.

More details are at www.cai-padelval.org. Then at the home page, click on Programs & Events; then click on Gold Star Communities.

BENEFITS:

- The Gold Star achievement by a community promotes the fact that your community is financially healthy with adequate reserves for future needs.

- The Gold Star achievement by your community underscores the fact that your community is managed utilizing the best practices in Community Association management.

IDEA #9

Discussion of better legal methods for termination of aging, failing Associations

Sometimes, state laws and governing documents are written with the assumption that the buildings of the Association will go on forever.

But buildings have an expected useful life, especially if the buildings are not well constructed to begin with or not well maintained in the meantime.

If there are provisions in the governing documents that state an 80% or even 100% yes vote of the owners is needed to end the association, that may not be an obtainable vote total and therefore not in the best interests of the owners of that Association.

Regarding realistic vote totals, consider the number of elections for local, state and even federal elections that are decided with only 15 to 40% total voter turn out.

And Association governing documents may state you need 80% to 100% of the owners voting and they all have to vote yes. (Not likely to happen.) Possibly a 66% yes vote of all owners to end the Association is a more realistic super majority for the drastic action of ending the Association.

BENEFITS:

As Association properties increase both in number and age in the United States, we, as a society, need to discuss fair, sound methods to "wind down" aging and failing Associations.

This could help to minimize the life disruptions for the final Association owners who remain with the property at the end of its useful life.

Part Two
Samples and Appendices

For All Five Property Examples

- Property overview
- Annual budget
- Monthly income statement
- Monthly balance sheet
- Monthly accounts receivable report

- Reserve Study (condensed version)
- Preventive-maintenance check list
- List of major structural renovation expenses for a "same neighborhood" single-family home
- Who does what? (Thumbnail list of job titles)

In-Depth Example A
Two- or Three-Story Stacked Flats
Neighbors live above or below you.

In-Depth Example B
Townhome / Patio Home
Neighbors live alongside you.

In-Depth Example C
Mid-rise
Four-to-eight stories, includes elevators.

In-Depth Example D
High-rise
Nine+ stories.

In-Depth Example E
Home Owner Association (HOA)
Detached, Single-family Homes
Owner responsible for exterior maintenance to his or
her own home, but reserves are still needed to
maintain community property.

Example A:
Two- or Three-Story Stacked Flats

Neighbors live above or below you.

Maintenance and Financial Planning Documentation

Financial PRO and CON overview of this housing type example

PRO
Affordability

Often, this condominium type is a converted apartment building. The initial purchase price may be:

- A lower cost than a single-family home in the same neighborhood.
- A lower cost than a newer condominium structure, which was built as condominiums.

CON
Much deferred maintenance

If a developer converted an old apartment building to condominium units, without a full renovation, there are looming capital costs that owners may not be able to afford.

Low financial reserves

With the struggle to continue with needed replacement of worn-out capital equipment, reserves are often low to non-existent.

Low-income residents, with few assets

With the low cost for a dwelling, owners often do not realize that ongoing renovations are necessary. With extremely limited incomes and assets, some may not have the capital for upgrading worn-out infrastructure elements.

Brief data for this property example

Number of buildings in the complex	6
Total number of housing units in the complex	24
Year(s) built	1962–1964
Quality level of original construction	Above average
Maintenance level since construction	Below average
Cost range for reserve study	$2,000 to $3,000+
Cost range for reserve study update	$1,500 to $2,500+
Current reserve account balance	**$150,000**
Recommended reserve account balance	**$392,661**

In this example:

Current monthly fee per sample unit $225*

Based on reserve study and operating budget analysis

Current monthly fee underfunding per sample unit $91

(This is the accumulating deficit per unit, per month, for this sample budget year.)

A Reserve Study, based on the specific components at your Association, is critical for determining an adequate monthly fee.

* In Condominium Associations with units of different sizes, it is customary to base the monthly fee on a cost-per-square-foot per condominium.

DISCLAIMER — Each property is unique. Therefore, each property budget is unique, based on local conditions and local laws. Do not use these budget figures from this specific yet theoretical example for your own property.

In this example, monthly fee includes:

Utility costs
- Water for all units
- Electricity and gas for common areas

Building and grounds expense
- Spring and fall roofing repairs, roof gutter and downspout cleaning
- Drywall and painting in common areas
- Common area plumbing repairs
- Hallway and basement cleaning
- Pest control for outside of buildings and basements
- Lawn care, tree trimming, fall leaf removal, snow and ice removal

Insurance
- Exterior and common area insurance (you still need to have homeowner's insurance for interior and contents)

Administrative services
- Ongoing, engineer-supervised renovation of buildings
- Off-site Community Manager services of taking phone calls and handling resident issues
- Bookkeeping and monthly invoice payments

Financial reserve expense
- Systematic savings for large capital expenses such as plumbing replacement, roof replacement, etc.

Actual reserves on hand vs. reserves called for in Reserve Study

NECESSARY FINANCIAL RESERVES

E   F

Consider raising reserve levels in order to have cash on hand for anticipated repairs and replacements.

100%
90%
70%
50%
30%
10%
0

Financial Reserves

38% funded

Sample Annual Budget

Fiscal Year — January 1 through December 31

Income	current year	% of budget	$ per month
Monthly assessments	$64,800	97.5%	$225.00
Special assessments	0	0.0%	0.00
Interest income	1,635	2.5%	5.68
Total income	**$66,435**	**100.0%**	**$230.68**

Operating Expenses (ongoing expenses that occur each year)

Bldgs & Grounds Expense			
Bldg maintenance and repairs	$5,300	5.7%	$18.40
Roof / gutter maintenance	635	0.7%	2.20
Painting	2,000	2.2%	6.94
Plumbing repairs	2,200	2.4%	7.64
Carpentry	600	0.6%	2.08
Cleaning	3,500	3.8%	12.15
Pest control	1,650	1.8%	5.73
Lawncare services	8,000	8.6%	27.78
Arborist (for large trees)	1,500	1.6%	5.21
Tree and plant replacements	600	0.6%	2.08
Snow removal	2,000	2.2%	6.94
Sanitation fees	620	0.7%	2.15
Total bldgs & grounds expense	**$28,605**	**30.9%**	**$99.32**

Administrative Expense			
Management fee	$4,896	5.3%	$17.00
Office supplies	2,000	2.2%	6.94
Accounting fees	600	0.6%	2.08
Legal fees	1,500	1.6%	5.21
Engineering / other professional fees	6,500	7.0%	22.57
Insurance	7,200	7.8%	25.00
Local taxes and fees	300	0.3%	1.04
Doubtful account expense	2,000	2.2%	6.94
Total administrative expense	**$24,996**	**27.0%**	**$86.79**

Insight

Underfunding the reserves can lead to:

- Special assessments, if permitted by bylaws or state laws
- Neglected maintenance
- Lower property values
- More difficulty selling badly maintained property

Sample Annual Budget

Fiscal Year — January 1 through December 31

Operating Expenses (cont.)

Utility Expense	current year	% of budget	$ per month
Gas and electric	$2,361	2.5%	$8.20
Water and sewer	7,315	7.9%	25.40
Total utilities expense	**$9,676**	**10.5%**	**$33.60**
Total operating expenses	**$63,277**	**68.3%**	**$219.71**

Reserve Expense Allocations (The amounts listed below are added to each year, into interest-bearing accounts, in preparation for high-cost, anticipated major repairs or replacements.)

	current year	% of budget	$ per month
Site components	$1,085	1.2%	$3.77
Plumbing	1,164	1.3%	4.04
Building systems	732	0.8%	2.54
Building stairwells	177	0.2%	0.61
Total reserve expense allocations	**$3,158**	**3.4%**	**$10.97**
Reserves not funded	$26,154	28.2%	$90.81
Total operating exp. & reserve alloc.	**$92,589**	**100.0%**	**$321.49**

**Annual budget will have shortfall
due to reserves not being fully funded**

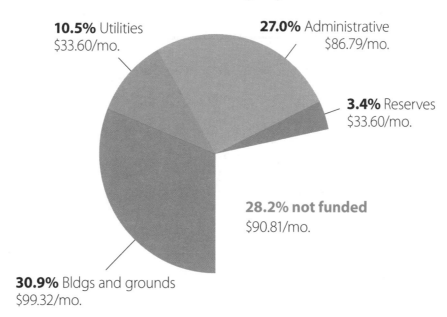

10.5% Utilities
$33.60/mo.

27.0% Administrative
$86.79/mo.

3.4% Reserves
$33.60/mo.

28.2% not funded
$90.81/mo.

30.9% Bldgs and grounds
$99.32/mo.

Sample Monthly Income Statement

Month Ending July 31, 2010

Income	Monthly actual	Monthly budget	YTD actual	YTD budget	YTD variance	Annual budget
Monthly assessments	$5,400	$5,400	$37,800	$37,800	$0	$64,800
Special assessments	0	0	0	0	0	0
Interest income	129	136	892	954	-62	1,635
Other income	0	0	0	0	0	0
Total income	**$5,529**	**$5,536**	**$38,692**	**$38,754**	**-$62**	**$66,435**

Operating Expenses (ongoing expenses that occur each year)

Bldgs and Grnds Exp						
Bldg maintenance / repairs	$446	$442	$3,154	$3,092	$62	$5,300
Roof / gutter maintenance	56	53	389	370	19	635
Painting	153	167	1,097	1,167	-70	2,000
Plumbing repairs	167	183	1,194	1,283	-90	2,200
Carpentry	51	50	354	350	4	600
Cleaning	280	292	1,980	2,042	-61	3,500
Pest control	125	138	866	963	-96	1,650
Lawncare services	853	667	5,600	4,667	933	8,000
Arborist	124	125	849	875	-26	1,500
Tree replacements	47	50	315	350	-35	600
Snow removal	157	167	1,213	1,167	47	2,000
Sanitation fees	49	52	376	362	14	620
Total bldgs and grnds exp	**$2,508**	**$2,384**	**$17,386**	**$16,686**	**$700**	**$28,605**

Administrative Expense						
Management fee	$400	$408	$2,913	$2,856	$57	$4,896
Office supplies	167	167	1,225	1,167	58	2,000
Accounting fees	48	50	329	350	-21	600
Legal fees	114	125	814	875	-61	1,500
Eng / other professional fees	553	542	3,830	3,792	38	6,500
Insurance	576	600	4,074	4,200	-126	7,200
Local taxes / fees	24	25	170	175	-5	300
Doubtful account expense	160	167	1,132	1,167	-35	2,000
Total admin expense	**$2,040**	**$2,083**	**$14,486**	**$14,581**	**-$95**	**$24,996**

Sample Monthly Income Statement
Month Ending July 31, 2010

Operating Expenses (cont.)	**Monthly actual**	**Monthly budget**	**YTD actual**	**YTD budget**	**YTD variance**	**Annual budget**
Utility Expense						
Gas and electric	$199	$197	$1,405	$1,377	$28	$2,361
Water and sewer	646	610	4,480	4,267	213	7,315
Total utility expense	**$845**	**$806**	**$5,885**	**$5,644**	**$241**	**$9,676**
Total operating expenses	**$5,393**	**$5,273**	**$37,757**	**$36,912**	**$846**	**$63,277**

Reserve Expense Allocations (The amounts listed below are added to each year, into interest-bearing accounts, in preparation for high-cost, anticipated major repairs or replacements.)

	Monthly actual	**Monthly budget**	**YTD actual**	**YTD budget**	**YTD variance**	**Annual budget**
Site components	$823	$839	$5,993	$5,876	$118	$10,073
Plumbing	900	900	6,618	6,303	315	10,805
Building systems	515	566	3,725	3,963	-238	6,794
Building stairwells	139	137	890	957	-67	1,640
Total reserve expense alloc.	**$2,378**	**$2,443**	**$17,227**	**$17,099**	**$128**	**$29,312**
Total operating expense & reserve allocations	**$7,771**	**$7,716**	**$54,984**	**$54,010**	**$973**	**$92,589**
Net income (loss)	**-$2,241**	**-$2,180**	**-$16,292**	**-$15,257**	**-$1,035**	**-$26,154**

Insight

What you learn from an income statement:

In a business, the income statement shows the profit or loss for the month (or the year, if an annual statement).

The income statement sometimes is known as the profit and loss statement.

In a Community Association, this summary shows how actual spending is progressing, compared with the original estimated budget for the year.

Keep in mind, the annual budget is a best guess and a guideline for what will happen during the year.

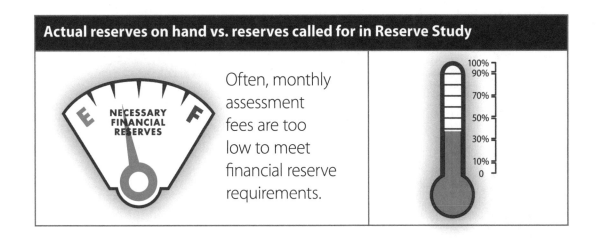

Actual reserves on hand vs. reserves called for in Reserve Study

Often, monthly assessment fees are too low to meet financial reserve requirements.

NECESSARY FINANCIAL RESERVES

E   F

Sample Monthly Balance Sheet

Month Ending July 31, 2010

Assets	
Cash in checking (operating checking)	$23,895
Cash in reserve money market account	58,750
Cash in certificates of deposit — reserves	95,000
Assessments receivable	4,590
Prepaid expenses (insurance, taxes, etc.)	2,985
Total assets	**$185,220**
Liabilities and fund balances	
Prepaid owner assessments	$4,218
Accounts payable — operating	3,895
Accounts payable — reserves	3,750
Total liabilities	**$11,863**
Fund balances (equity)	
Operating fund	$23,357
Reserve fund	150,000
Total fund balances	**$173,357**
Total liabilities and fund balances	**$185,220**

Actual reserves on hand vs. reserves called for in Reserve Study

Often, monthly assessment fees are too low to meet financial reserve requirements.

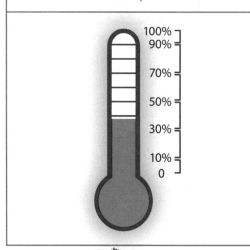

Insight

What you learn from a balance sheet:

The balance sheet is a "snapshot" statement of the assets and liabilities of the Association at a specific date, usually the last day of each month.

Each month, you will see at a glance, the net worth of the Association.

Keep in mind that you must subtract from that total any monthly fees that are late and still owed to the Association.

Sample Monthly Accounts Receivable Report

Month Ending July 31, 2010

Owner Name	Amount	Current	30 Days	60 Days	90 Days
Adrianowicz	2,890	25	250	250	2,365
Krombeen	525	25	250	250	0
Grimes	275	25	250	0	0
Walker	275	25	250	0	0
Gentry	275	25	250	0	0
Anderson	275	25	250	0	0
Thomas	50	25	25	0	0
Scott	25	25	0	0	0
Totals	**$4,590**	**$200**	**$1,525**	**$500**	**$2,365**

 **Warning!**

Monthly fee collections are the *lifeblood* for the financial health of your Association and therefore for your property values.

The collection policy of your Association must be clear to owners, along with other information when new owners move in.

Some owners, while pressed hard for credit card debt and mortgage payments, especially during economic recessions, think the monthly Association dues might not be as urgent to pay. But that is an incorrect assumption.

Review the accounts receivable at least monthly. When collections spiral out of control, the maintenance of the Association can suffer.

 **Best Scenario**

Have a payment and collections policy.

SAMPLE COLLECTION POLICY
- Monthly payments due by first of month.
- 10 days late - Late letter (or late charge, if permitted by governing documents and local state law).
- 30 days late - More urgently worded late letter.
- 60 days late - Account turned over to a collections attorney, with attorney fees to be paid by the late-paying owner. At the county courthouse, a lien is filed against the property.

COLLECTION LETTERS ARE BEST HANDLED BY COMMUNITY ASSOCIATION LAWYER
- Collections are best handled by a hired outside third party. Often, this is the Community Association lawyer, who will comply with the Federal Fair Debt Collections Act.

Sample Reserve Study (condensed version)
Two- or Three-Story Stacked Flats

Neighbors live above or below you.

Sample Reserve Study (condensed version)

Some thoughts as you review this sample Reserve Study

Warning!

Condominium "conversions" can be old, worn-out apartment buildings, recently "flipped" with just fresh paint.

Condominium **conversions** mean that a building has been **converted** through a legal filing, to a multiple-owner, condominium form of ownership.

Unless there has been a complete renovation of major systems, such as plumbing, electrical wiring, roofs and windows, this property can become a financial disaster waiting to happen.

Best Scenario

Contingency reserves are extra reserves

A Reserve Study provides a "best guess" for what may happen in the future at a property. However, it is seldom possible to anticipate every expense/replacement that will be incurred.

Therefore, for example, the California Department of Real Estate (DRE) recommends extra reserve amounts based on their experience with property maintenance costs.

Property type	Minimum extra in contingency reserves
All properties	**3% extra**
Conversion from apartment building	**5% extra**
High-rise building (over 70 feet tall)	**10% extra**

Warning!

Sometimes, long-term infrastructure costs are not yet included in the current reserve study.

In the few states that mandate a reserve study, periodic updates of the reserve study, from every 1 to 5 years, are also mandated.

Major infrastructure components, slated to last more than 20 to 30 years, are often not included in the cost of future capital needs. That is because the current estimated useful life of the component extends beyond the 20- to 30-year time range of the current Reserve Study.

Currently, among prominent reserve study practitioners, there is not consensus yet on when to start adding in the replacement cost of longer-life infrastructure components.

One school of thought is that in the periodic Reserve Study updates, when a major component starts to show signs of premature failure, it is time to include funding plans for that component in the next updated Reserve Study.

Be Aware.

Here is the potential danger to consumers and why periodically updated reserve studies are so important to you.

If faulty major components are found – for example, deteriorating plumbing pipes, electrical wiring, foundations, etc. – the infrastructure replacement costs can be very high. If there is only a short time to ramp up funding for those expensive infrastructure components, the special assessment costs for infrastructure repairs can be very high.

Sample Reserve Study (condensed version)
Condition Assessment

 **Best Scenario**

The persuasive power of on-site digital photos

Reserve Studies often contain color digital photos of deferred maintenance problem areas. Because deferred maintenance happens slowly, it is easy to walk past gradually worsening problems everyday and not notice. Digital photos help bring the problem into focus with the goal of convincing owners to *act now* to fix the problems.

A galvanized iron plumbing pipe, rusting from the inside out, is perilously close to bursting.

Pinhole leaks occurring in copper pipe can cause extensive water damage, can lead to cancellation of insurance, and should be repaired.

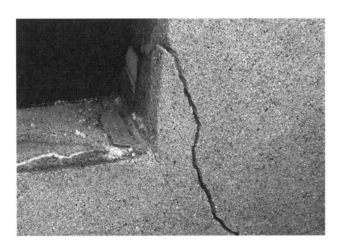

Foundation and settlement cracks can be an indicator of larger underlying problems, which must be addressed.

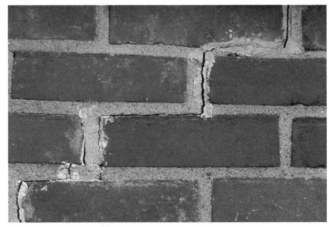

Deteriorating mortar between bricks can be repaired by repointing the bricks. This reduces damaging water intrusion.

 DISCLAIMER — Do not base your monthly fees or reserves on this specific yet theoretical example. Each property is unique, subject to local conditions and local laws. Budget funds for your Association's custom-created, professional Reserve Study.

Sample Reserve Study (condensed version)

Condition Assessment

Asphalt should be seal coated every 3 to 5 years. This extends the life of the asphalt. Cleaning and crack repair should be performed first.

Parking areas with extensive cracking or deterioration that cannot be made watertight should be cut out and patched.

Some wooden components at the property are in very poor condition. When replacing these elements, consider low-maintenance synthetic or cementitious products.

Ornamental ironwork will rust without continuous painting. At the base, tapering with caulking can reduce unsightly and damaging rusting.

Sample Reserve Study (condensed version)

Executive Summary

Major component parts and estimated remaining useful life of components

Component	Approximate quantity	Useful life of component (years)	Remaining useful life of component (years)	Replacement costs for 30 years without inflation factor
Plumbing				
Domestic water lines	All	25	0	$200,000
Sanitary lines	All	35	5	$80,000
Stormwater management		Up to 50	Components expire at planned staggered dates	$7,500
Paving				
Asphalt seal coat	37,400 sq ft	5	3	$44,880
Asphalt pavement, mill and overlay	37,400 sq ft	20	3	$104,720
Concrete curb and gutters (*At 3 milestone dates, replace 60% of systems*)	420 linear ft	Up to 60	Components expire at planned staggered dates	$28,560
Concrete sidewalks (*At 10 milestone dates, replace 60% of the system*)	390 linear ft	Up to 60	Components expire at planned staggered dates	$16,575
Concrete steps (*At 10 milestone dates, replace 60% of the system*)	10	Up to 60	Components expire at planned staggered dates	$7,500

Sample Reserve Study (condensed version)

Executive Summary

Major component parts and estimated remaining useful life of components (continued)

Component	Approximate quantity	Useful life of component (years)	Remaining useful life of component (years)	Replacement costs for 30 years without inflation factor
Roofing components				
Shingle roofs	12,400 sq ft	25	23	$58,900
Gutters and downspouts	860 linear ft	25	23	$5,590
Chimney caps	6	25	23	$4,800
Other exterior components				
Repoint brick work (*At 5 milestone dates, replace 50% of surfaces*)	5,500 sq ft	Up to 50	Components expire at planned staggered dates	$41,250
Trim and shutters	2,800 sq ft	25	0	$29,400
Building caulking	1,800 sq ft	5	0	$21,600
Building stairwells				
Fire alarm system	6	20	0	$30,000
Outside entry doors	6	25	0	$13,200
Carpet	1,200 sq ft	15	15	$4,800
Mailboxes	24	45	5	$3,840
Common interior lights	24	15	15	$3,000
Stairwell windows	6	25	0	$5,400
Emergency and exit lights	18	15	15	$1,710
Entry lights	6	15	15	$1,050
Other site components				
Wooden site components (*At 5 milestone dates, replace 100% of components*)	100	Up to 25	Components expire at planned staggered dates	$27,000
Site lights, poles	7	30	0	$10,500
Site lights, heads	7	15	0	$6,300

DISCLAIMER — Do not base your monthly fees or reserves on this specific yet theoretical example. Each property is unique, subject to local conditions and local laws. Budget funds for your Association's custom-created, professional Reserve Study.

Sample Reserve Study (condensed version)

Executive Summary

Components that may be **EXCLUDED** from the Reserve Study calculations

Insight

Components that are left out of the custom Reserve Study will vary from community to community, based on Association governing documents and other local existing conditions. Examples are listed in the table below.

Type of excluded component	Definition	Examples
Unit owner responsibility Component exclusion	Based on your association's governing documents, some components are a unit owner responsibility.	Windows, garage doors, unit doors
Long-life Component exclusion	Some long-lasting infrastructure components are not yet included in the most current Reserve Study, because the expected useful life of the component extends beyond the 20- to 30-year range of the Reserve Study.	Plumbing pipes, electrical wiring, foundations
Utility Component exclusion	Some components might be maintained by the local utility company.	Primary electric feeds, telephone cables, gas mains and meters
Maintenance and repair Component exclusion	Some components can have ongoing preventive maintenance and repair. This repair cost is an operating expense and not a capital reserve expense.	Operating expense example: • Annual or semi-annual roof inspection and repair Reserve expense example: • Replacing the whole roof
Below threshold cost Component exclusion	If the reserve component is below a certain dollar amount, it is not included in the Reserve Study.	Some Reserve Studies only include components that cost at least $500 or $1,000 to replace. If the component is less than the threshold amount, it is often counted as an operating expense.
Government funded Component exclusion	If a local government maintains and replaces certain components, then these components are left out of the Reserve Study.	Street paving, sidewalks, storm water management

Sample Reserve Study (condensed version)

Executive Summary

Components **EXCLUDED** from the Stacked Flats example Reserve Study

Unit owner responsibility component exclusions

- Unit windows
- Unit doors
- Unit interior
- Domestic water pipes serving one unit
- Sanitary sewers serving one unit
- Electrical wiring serving one unit
- Domestic water pipes serving one unit
- Sanitary sewers serving one unit
- Electrical wiring serving one unit

Long-life component exclusions

- Exterior brick veneer
- Building foundations
- Concrete floor slabs (interior)
- Wall, floor and roof structure
- Common element electrical services
- Electrical wiring

Utility component exclusions

- Primary electric feeds
- Electric transformers
- Cable TV systems and structures
- Telephone cables and structures
- Gas mains and meters

Maintenance and repair component exclusions

- Cleaning of asphalt pavement
- Crack sealing of asphalt pavement
- Painting of curbs
- Striping and numbering of parking spaces
- Landscaping and site grading
- Exterior painting
- Janitorial service
- Repair services
- Partial replacements

Below-threshold cost component exclusions

- Miscellaneous signage
- Bench
- Hose bib
- Fire extinguisher cabinet

Government-funded component exclusions

- Government roadways and parking
- Government sidewalks and curbs
- Government lighting
- Government storm water management

Sample Reserve Study (condensed version)

Estimated Reserve Fund Expenditures 2008 through 2037

2008

$3,315	Concrete sidewalks — 6% of total project
$1,050	Reset pavers — 20% of total project
$1,500	Concrete steps — 6% of total project
$3,150	Site lights — heads
$10,500	Site lights — poles
$100,000	Domestic water lines
$2,500	Stormwater mgmt. — 10% of total project
$13,750	Repoint brickwork — 10% of total project
$14,700	Trim and shutters
$3,600	Building caulking
$6,600	Entry doors
$2,700	Stairwell windows
$15,000	Fire alarm system
$178,365	Total reserve expenses for year

2009

$4,500	Wooden site components — 20% of total project
$4,500	Total reserve expenses for year

2010

No reserve expenditures planned for this year

$0	Total reserve expenses for year

2011

$7,480	Asphalt seal coat
$52,360	Asphalt pavement — mill and overlay
$14,280	Concrete curb and gutter — 20% of total project
$1,050	Reset pavers — 20% of total project
$4,080	Iron railings
$79,250	Total reserve expenses for year

2012

$1,800	Entrance sign
$1,800	Total reserve expenses for year

2013

$80,000	Sanitary lines
$3,600	Building caulking
$3,840	Mailboxes
$87,440	Total reserve expenses for year

Insight

Operating expense versus reserve expenses.

Operating expenses are:

Ongoing, annual expenses, which often arrive as predictable monthly invoices, such as:

- Lawn care services
- Property management and bookkeeping services
- Ordinary, minor repairs
- Insurance, etc.

Reserve expenses are:

Higher-cost, major repairs and replacements, such as:

- Roof replacement
- Foundation repairs
- Siding replacement
- Parking area resurfacing
- Street repaving

Sample Reserve Study (condensed version)

Estimated Reserve Fund Expenditures 2008 through 2037

2014

$3,315	Concrete sidewalks — 6% of total project
$1,050	Reset pavers — 20% of total project
$1,500	Concrete steps — 6% of total project
$4,500	Wooden site components — 20% of total Project
$10,365	Total reserve expenses for year

2015

No reserve expenditures planned for this year

$0	Total reserve expenses for year

2016

$7,480	Asphalt seal coat
$7,480	Total reserve expenses for year

2017

$1,050	Reset pavers — 20% of total project
$1,050	Total reserve expenses for year

2018

$2,500	Stormwater mgmt. — 10% of total project
$13,750	Repoint brickwork — 10% of total project
$3,600	Building caulking
$19,850	Total reserve expenses for year

2019

$4,500	Wooden site components — 20% of total project
$4,500	Total reserve expenses for year

2020

$3,315	Concrete sidewalks — 6% of total project
$1,050	Reset pavers — 20% of total project
$1,500	Concrete steps — 6% of total project
$5,865	Total reserve expenses for year

2021

$7,480	Asphalt seal coat
$7,480	Total reserve expenses for year

2022

No reserve expenditures planned for this year

$0	Total reserve expenses for year

2023

$1,050	Reset pavers — 20% of total project
$3,150	Site lights — heads
$3,600	Building caulking
$1,050	Entry lights
$4,800	Carpet
$3,000	Common interior lights
$1,710	Emergency and exit lights
$18,360	Total reserve expenses for year

2024

$4,500	Wooden site components — 20% of total project
$4,500	Total reserve expenses for year

2025

No reserve expenditures planned for this year

$0	Total reserve expenses for year

Sample Reserve Study (condensed version)

Estimated Reserve Fund Expenditures 2008 through 2037

2026

$7,480	Asphalt seal coat
$3,315	Concrete sidewalks — 6% of total project
$1,050	Reset pavers — 20% of total project
$1,500	Concrete steps — 6% of total project
$13,345	Total reserve expenses for year

2027

No reserve expenditures planned for this year

$0	Total reserve expenses for year

2028

$2,500	Stormwater mgmt. — 10% of total project
$13,750	Repoint brickwork — 10% of total project
$3,600	Building caulking
$15,000	Fire alarm system
$34,850	Total reserve expenses for year

2029

$1,050	Reset pavers
$4,500	Wooden site components — 20% of total project
$5,550	Total reserve expenses for year

2030

No reserve expenditures planned for this year

$0	Total reserve expenses for year

2031

$7,480	Asphalt seal coat
$52,360	Asphalt pavement — mill and overlay
$14,280	Concrete curb and gutter — 20% of total project
$58,900	Shingle roofs
$5,590	Gutters and downspouts
$4,800	Chimney caps
$143,410	Total reserve expenses for year

2032

$3,315	Concrete sidewalks — 6% of total project
$1,050	Reset pavers — 20% of total project
$1,500	Concrete steps — 6% of total project
$1,800	Entrance sign
$7,665	Total reserve expenses for year

2033

$100,000	Domestic water lines
$14,700	Trim and shutters
$3,600	Building caulking
$6,600	Entry doors
$2,700	Stairwell windows
$127,600	Total reserve expenses for year

Sample Reserve Study (condensed version)

Estimated Reserve Fund Expenditures 2008 through 2037

2034

$4,500	Wooden site components — 20% of total project
$4,500	Total reserve expenses for year

2035

$1,050	Reset pavers — 20% of total project
$1,050	Total reserve expenses for year

2036

$7,480	Asphalt seal coat
$4,080	Iron railings
$11,560	Total reserve expenses for year

2037

No reserve expenditures planned for this year

$0	Total reserve expenses for year

30-year TOTAL needed for reserve expenses:

$780,355

Sample Reserve Study (condensed version)

Estimated Reserve Fund Expenditures by Year

2008 through 2037

Insight

Often, capital expenditures can vary dramatically from year to year, as shown below.

The black line near the bottom of the graph shows the average annual expenditure of money.

As the property ages, it generally costs more to maintain. That is because:

- More building components will reach the end of their useful life and must be replaced.
- Future expenditures are often figured with an estimated inflation rate such as 3% per year.

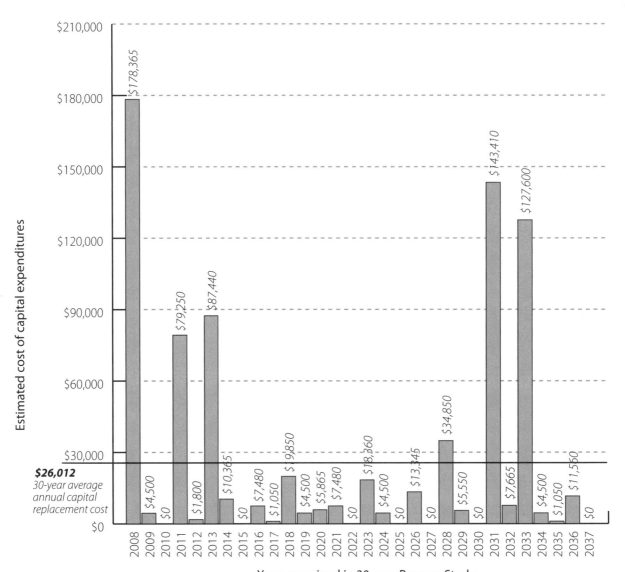

$26,012
30-year average annual capital replacement cost

Estimated cost of capital expenditures

Years examined in 30-year Reserve Study

Sample Reserve Study (condensed version)

Estimated Reserve Fund Expenditures by Category

2008 through 2037

30-year total needed for reserve expenses: **$780,335**

30-year average annual spending for reserve expenses: **$26,011**

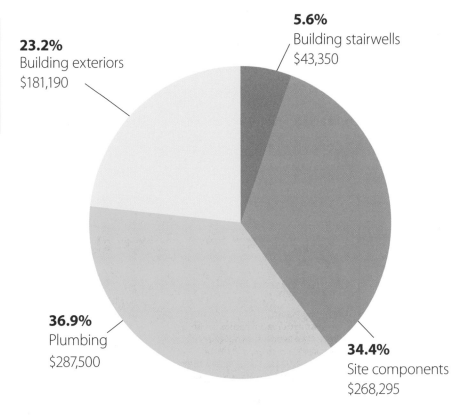

5.6%
Building stairwells
$43,350

23.2%
Building exteriors
$181,190

36.9%
Plumbing
$287,500

34.4%
Site components
$268,295

Site Components

Asphalt seal coat	$44,880
Asphalt pavement, mill and overlay	104,720
Concrete curb and gutter	28,560
Concrete sidewalks	16,575
Reset pavers	10,500
Concrete steps	7,500
Iron railings	8,160
Wooden site components	27,000
Entrance sign	3,600
Site lights, heads	6,300
Site lights, poles	10,500
TOTAL	**$268,295**

Plumbing

Domestic water lines	$200,000
Sanitary lines	80,000
Stormwater management	7,500
TOTAL	**$287,500**

Building Stairwells

Carpet	$4,800
Mailboxes	3,840
Common interior lights	3,000
Emergency and exit lights	1,710
Fire alarm system	30,000
TOTAL	**$43,350**

Building Exteriors

Shingle roofs	$58,900
Gutters and downspouts	5,590
Chimney caps	4,800
Repoint brickwork	41,250
Trim and shutters	29,400
Building caulking	21,600
Outside entry doors	13,200
Stairwell windows	5,400
Entry lights	1,050
TOTAL	**$181,190**

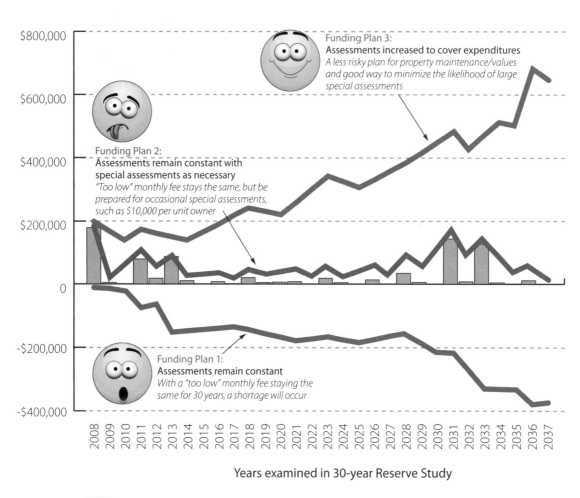

Sample Reserve Study (condensed version)

Three Alternative Funding Plans vs. Component Costs

2008 through 2037

Warning!

Often in a professional Reserve study, various funding plans are charted. For example, if the monthly maintenance fee starts too low at the beginning of the development and is never raised, there can be dire financial consequences.

Funding Plan 3:
Assessments increased to cover expenditures
A less risky plan for property maintenance/values and good way to minimize the likelihood of large special assessments

Funding Plan 2:
Assessments remain constant with special assessments as necessary
"Too low" monthly fee stays the same, but be prepared for occasional special assessments, such as $10,000 per unit owner

Funding Plan 1:
Assessments remain constant
With a "too low" monthly fee staying the same for 30 years, a shortage will occur

Years examined in 30-year Reserve Study

☐ Estimated cash needs
▬ **Funding Plan 1:** Assessments remain constant throughout 30-year projection
▬ **Funding Plan 2:** Assessments remain constant with special assessments as necessary
▬ **Funding Plan 3:** Assessments increased to cover expenditures

Sample Reserve Study (condensed version)

Cash-Flow Analysis

2008 through 2037

Just as in a business, having cash available to cover expenses each year is necessary for economic survival. Positive cash flow usually does not happen by accident.

Often in Reserve Studies, there is a cash-flow analysis that projects cash availability with an overlay of:

- Reserve expenditures
- Reserve contributions
- Cash on hand

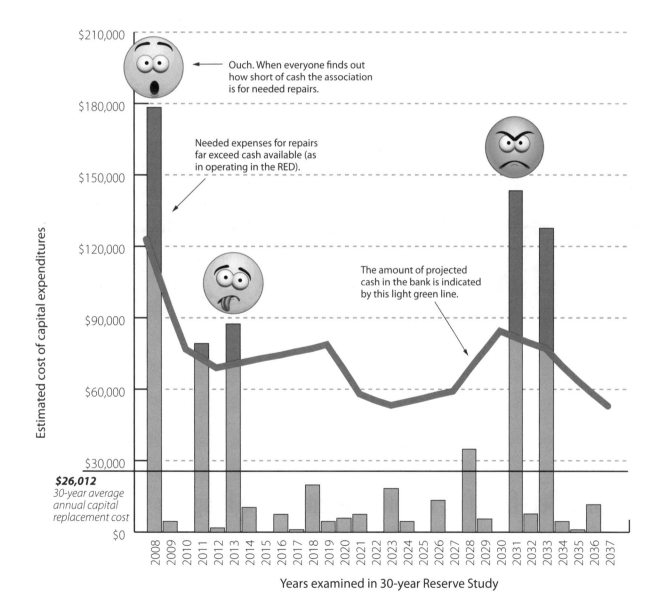

Ouch. When everyone finds out how short of cash the association is for needed repairs.

Needed expenses for repairs far exceed cash available (as in operating in the RED).

The amount of projected cash in the bank is indicated by this light green line.

Estimated cost of capital expenditures

$26,012
30-year average annual capital replacement cost

Years examined in 30-year Reserve Study

Sample Preventive-Maintenance Check List
Executive Summary

Roof Flashing
Water leaks frequently occur in the flashing area, where the roof sections join.

Chimney Crowns
Cracking naturally occurs here, over time, allowing damaging water leaks.

Roof Shingles
Water damage can occur from routine high winds, which cause single nails to pop up, giving water a chance to leak inside.

Gutter Screens
These provide good value, especially in areas with mature trees.

Foundation
After a hard rain, check to see if water is pooling at any foundations. (Grade dirt so water drains *away* from foundations.)

Exterior Painting
Consider annual touch-up painting, in between regular multiple-year painting cycles.

Downspouts
Leaves and seedlings lodged in downspouts cause water to back up in the drainage system.

Cost-Saving Benefits of a Preventive-Maintenance Program

A preventive-maintenance checklist helps you to manage your property.

By carefully prolonging the life of building components, and systematically monitoring those components at least each spring and fall, you can help reduce the frequency of expensive, unanticipated emergency repairs.

Sample Preventive-Maintenance Check List

Property Map (Overview of Property)

Ideas

Clearer communication with vendors by providing:

1. Map of property
2. Digital photos of problem areas

If you do not have a map of your property,

1. Check for a copy of the plat, on file at the county courthouse.
2. Go to *www.googlearth*, key in your address, pull up a satellite view of the property, and trace over it for accurate sizing.

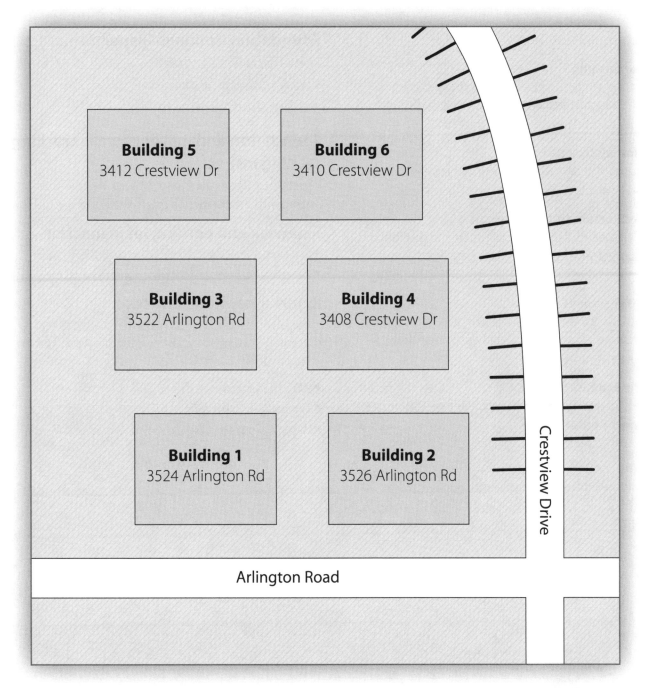

Building 5
3412 Crestview Dr

Building 6
3410 Crestview Dr

Building 3
3522 Arlington Rd

Building 4
3408 Crestview Dr

Building 1
3524 Arlington Rd

Building 2
3526 Arlington Rd

Crestview Drive

Arlington Road

Sample Preventive-Maintenance Check List

This list *does not* include monthly, weekly and daily check lists for your building.

Spring

Roof inspection

(Especially on roofs, all inspections and repairs should be performed by an insured, qualified roofing contractor.)

Roof shingles

Check for nail pop-ups on shingles, which are caused by routine high winds. Nail pop-ups cause shingle roof nails to loosen and allow water to leak inside.

Roof flashing

Roof flashing occurs where one roofing section joins another roofing section, chimney, attic exhaust fan vent, etc. This is a prime area for leaks to occur.

Chimney crowns

Cracking naturally occurs at the top of chimneys, which allows water to leak in.

Roof gutters and downspouts

Spring seedlings can clog roof gutters and downspouts. A clogged downspout can cause water to back up in the drainage system.

Gutter screens

Even with gutter screens protection, fine debris should be removed from inside the roof gutter every four to five years.

Attic exhaust fans

Check power ventilator, belts and thermometer on attic exhaust fans.

Outside, ground-level water drains

Check outside, ground-level water drains for leaves or blockage.

Basements

- Signs of water entering foundation cracks?

Foundation drainage inspection

After a hard rain, check to see if:

- Water is pooling at any foundations.
- Water leaks in basements.

Foundation and masonry walls cracking/settling inspection

Inspect foundations and masonry (brick walls) for cracking or settling, which can allow water into the building envelope.

Sidewalk and parking lot inspection

- Review sidewalk condition for new cracks, leveling.
- Review parking lot condition for new cracks, leveling.

Exterior painted surfaces

Possible annual touch-up painting, in between every four- to seven-year painting cycle, to extend life of paint job and protect wood surfaces.

- Wood fluting around doorways
- Exterior door paint condition
- Wrought iron railing paint condition

Sample Preventive-Maintenance Check List

This list *does not* include monthly, weekly and daily check lists for your building.

Fall

Roof inspection

Since fall leaves will be cleaned from gutters and downspouts, inspect roofs, as in springtime, for:

- Roof shingles (look for shingle nail pop-ups)
- Roof flashing
- Chimney crowns

Roof gutters and downspouts

Clean leaves from roof gutters and downspouts by November 1 and again on December 1.

Winterizing and shutting down

- Bring outside water hoses inside to basement.
- Turn off water to outside faucets to prevent freezing.

Fall preventive-maintenance procedures same as spring preventive-maintenance procedures for the following categories:

- Outside, ground-level water drains
- Basements
- Foundation drainage inspection

Basements and hallways

- Test public area smoke detectors.
- In public areas, note any unauthorized infrastructure changes, such as electrical, plumbing, and HVAC.

Major Structural Renovation Expenses Reserve Cost Comparison

Detached, Single-Family Home

In same neighborhood as Stacked Flat Condominium Association and same time of construction

Brief data for this property example

Year built	1962
Quality level of original construction	Above average
Maintenance level since construction	Average
Have any major systems (plumbing, wiring, HVAC) been replaced since construction in 1962?	Central air conditioning installed for the first time in 1976
Cost range for reserve study for a single-family home	$1,500 to $3,000

Insight

What are the major repair and replacement costs for a single-family home?

Most home owners know that major repair and replacement costs for a single-family home represent large future outlays of cash, but few have taken the time to create a Reserve Study for a single-family home.

In the list at the right, are projected major repair and replacement costs for a single family home, in the same neighborhood, constructed at the same time as the Reserve Study for the sample Association property in this section.

This list is presented to readers merely as food for thought, and not for the purposes of a direct comparison of costs between a single-family home and a condominium.

Home owner costs that are not included in the list at right, are the additional day-to-day operating expenses for a single-family home such as removal of leaves from roof gutters, lawn care, snow removal, exterior painting, and other routine minor home repairs.

DISCLAIMER—Life expectancy of component parts will vary based on many factors, such as:
- Quality level of original components
- Local climate conditions
- Interim preventive maintenance if applicable

DISCLAIMER—Actual renovation costs can vary widely based on many factors, such as:
- Local availability of skilled labor
- Quality of component parts used
- Current worldwide demand for raw materials

Major Structural Renovation Expenses Reserve Cost Comparison

Detached, Single-Family Home

Component	Approximate quantity	Useful life of component (years)	Remaining useful life of component (years)	Current average replacement cost	Future average replacement cost
Exterior building elements					
Gutters and downspouts	220 linear ft	15 to 20	7	$1,980	$2,519
Roof, asphalt shingles	23 squares	15 to 20	7	$7,360	$9,364
Walls, masonry, inspections and partial repointing	1,100 sq ft	8 to 12	6	$1,100	$1,698
Windows, frames, paint finishes and sealants	270 sq ft	4 to 6	1	$945	$1,332
Windows and doors, replacement	270 sq ft	45 to 55	6	$9,450	$11,616
Building services elements					
Electrical system, upgrade	1 each	to 75+	28	$9,000	$23,582
Piping, partial replacements	1 each	to 75+	23	$6,000	$13,237
Split system heating and cooling unit	1 system	15 to 20	13	$5,000	$7,820
Water heater	1 each	12 to 15	5	$800	$1,218
Property site elements					
Concrete sidewalk and patio, partial replacements	75 sq ft	to 65	8	$713	$1,131
Railings, metal	28 linear ft	to 40	30	$1,260	$3,537

Who Does What?

Executive summary of volunteer and paid positions to operate the property

Owners to volunteer to serve on the Board of Directors

- President
- Treasurer
- Secretary
- At-large board members

Off-site property management firm

If no outside property management firm is hired, the property is referred to as "self-managed" by volunteers within the Association.

Key staff positions often provided by an off-site Property Management firm may include:

- Community manager
- Customer service coordinator
- Maintenance coordinator
- Bookkeeper

Full-time on-site manager and staff

Often, at larger developments and more upscale developments, a full-time site manager and staff are hired.

Paid part-time outside vendors

Financial and mechanical planning services

- Reserve specialist and staff

Mechanical planning services

- Consulting mechanical engineer

Financial and tax-filing services

- Certified public accountant and staff
- Banking services

Legal services

- Attorney and staff
- Usually has experience as a real estate attorney, as well as community association experience

Insurance services

- Insurance agent and staff

Trade and crafts persons

- Roofing crew
- Plumbing crew
- Electrical crew
- "Handyman" for routine day-to-day repairs
- Painting crew
- Concrete and masonry crew (for sidewalk, foundation and masonry repairs)
- Asphalt and paving crew

Grounds services

- Lawn care crew
- Arborist crew for large tree trimming
- Snow removal crew
- Pest control
- Cleaning / janitorial services
- Trash removal services

Warning!

All vendors must submit annual proof of insurance form(s)

All vendors should be fully insured and submit the annual proof of insurance forms for your records. This insurance includes workers comp, liability and whatever is mandated by laws in your state.

Example B:
Townhome / Patio Home

Neighbors live alongside you.

Maintenance and Financial Planning Documentation

Financial PRO and CON overview of this housing type example

PRO

Affordability, *but with qualifications*

Sometimes, this type of housing is more affordable to both buy and maintain than a single-family home of a similar age and number of square feet, in the same neighborhood.

Maintenance costs are pooled among all the owners, which allows volume discounts from the economy of scale, especially in larger associations, such as this example.

No one living above or below you

Noise from neighbors is an ongoing issue to be worked through in association living. There is still the issue of possible noise from neighbors on either side of you, from your shared wall, but there is no one living above or below you.

Large association benefits, *in this example*

Large associations with adequate budgets often have:

- Clubhouse, pool, tennis court and other amenities
- Full-time, on-site management and maintenance staff

CON

Interior unit mechanical system repair costs

Owner is often completely responsible for all interior mechanical system maintenance, up to and including repair and replacement of heating and cooling systems, deteriorating plumbing pipes, electrical wiring, etc. Check your governing documents.

Brief data for this property example

Number of buildings in the complex	45
Total number of housing units in the complex	240
Year(s) built	1976–1980
Other major buildings/ facilities in the complex	• Clubhouse / recreational building • 3 pools, 3 tennis courts • Gym / spa / rest rooms • On-site office
Quality level of original construction	Average
Maintenance level since construction	Average
Cost range for reserve study	$1,850 to $2,750
Cost range for reserve study update with site visit	$1,500 to $2,000
Cost range for reserve study update without site visit	$600 to $1,000
Current reserve account balance	**$1,138,028**
Recommended reserve account balance	**$2,406,639**

In this example:

Current monthly fee per sample unit $325*

Based on reserve study *and* operating budget analysis

Current monthly fee *underfunding* per sample unit $37

(This is the accumulating deficit per unit, per month, for this sample budget year.)

A Reserve Study, based on the specific components at your Association, is critical for determining an adequate monthly fee.

* *In Condominium Associations with units of different sizes, it is customary to base the monthly fee on a cost-per-square-foot per condominium.*

DISCLAIMER — Each property is unique. Therefore, each property budget is unique, based on local conditions and local laws. Do not use these budget figures from this specific yet theoretical example for your own property.

Monthly fee includes:

Utility costs
- For clubhouse / recreational building, pool area, outdoor lighting

Building and grounds expense
- Spring and fall roofing repairs, roof gutter and downspout cleaning
- Common area repairs
- Pest control for outside of buildings and common areas.
- Lawn care, landscaping, bush trimming, tree trimming, pool maintenance
- Garbage removal

Insurance
- Exterior and common area insurance (You still need to have homeowner's insurance for interior and contents.)

Administrative services
- Management services including taking phone calls from owners, handling resident issues, long-range planning, vendor bidding for maintenance projects and vendor job oversight
- Bookkeeping and monthly invoice payments
- CPA-produced tax returns and trial balance

Financial reserve expense
- Systematic savings for large capital expenses such as roof replacement, siding replacement, exterior painting, wood fence replacement, street repaving and more

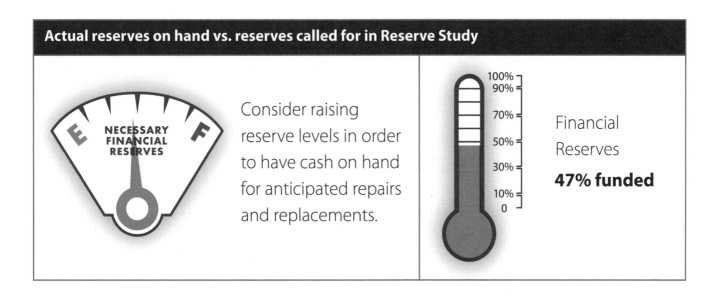

Actual reserves on hand vs. reserves called for in Reserve Study

Consider raising reserve levels in order to have cash on hand for anticipated repairs and replacements.

Financial Reserves **47% funded**

Sample Annual Budget

Fiscal Year — January 1 through December 31

Income	current year	% of budget	$ per month
Monthly Assessments	$1,044,706	99.4%	$362.75
Special assessments	0	0.0%	0.00
Interest income	150	0.0%	0.05
Other income	6,000	0.6%	2.08
Total income	**$1,050,856**	**100.0%**	**$364.88**

Operating Expenses (ongoing expenses that occur each year)

Buildings Expense	current year	% of budget	$ per month
Maintenance salaries	$112,320	9.6%	$39.00
Payroll taxes / workers' comp	19,094	1.6%	6.63
Health insurance — employees	13,200	1.1%	4.58
Building repairs	16,000	1.4%	5.56
Roof / gutter repairs	5,000	0.4%	1.74
Plumbing / electrical repairs	4,000	0.3%	1.39
Maintenance supplies	16,000	1.4%	5.56
Cleaning / janitorial	5,200	0.4%	1.81
Pest control	6,300	0.5%	2.19
Clubhouse	6,300	0.5%	2.19
Water & sewer	100,800	8.6%	35.00
Electric — common areas	32,136	2.8%	11.16
Trash / refuse pickup	47,250	4.1%	16.41
Total buildings expense	**$383,600**	**32.9%**	**$133.19**

Grounds Expense	current year	% of budget	$ per month
Groundskeeping salaries	$99,840	8.6%	$34.67
Payroll taxes / workers' comp	16,973	1.5%	5.89
Health insurance — employees	13,200	1.1%	4.58
Tree pruning	10,000	0.9%	3.47
Arborist / consultant	1,000	0.1%	0.35
Plant / tree replacement	5,000	0.4%	1.74
Irrigation repairs	4,000	0.3%	1.39
Pool service / repairs	7,200	0.6%	2.50
Gas — pool heating	8,400	0.7%	2.92
Tennis court repairs	600	0.1%	0.21
Street sweeping	5,700	0.5%	1.98
Sealcoat streets, etc.	2,030	0.2%	0.70
Total grounds expense	**$173,943**	**14.9%**	**$60.40**

Insight

Underfunding the reserves can lead to:

- Special assessments, if permitted by bylaws or state laws
- Neglected maintenance
- Lower property values
- More difficulty selling badly maintained property

DISCLAIMER — Each property is unique. Therefore, each property budget is unique, based on local conditions and local laws. Do not use these budget figures from this specific yet theoretical example for your own property.

Sample Annual Budget

Fiscal Year — January 1 through December 31

Operating Expenses (cont.)

Insurance & Administration	current year	% of budget	$ per month
Bldg / common area insurance	$195,250	16.7%	$67.80
Management contract	50,918	4.4%	17.68
Office / postage / printing	8,000	0.7%	2.78
Local taxes and fees	600	0.1%	0.21
Legal	8,000	0.7%	2.78
Accounting / other professional	4,800	0.4%	1.67
Doubtful account expense	20,000	1.7%	6.94
Total insurance & administration	**$287,568**	**24.7%**	**$99.85**
Total operating expense	**$845,112**	**72.5%**	**$293.44**

Reserve Expense Allocations (The amounts listed below are added to each year, into interest-bearing accounts, in preparation for high-cost, anticipated major repairs or replacements.)

	current year	% of budget	$ per month
Roofs / decks / gutters	$37,049	3.2%	$12.86
Siding — wood	48,753	4.2%	16.93
Siding — shingle	51,333	4.4%	17.82
Other structure	3,572	0.3%	1.24
Painting	31,328	2.7%	10.88
Mechanical / plumbing	2,884	0.2%	1.00
Electrical	7,100	0.6%	2.47
Flooring	1.252	0.1%	0.43
Pool / spa	3,970	0.3%	1.38
Tennis court	952	0.1%	0.33
Landscape / paving / fences	11,662	1.0%	4.05
Recreation facilities	4,999	0.4%	1.74
Miscellaneous	478	0.0%	0.17
Contingency reserve	412	0.0%	0.14
Total reserve expense allocations	**$205,744**	**17.7%**	**$71.44**
Reserves not funded	**$115,594**	**9.9%**	**$40.14**
Total operating exp. & reserve alloc.	**$1,166,450**	**100.0%**	**$405.02**

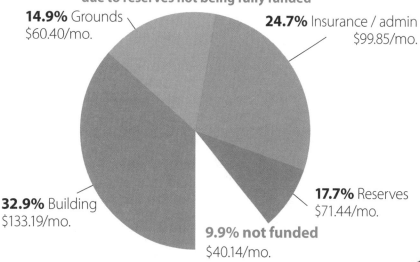

**Annual budget will have shortfall
due to reserves not being fully funded**

14.9% Grounds
$60.40/mo.

24.7% Insurance / admin
$99.85/mo.

32.9% Building
$133.19/mo.

17.7% Reserves
$71.44/mo.

9.9% not funded
$40.14/mo.

Sample Monthly Income Statement

Month Ending July 31, 2009

Income	Monthly actual	Monthly budget	YTD actual	YTD budget	YTD variance	Annual budget
Monthly assessments	$78,120	$78,120	$546,840	$546,840	$0	$937,440
Special assessments	0	0	0	0	0	0
Interest income	10	17	85	117	-32	200
Other income	335	417	3,201	2,917	284	5,000
Total income	**$78,465**	**$78,553**	**$550,126**	**$549,873**	**$253**	**$942,640**

Operating Expenses (ongoing expenses that occur each year)

Building Expense	Monthly actual	Monthly budget	YTD actual	YTD budget	YTD variance	Annual budget
Maintenance salaries	$8,875	$9,000	$63,250	$63,000	$250	$108,000
Payroll taxes / workers' comp	1,400	1,440	10,200	10,080	120	17,280
Health ins. — employees	1,125	1,000	7,450	7,000	450	12,000
Building repairs	1,800	1,250	8,000	8,750	-750	15,000
Roof / gutter repairs	0	417	4,020	2,917	1,103	5,000
Plumbing / electrical repairs	625	333	3,050	2,333	717	4,000
Maintenance supplies	975	1,250	7,700	8,750	-1,050	15,000
Cleaning / janitorial	400	417	3,050	2,917	133	5,000
Pest control	250	500	2,000	3,500	-1,500	6,000
Clubhouse	550	500	4,268	3,500	768	6,000
Water & sewer	8,700	8,000	58,100	56,000	2,100	96,000
Electric — common areas	2,825	2,600	19,420	18,200	1,220	31,200
Trash / refuse pickup	3,725	3,750	25,950	26,250	-300	45,000
Total buildings expense	**$31,250**	**$30,457**	**$216,458**	**$213,197**	**$3,261**	**$365,480**

Grounds Expense	Monthly actual	Monthly budget	YTD actual	YTD budget	YTD variance	Annual budget
Groundskeeping salaries	$8,115	$8,000	$56,840	$56,000	$840	$96,000
Payroll taxes / workers' comp	1,300	1,280	9,240	8,960	280	15,360
Health ins. — employees	1,125	1,000	7,500	7,000	500	12,000
Tree pruning	0	667	6,000	4,667	1,333	8,000
Arborist / consultant	0	83	0	583	-583	1,000
Plant / tree replacement	900	417	2,500	2,917	-417	5,000
Irrigation repairs	880	292	2,040	2,042	-2	3,500
Pool service / repairs	575	550	3,950	3,850	100	6,600
Gas — pool heating	350	667	3,500	4,667	-1,167	8,000
Tennis court repairs	0	50	0	350	-350	600
Street sweeping	450	450	3,150	3,150	0	5,400
Snow removal	0	0	0	0	0	0
Sealcoat streets, etc.	0	133	0	933	-933	1,600
Total grounds expense	**$13,695**	**$13,588**	**$94,720**	**$95,118**	**-$398**	**$163,060**

Insight

What you learn from an income statement:

In a business, the income statement shows the profit or loss for the month (or the year, if an annual statement).

The income statement sometimes is known as the profit and loss statement.

In a Community Association, this summary shows how actual spending is progressing, compared with the original estimated budget for the year.

Keep in mind, the annual budget is a best guess and a guideline for what will happen during the year.

DISCLAIMER — Each property is unique. Therefore, each property budget is unique, based on local conditions and local laws. Do not use these budget figures from this specific yet theoretical example for your own property.

Sample Monthly Income Statement

Month Ending July 31, 2009

Operating Expenses (cont.) **Insurance & Administration**	**Monthly actual**	**Monthly budget**	**YTD actual**	**YTD budget**	**YTD variance**	**Annual budget**
Bldg / common area ins.	$15,550	$14,792	$109,250	$103,542	$5,708	$177,500
Management contract	4,080	4,080	28,560	28,560	0	48,960
Office / postage / printing	609	650	4,603	4,552	51	7,803
Local taxes and fees	0	50	500	350	150	600
Legal	1,225	667	5,950	4,667	1,283	8,000
Acctg / other professional	0	375	3,000	2,625	375	4,500
Doubtful acct expense	3,250	500	11,500	3,500	8,000	6,000
Total insurance & admin.	**$24,714**	**$21,114**	**$163,363**	**$147,795**	**$15,568**	**$253,363**
Total operating expenses	**$69,659**	**$65,159**	**$474,541**	**$456,110**	**$18,431**	**$781,903**

Reserve Expense Allocations (The amounts listed below are added to each year, into interest-bearing accounts, in preparation for high-cost, anticipated major repairs or replacements.)

	Monthly actual	**Monthly budget**	**YTD actual**	**YTD budget**	**YTD variance**	**Annual budget**
Roofs / decks / gutters	$2,412	$2,412	$16,884	$16,884	$0	$28,944
Siding — wood	3,174	3,174	22,218	22,218	0	38,088
Siding — shingle	3,342	3,342	23,394	23,394	0	40,104
Other structure	233	233	1,628	1,628	0	2,791
Painting	2,040	2,040	14,277	14,277	0	24,475
Mechanical / plumbing	188	188	1,314	1,314	0	2,253
Electrical	462	462	3,236	3,236	0	5,547
Flooring	82	82	571	571	0	978
Pool / spa	258	258	1,809	1,809	0	3,102
Tennis court	62	62	434	434	0	743
Landscape / paving / fences	755	755	5,287	5,287	0	9,064
Recreation facilities	325	325	2,278	2,278	0	3,905
Miscellaneous	31	31	218	218	0	374
Contingency reserve	31	31	215	215	0	368
Total reserve expense alloc.	**$13,395**	**$13,395**	**$93,763**	**$93,763**	**$18,431**	**$160,737**
Total operating expense & reserve allocations	**$83,054**	**$78,553**	**$568,304**	**$549,873**	**-$18,178**	**$942,640**
Net income (loss)	**-$4,589**	**$0**	**-$18,178**	**$0**	**-$18,178**	**$0**

Actual reserves on hand vs. reserves called for in Reserve Study

NECESSARY FINANCIAL RESERVES

E   F

Often, monthly assessment fees are too low to meet financial reserve requirements.

100%
90%
70%
50%
30%
10%
0

Sample Monthly Balance Sheet

Month Ending July 31, 2009

Assets	
Cash in checking (operating checking)	$12,065
Cash in reserve money market account	139,028
Cash in certificates of deposit — reserves	1,000,000
Assessments receivable	23,965
Prepaid expenses (insurance, taxes, etc.)	5,250
Total assets	**1,180,308**
Liabilities and fund balances	
Prepaid owner assessments	$9,625
Accounts payable — operating	8,335
Accounts payable — reserves	1,000
Total liabilities	**$18,960**
Fund balances (equity)	
Operating fund	$23,320
Reserve fund	1,138,028
Total fund balances	**1,161,348**
Total liabilities and fund balances	**$1,180,308**

Actual reserves on hand vs. reserves called for in Reserve Study

Often, monthly assessment fees are too low to meet financial reserve requirements.

Insight

What you learn from a balance sheet:

The balance sheet is a "snapshot" statement of the assets and liabilities of the Association at a specific date, usually the last day of each month.

Each month, you will see at a glance, the net worth of the Association.

Keep in mind that you must subtract from that total any monthly fees that are late and still owed to the Association.

Sample Monthly Accounts Receivable Report

Month Ending July 31, 2009

Owner Name/Address	Amount	Current	30 Days	60 Days	90 Days
John Smith — 4211 Fairfield Place	325.50		325.50		
Jane Doe — 4323 Vista Court	651.00			651.00	
Richard & Ann Jones — 4424 Avon Place	3,906.00				3,906.00
Sarah Sabatino — 4123 LaRosa Court	651.00			651.00	
Eric & Karen Costas — 4222 Fiesta Place	325.50			325.50	
James Cohen — 4343 San Marcos Circle	325.50		325.50		
Katherine Wyatt — 4423 Fairfield Place	325.50		325.50		
Amanda Attarzadeh — 4121 Vista Court	325.50		325.50		
Margaret Hunter — 4420 Avon Place	325.50			325.50	
Olivia Flores — 4125 LaRosa Court	651.00			651.00	
Kim Hughes — 4333 Fiesta Place	1,953.00				1,953.00
Martha Ryan — 4424 San Marcos Circle	325.00		325.00		
(Page 2 of Receivable Report not shown)	$14,200.00		$5,532.50	$1,692.00	$6,650.00
Total Accounts Receivable	**$23,965.00**		**$7,160.00**	**$4,296.00**	**$12,509.00**

Warning!

Monthly fee collections are the *lifeblood* for the financial health of your Association and therefore for your property values.

The collection policy of your Association must be clear to owners, along with other information when new owners move in.

Some owners, while pressed hard for credit card debt and mortgage payments, especially during economic recessions, think the monthly association dues might not be as urgent to pay. But that is an incorrect assumption.

Review the accounts receivable at least monthly. When collections spiral out of control, the maintenance of the Association can suffer.

Best Scenario

Have a payment and collections policy.

SAMPLE COLLECTION POLICY
- Monthly payments due by first of month.
- 10 days late - Late letter (or late charge, if permitted by governing documents and local state law).
- 30 days late - More urgently worded late letter.
- 60 days late - Account turned over to a collections attorney, with attorney fees to be paid by the late-paying owner. At the county courthouse, a lien is filed against the property.

COLLECTION LETTERS ARE BEST HANDLED BY COMMUNITY ASSOCIATION LAWYER
- Collections are best handled by a hired outside third party. Often, this is the Community Association lawyer, who will comply with the Federal Fair Debt Collections Act.

Sample Reserve Study (condensed version)
Townhome / Patio Home

Neighbors live alongside you.

Sample Reserve Study (condensed version)

Some thoughts as you review this sample Reserve Study

 **Best Scenario**

 **Warning!**

Contingency reserves are extra reserves

A reserve study provides a best guess for what may happen in the future at a property. However, it is seldom possible to anticipate every expense/replacement that will be incurred.

Therefore, for example, the California Department of Real Estate (DRE) recommends extra reserve amounts based on their experience with property maintenance costs.

Property type	Minimum extra in contingency reserves
All properties	**3% extra**
Conversion from apartment building	**5% extra**
High-rise building (over 70 feet tall)	**10% extra**

Sometimes, long-term infrastructure costs are not yet included in the current Reserve Study.

In the few states that mandate a Reserve Study, periodic updates of the Reserve Study, from every 1 to 5 years, are also mandated.

Major infrastructure components, slated to last more than 20 to 30 years, are often not included in the cost of future capital needs. That is because the current estimated useful life of the component extends beyond the 20- to 30-year time range of the current Reserve Study.

Currently, among prominent reserve study practitioners, there is not consensus yet on when to start adding in the replacement cost of longer-life infrastructure components.

One school of thought is that in the periodic Reserve Study updates, when a major component starts to show signs of premature failure, it is time to include funding plans for that component in the next updated Reserve Study.

Be aware.

Here is the potential danger to consumers and why periodically updated Reserve Studies are so important to you.

If faulty major components are found – for example, deteriorating plumbing pipes, electrical wiring, foundations, etc. – the infrastructure replacement costs can be very high. If there is only a short time to ramp up funding for those expensive infrastructure components, the special assessment costs for infrastructure repairs can be very high.

Sample Reserve Study (condensed version)
Condition Assessment

 ✓ **Best Scenario**

The persuasive power of on-site digital photos

Reserve Studies often contain color digital photos of deferred-maintenance problem areas. Since deferred maintenance happens slowly, it is easy to walk past gradually worsening problems everyday and not notice. Digital photos help bring the problem into focus with the goal of convincing owners to *act now* to fix the problems.

Deteriorated paint on wood siding will lead to warping, cupping and deterioration of the wood. This deterioration allows for water intrusion and mold.

Deteriorated paint on wood railings will accelerate degradation of the wood, as well as increase the cost of future paint preparation.

Deteriorated paint on wood fencing and missing boards will lead to premature degradation of fencing, resulting in costly early replacement and loss of privacy.

Inoperable sump pump may allow flooding and water damage during heavy rains.

DISCLAIMER — Do not base your monthly fees or reserves on this specific yet theoretical example. Each property is unique, subject to local conditions and local laws. Budget funds for your Association's custom-created, professional Reserve Study.

Sample Reserve Study (condensed version)
Condition Assessment

Deteriorated composition shingle roofing may promote damage to roofing structure (such as the supporting roof trusses below the shingles) as well as leakage and damage to units under the roof.

Missing and damaged waterline pool tile is more of an aesthetic issue, but continued degradation could harm plaster, the filtration system and users of the pool.

Vertically displaced concrete flatwork can likely be a trip hazard causing legal exposure to the association.

Cracked brick siding could be indicative of structural problems. It will also allow for moisture intrusion and potential damage to the structure. Water intrusion can also open the possibility of mold problems.

Sample Reserve Study (condensed version)

Executive Summary

Major component parts and estimated remaining useful life of components

Component	Approximate quantity	Useful life of component (years)	Remaining useful life of component (years)	Replacement costs for 30 years with inflation factor of 2.85% annually
Roof replacement				
Buildings 1 through 11	89,750 sq ft	30	21	$588,229
Buildings 12 through 22	89,750 sq ft	30	22	$588,229
Buildings 23 through 33	89,750 sq ft	30	23	$588,229
Buildings 34 through 44	89,750 sq ft	30	24	$588,229
Clubhouse / rec building	2,800 sq ft	30	25	$0*
Gutters and downspouts	45 buildings	35	1	$0*
Structural				
Siding — wood	162,450 sq ft	40	25	$3,068,697
Siding — shingle	162,450 sq ft	35	19	$2,239,504
Wood arbors	14,750 sq ft	30	20	$219,804
Foundations / structural frame	45 buildings	30+	30+	0*
Structural pest control	6,059,700 cu ft	N/A	N/A	0*
Painting				
Exterior flatwork	357,350 sq ft	4	2	$6,482,099
Doors	615 sides	5	3	$548,594
Wood fencing	56,550 sq ft	4	2	$613,111

*Please refer to Warning icon on page 101.

Sample Reserve Study (condensed version)

Executive Summary

Major component parts and estimated remaining useful life of components (continued)

Component	Approximate quantity	Useful life of component (years)	Remaining useful life of component (years)	Replacement costs for 30 years with inflation factor of 2.85% annually
Landscape / paving				
Wood fencing	5,650 sq ft	12	10	$1,655,504
Asphalt overlay (streets and driveways)	63,150 sq ft	20	12	$137,130
Asphalt seal coat	63,150 sq ft	5	5	$78,861
Concrete block walls	Lifetime	30+	30+	0*
Concrete flatwork	Lifetime	30+	30+	0*
Irrigation system time clocks	9 time clocks	10	5	$64,752
Electrical				
Lighting — buildings	990 fixtures	20	10	$124,542
Lighting — street (fixtures)	15 fixtures	25	0	$33,952
Lighting — street (posts)	15 posts	N/A	N/A	$12,750
Lighting — tennis courts	24 fixtures	25	16	$28,212
Pool / spa				
Acrylic decks — resurface	6,900 sq ft	20	10	$73,163
Acrylic decks — coating	6,900 sq ft	10	5	$56,783
Fiberglass pools (#1 and #2)	3,000 sq ft	15	10	$73,019
Coping / tile	460 ln ft	20	8	$57,910
Furniture — replace	83 items	15	5	$49,663
Furniture — refurbish	83 items	5	0	$39,888
Clubhouse / rec building				
Carpet	390 sq yds	8	0	$60,992
A/C coils	5 coils	24	0	$39,543
A/C condensers	5@ 3–3.5 tons	12	3	$64,068

*Please refer to Warning icon on page 101.

Sample Reserve Study (condensed version)
Executive Summary
Components that may be **EXCLUDED** from the Reserve Study calculations

Components that are left out of the custom Reserve Study will vary from community to community, based on Association governing documents and other local existing conditions. Examples are listed in the table below.

Type of excluded component	Definition	Examples
Unit owner responsibility Component exclusion	Based on your association's governing documents, some components are a unit owner responsibility.	Windows, garage doors, unit doors
Long-life Component exclusion	Some long-lasting infrastructure components are not yet included in the most current Reserve Study, because the expected useful life of the component extends beyond the 20- to 30-year range of the Reserve Study.	Plumbing pipes, electrical wiring, foundations
Utility Component exclusion	Some components might be maintained by the local utility company.	Primary electric feeds, telephone cables, gas mains and meters
Maintenance and repair Component exclusion	Some components can have ongoing preventive maintenance and repair. This repair cost is an operating expense and not a capital reserve expense.	Operating expense example: • Annual or semi-annual roof inspection and repair Reserve expense example: • Replacing the whole roof
Below threshold cost Component exclusion	If the reserve component is below a certain dollar amount, it is not included in the Reserve Study.	Some Reserve Studies only include components that cost at least $500 or $1,000 to replace. If the component is less than the threshold amount, it is often counted as an operating expense.
Government funded Component exclusion	If a local government maintains and replaces certain components, then these components are left out of the Reserve Study.	Street paving, sidewalks, storm water management

DISCLAIMER — Do not base your monthly fees or reserves on this specific yet theoretical example. Each property is unique, subject to local conditions and local laws. Budget funds for your Association's custom-created, professional Reserve Study.

Sample Reserve Study (condensed version)

Executive Summary

Components **EXCLUDED** from the Townhome / Patio Home example Reserve Study

Unit owner responsibility component exclusions

- Unit windows
- Unit doors
- Unit interior
- Garage doors
- Heating, ventilating and air conditioning (HVAC) equipment that is inside the individual unit

Long-life component exclusions

- Foundations / structural frame
- Chain link fencing
- Concrete block walls
- Concrete flatwork

Utility component exclusions

- Primary electric feeds
- Electric transformers
- Cable TV systems and structures
- Telephone cables and structures
- Gas mains and meters

Maintenance and repair component exclusions

- Structural pest control
- Utility doors
- Parking stripes
- Curb painting

Below-threshold cost component exclusions

- Reserve expenditures that are less than $300 are not included

Government-funded component exclusions

- Government roadways and parking
- Government sidewalks and curbs
- Government lighting
- Government stormwater management

Sample Reserve Study (condensed version)

Estimated Reserve Fund Expenditures 2008 through 2037

2008

$5,750	Mechanical — furnaces
$13,350	Mechanical — evaporative coils
$600	Plumbing — circulation pump
$1,300	Plumbing — water heater
$5,500	Electrical — lighting — yard
$11,250	Electrical — street — fixtures
$12,750	Electrical — lighting — street (posts)
$10,550	Flooring — carpet
$6,800	Pool / spa — furniture — refurbish
$8,100	Tennis court — playing surfaces
$2,400	Tennis court — windscreen
$16,000	Recreation facilities — saunas — refinish
$1,550	Recreation facilities — saunas — heaters
$300	Recreation facilities — billiard table
$4,813	Contingency reserve
$101,063	Total reserve expenses for year

2009

$1,080	Plumbing — drinking fountain — chilled
$54	Contingency reserve
$1,134:	Total reserve expenses for year

2010

$644,712	Paint — exterior flatwork
$60,981	Paint — wood fencing
$2,856	Pool / spa — fiberglass — spa
$1,957	Pool / spa — motors
$1,111	Tennis courts — nets
$35,581	Contingency reserve
$747,198	Total reserve expenses for year

2011

$62,554	Paint — doors
$8,921	Paint — interior flatwork
$2,775	Paint — wallpaper
$8,594	Paint — ironwork
$14,686	Mechanical — condensers
$979	Flooring — vinyl
$6,255	Recreation facilities — restrooms
$5,238	Contingency reserve
$110,002	Total reserve expenses for year

2012

$2,070	Pool / spa — pumps
$4,363	Landscape / paving
$18,461	Recreation facilities — furnishings
$1,245	Contingency reserve
$26,139	Total reserve expenses for year

2013

$13,925	Pool / spa — acrylic decks — coating
$1,093	Paint — parking stripes
$806	Paint — curb
$2,531	Plumbing — drinking fountain — non-chilled
$2,590	Pool / spa — coping joint
$1,449	Pool / spa — chlorinators
$19,678	Pool / spa — furniture replace
$9,321	Tennis court — playing surfaces
$11,679	Landscape / paving — asphalt seal coat
$15,881	Landscape / paving — irrigation system — time clocks
$10,069	Recreation facilities — office equipment
$4,451	Contingency reserve
$93,464	Total reserve expenses for year

Insight

Operating expense versus reserve expenses.

Operating expenses are:

Ongoing, annual expenses, which often arrive as predictable monthly invoices, such as:

- Lawn care services
- Property management and bookkeeping services
- Ordinary, minor repairs
- Insurance, etc.

Reserve expenses are:

Higher-cost, major repairs and replacements, such as:

- Roof replacement
- Foundation repairs
- Siding replacement
- Parking area resurfacing
- Street repaving

Sample Reserve Study (condensed version)

Estimated Reserve Fund Expenditures 2008 through 2037

2014

$721,354	Paint — exterior flatwork
$68,230	Paint — wood fencing
$5,858	Flooring — tile
$39,772	Contingency reserve
$835,214	Total reserve expenses for year

2015

$1,582	Plumbing — water heater
$5,114	Pool / spa — filters
$2,252	Pool / spa — motors
$1,278	Tennis court — nets
$23,127	Recreation facilities — gym equipment
$5,601	Recreation facilities — kitchen
$7,363	Miscellaneous — directory boards
$1,644	Miscellaneous — washer / dryer
$2,398	Contingency reserve
$50,359	Total reserve expenses for year

2016

$71,983	Paint — doors
$9,890	Paint — wood fencing
$13,208	Flooring — carpet
$21,031	Pool / spa — coping / tile
$11,079	Pool / spa — heaters
$3,003	Tennis court — windscreen
$6,510	Contingency reserve
$136,704	Total reserve expenses for year

2017

$7,340	Pool / spa — plaster
$2,253	Landscape / paving — wrought iron
$480	Contingency reserve
$10,073	Total reserve expenses for year

2018

$73,163	Pool / spa — acrylic decks — resurface
$807,108	Paint — exterior flatwork
$76,341	Paint — wood fencing
$1,258	Paint — parking stripes
$928	Paint — curb
$795	Plumbing — circulation pump
$124,542	Electrical — lighting — building
$28,932	Pool / spa — fiberglass — pool (#1 and #2)
$9,005	Pool / spa — furniture — refurbish
$10,726	Tennis court — playing surfaces
$13,440	Landscape / paving — asphalt seal coat
$689,587	Landscape / paving — wood fencing
$398	Recreation facilities — billiard table
$12,381	Recreation facilities — manager's apartment
$92,430	Contingency reserve
$1,941,034	Total reserve expenses for year

2019

$11,167	Paint — interior flatwork
$3,474	Paint — wallpaper
$732	Contingency reserve
$15,373	Total reserve expenses for year

2020

$3,782	Pool / spa — fiberglass — spa
$2,592	Pool / spa — motors
$1,470	Tennis court — nets
$137,130	Landscape / paving — asphalt overlay
$7,249	Contingency reserve
$153,223	Total reserve expenses for year

2021

$82,833	Paint — doors
$11,381	Paint — ironwork
$1,512	Plumbing — drinking fountain — chilled
$1,297	Flooring — vinyl
$3,243	Pool / spa — coping joint
$14,192	Miscellaneous — mailboxes
$3,601	Miscellaneous — signs
$5.903	Contingency reserve
$123,962	Total reserve expenses for year

2022

$903,506	Paint — exterior flatwork
$85,416	Paint — wood fencing
$1,925	Plumbing — water heater
$49,520	Contingency reserve
$1,039,917	Total reserve expenses for year

Sample Reserve Study (condensed version)

Estimated Reserve Fund Expenditures 2008 through 2037

2023

$18,440	Pool / spa — acrylic decks — coating
$1,448	Paint — parking stripes
$1,068	Paint — curb
$20,570	Mechanical — condensers
$8,457	Electrical — lighting — yard
$1,907	Pool / spa — chlorinators
$10,362	Pool / spa — furniture — refurbish
$12,342	Tennis court — playing surfaces
$15,466	Landscape / paving — asphalt seal coat
$21,027	Irrigation system — time clocks
$5,554	Contingency reserve
$116,641	Total reserve expenses for year

2024

$28,212	Electrical — lighting — tennis
$16,535	Flooring — carpet
$3,759	Tennis court — windscreen
$2,425	Contingency reserve
$50,931	Total reserve expenses for year

2025

$6,772	Pool / spa — filters
$2,983	Pool / spa — motors
$1,692	Tennis court — nets
$572	Contingency reserve
$12,019	Total reserve expenses for year

2026

$1,010,412	Paint — exterior flatwork
$95,318	Paint — doors
$13,097	Paint — ironwork
$95,570	Paint — wood fencing
$60,720	Contingency reserve
$1,275,117	Total reserve expenses for year

2027

$2,239,504	Structure — siding — shingle
$13,979	Paint — interior flatwork
$4,350	Wallpaper
$9,719	Pool / spa — plaster — pool (main)
$3,155	Pool / spa — pumps
$6,648	Landscape / paving — back flow preventors
$28,130	Recreation facilities — furnishings
$115,274	Contingency reserve
$2,420,759	Total reserve expenses for year

2028

$219,804	Structure — wood arbors
$1,666	Paint — parking stripes
$1,228	Paint — parking stripes
$10,082	Mechanical — furnaces
$1,053	Plumbing — circulation pump
$15,519	Pool / spa — heaters
$29,985	Pool / spa — furniture — replace
$14,203	Tennis court — playing surfaces
$17,797	Landscape / paving — asphalt seal coat
$15,344	Recreation facilities — office equipment
$28,055	Recreation facilities — saunas — refinish
$2,716	Recreation facilities — saunas — heaters
$527	Recreation facilities — billiard table
$17,899	Contingency reserve
$375,878	Total reserve expenses for year

2029

$2,352,918	Roof — composition shingle roof for residences and mailboxes
$2,343	Plumbing — water heater
$4,058	Pool / spa — coping joint
$117,966	Contingency reserve
$2,477,285	Total reserve expenses for year

2030

$1,130,530	Paint — exterior flatwork
$106,931	Paint — wood fencing
$5,010	Pool / spa — fiberglass — spa
$3,432	Pool / spa — motors
$1,947	Tennis court — nets
$965,917	Landscape / paving — wood fencing
$35,244	Recreation facilities — gym equipment
$11,222	Miscellaneous — directory boards
$2,505	Miscellaneous — washer / dryer
$113,137	Contingency reserve
$2,375,875	Total reserve expenses for year

DISCLAIMER — Do not base your monthly fees or reserves on this specific yet theoretical example. Each property is unique, subject to local conditions and local laws. Budget funds for your Association's custom-created, professional Reserve Study.

Sample Reserve Study (condensed version)

Estimated Reserve Fund Expenditures 2008 through 2037

2031

$109,686	Paint — doors
$15,072	Paint — ironwork
$1,717	Flooring — vinyl
$10,968	Recreation facilities — restrooms
$6,872	Contingency reserve
$144,315	Total reserve expenses for year

2032

$26,193	Mechanical — evaporative coils
$20,699	Flooring — carpet
$4,705	Tennis court — windscreen
$3,433	Landscape / paving — wrought iron
$2,752	Contingency reserve
$57,782	Total reserve expenses for year

2033

$24,418	Pool / spa — acrylic decks — coating
$3,068,697	Structure — siding wood
$1,917	Paint — parking stripes
$1,413	Paint — curb
$2,118	Plumbing — drinking fountain — chilled
$4,437	Plumbing — drinking fountain — non-chilled
$22,702	Electrical — lighting — street (fixtures)
$44,087	Pool / spa — fiberglass pool (#1 and #2)
$2,524	Pool / spa — chlorinators
$13,721	Pool / spa — furniture — refurbished
$16,345	Tennis court — playing surfaces
$20,479	Landscape / paving — asphalt seal coat
$27,844	Landscape / paving — irrigation system time clocks
$162,535	Contingency reserve
$3,413,237	Total reserve expenses for year

2034

$1,264,927	Paint — exterior flatwork
$119,642	Paint — wood fencing
$10,272	Flooring — tile
$69,742	Contingency reserve
$1,464,583	Total reserve expenses for year

2035

$17,499	Paint — interior flatwork
$5,447	Paint — wallpaper
$28,812	Mechanical — condensers
$8,967	Pool / spa — filters
$3,949	Pool / spa — motors
$2,240	Tennis court — nets
$9,822	Recreation facilities — kitchen
$3,837	Contingency reserve
$80,573	Total reserve expenses for year

2036

$126,220	Paint — doors
$17,343	Paint — ironwork
$2,854	Plumbing — water heater
$38,879	Pool / spa — coping / tile
$21,625	Miscellaneous — mailboxes
$5,488	Miscellaneous — signs
$10,520	Contingency reserve
$220,929	Total reserve expenses for year

2037

$12,872	Paint — exterior flatwork
$5,081	Paint — wood fencing
$898	Contingency reserve
$18,851	Total reserve expenses for year

30-year TOTAL needed for Reserve Expenses: $19,888,633

Sample Reserve Study (condensed version)

Estimated Reserve Fund Expenditures by Year

2008 through 2037

Insight

Often, capital expenditures can vary dramatically from year to year, as shown below.

The black line near the bottom of the graph shows the average annual expenditure of money.

As the property ages, it generally costs more to maintain. That is because:

- More building components will reach the end of their useful life and must be replaced.
- Future expenditures are often figured with an estimated inflation rate such as 3% per year.

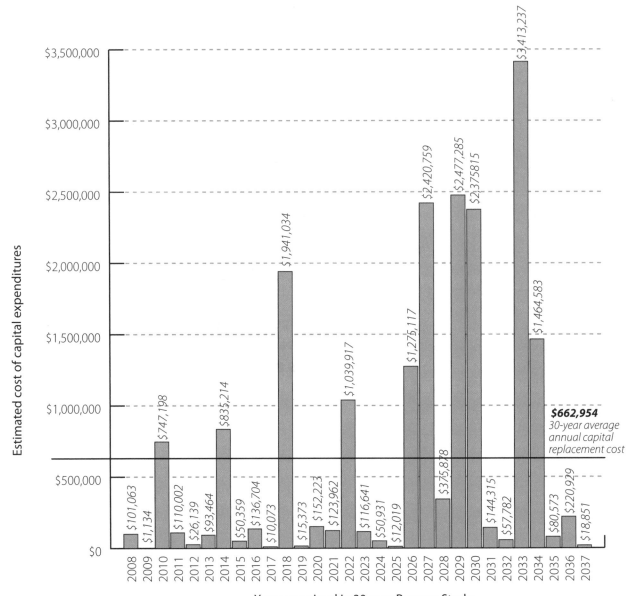

$662,954
30-year average annual capital replacement cost

Estimated cost of capital expenditures

Years examined in 30-year Reserve Study

DISCLAIMER — Do not base your monthly fees or reserves on this specific yet theoretical example. Each property is unique, subject to local conditions and local laws. Budget funds for your Association's custom-created, professional Reserve Study.

Sample Reserve Study (condensed version)

Estimated Reserve Fund Expenditures by Category

2008 through 2037

30-year total needed for reserve expenses: **$19,888,633**

30-year average annual spending for reserve expenses: **$662,954**

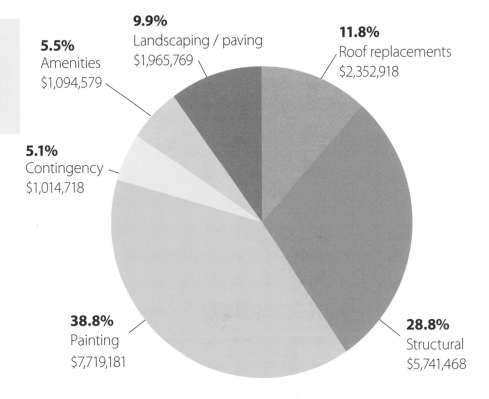

5.5% Amenities $1,094,579

9.9% Landscaping / paving $1,965,769

11.8% Roof replacements $2,352,918

5.1% Contingency $1,014,718

38.8% Painting $7,719,181

28.8% Structural $5,741,468

Painting	
Exterior flatwork	$6,482,099
Wood fencing	613,111
Doors	548,594
Ironwork	75,377
TOTAL	**$7,719,181**

Structural	
Siding wood	$3,068,697
Siding shingle	2,239,504
Wood arbors	219,804
Electrical	213,463
Foundations / structural frame	0
Structural pest control	0
Utility doors	0
TOTAL	**$5,741,468**

Roof Replacement	
Townhomes	$2,352,918
Clubhouse / rec bldg	0
Gutters and downspouts	0
TOTAL	**$2,352,918**

Landscape / Paving	
Wood fencing (replace)	$1,655,504
Asphalt overlay	137,130
Asphalt sealcoat	78,861
Irrigation system timeclocks	64,752
Backflow preventers	11,011
Parking stripes	7,382
Curb painting	5,443
Wrought iron (replace)	5,686
TOTAL	**$1,965,769**

Amenities	
Clubhouse / rec bldg	$504,796
Pool / spa	495,141
Tennis courts	94,642
TOTAL	**$1,094,579**

Contingency	
Contingency and misc.	$947,078
Mailboxes	35,817
Directory boards	18,585
Signs	9,089
Washer / dryer (rec bldg)	4,149
TOTAL	**$1,014,718**

Sample Reserve Study (condensed version)

Three Alternative Funding Plans vs. Component Costs

2008 through 2037

Warning!

Often in a professional Reserve study, various funding plans are charted. For example, if the monthly maintenance fee starts too low at the beginning of the development and is never raised, there can be dire financial consequences.

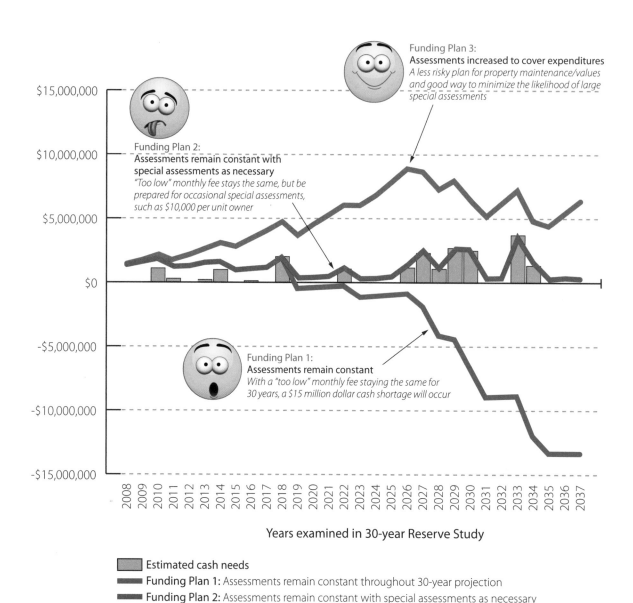

Funding Plan 3:
Assessments increased to cover expenditures
A less risky plan for property maintenance/values and good way to minimize the likelihood of large special assessments

Funding Plan 2:
Assessments remain constant with special assessments as necessary
"Too low" monthly fee stays the same, but be prepared for occasional special assessments, such as $10,000 per unit owner

Funding Plan 1:
Assessments remain constant
With a "too low" monthly fee staying the same for 30 years, a $15 million dollar cash shortage will occur

Years examined in 30-year Reserve Study

Estimated cash needs
Funding Plan 1: Assessments remain constant throughout 30-year projection
Funding Plan 2: Assessments remain constant with special assessments as necessary
Funding Plan 3: Assessments increased to cover expenditures

Sample Reserve Study (condensed version)
Cash-Flow Analysis
2008 through 2037

 Insight

Just as in a business, having cash available to cover expenses each year is necessary for economic survival. Positive cash flow usually does not happen by accident.

Often in Reserve Studies, there is a cash-flow analysis that projects cash availability with an overlay of:

- Reserve expenditures
- Reserve contributions
- Cash on hand

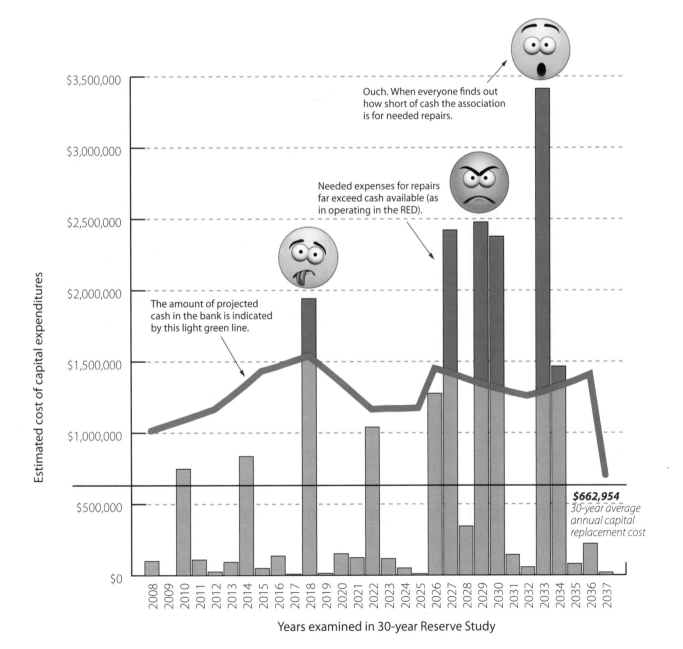

Ouch. When everyone finds out how short of cash the association is for needed repairs.

Needed expenses for repairs far exceed cash available (as in operating in the RED).

The amount of projected cash in the bank is indicated by this light green line.

$662,954
30-year average annual capital replacement cost

Estimated cost of capital expenditures

Years examined in 30-year Reserve Study

Sample Preventive-Maintenance Check List
Executive Summary

Roof shingles
At least annually, have roofs examined for replacement of missing and damaged shingles.

Roof flashing
All flashing should be examined at least annually and resealed with caulking mastic as necessary.

Roof gutters and downspouts
These should be checked at least each spring and fall for blockages from leaves, seedlings and other debris.

Roof maintenance contract
A maintenance contract with a licensed roofing contractor is strongly recommended.

Foundation
After a hard rain, check to see if water is pooling at any foundations. (Grade dirt so water drains *away* from foundations.)

Wood siding
Siding maintenance is important for aesthetics and also helps prevent termite infestation. In this climate and example, siding should be painted at least every 4 years.

Irrigation system
At least annually, garden services should clean sprinkler heads that can become clogged. This helps prevent premature death of shrubbery and ground cover.

Cost-Saving Benefits of a Preventive-Maintenance Program

A preventive-maintenance checklist helps you to manage your property.

By carefully prolonging the life of building components, and systematically monitoring those components at least each spring and fall, you can help reduce the frequency of expensive, unanticipated emergency repairs.

DISCLAIMER — Each property is unique. Therefore, each property Preventive Maintenance Check List is unique, based on local conditions and local laws. Do not use this example list for your own property.

Sample Preventive-Maintenance Check List
Property Map (Overview of Property)

Ideas

Clearer communication with vendors by providing:

1. Map of property
2. Digital photos of problem areas

If you do not have a map of your property,

1. Check for a copy of the plat, on file at the county courthouse.

2. Go to *www.googlearth*, key in your address, pull up a satellite view of the property, and trace over it for accurate sizing.

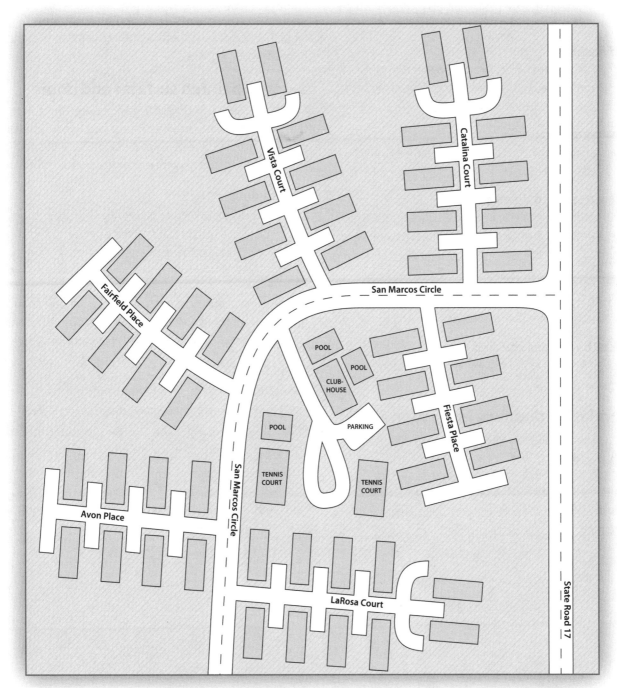

Sample Spring / Fall Preventive-Maintenance Check List

This list *does not* include monthly, weekly or daily check lists for common areas.

Roof inspection

Especially on roofs, all inspections and repairs should be performed by a licensed, insured, qualified roofing contractor.

Roof shingles

Check for missing and damaged shingles, especially after windy weather and prior to the rainy season.

Roof flashing

Roof flashing occurs where one roofing section joins another roofing section, chimney, attic exhaust fan vent, etc. This is a prime area for leaks to occur.

Chimney crowns

Cracking naturally occurs at the top of chimneys, which allows water to leak in.

Roof gutters and downspouts

Spring seedlings and fall leaves can clog roof gutters and downspouts. A clogged downspout can cause water to back up in the drainage system.

Gutter screens

Even with gutter screen protection, fine debris should be removed from inside the roof gutter every 4 to 5 years.

Attic exhaust fans checked

Check power ventilator, belts and thermometer on attic exhaust fans.

Foundation drainage inspection

Drainage should be directed away from the structure. Grade so that water drains away from foundations. All grading at foundations should slope away from the structures, so that rainwater is directed away from the structures. This is especially good to check after a hard rain.

Pest control

Follow local codes. In California for example, state statutes recommend annual inspections be performed to discover any infestation in its early stages before it becomes a serious problem.

A regular on-going maintenance program should be established with a reputable licensed pest control operator. Programs range from monthly spraying for pests to quarterly inspections for termites.

Exterior painted surfaces and doors

Possible annual touch-up painting, in between every 4- to 7-year painting cycles, to extend life of paint job and protect wood surfaces. All peeling paint should be sanded/scraped and bare areas properly primed prior to any finish paint.

Wood siding

Check for cracks and splits in siding. Any protruding nails should be redriven and sealed. (In this example, siding should be regularly painted at least every 4 years.)

Arbors

Examine for potential decay as part of regular pest control maintenance program. Repainting or staining is advocated at 4-year intervals for longevity of this component.

Wood fencing

Annual touch up painting of peeling and damaged surfaces with complete repainting or restaining at least every four years.

All peeling paint should be sanded/scraped and bare areas property primed prior to any finish painting. Any splits and cracks should be sealed with appropriate materials. This helps with aesthetics but also protects the wood fence itself and helps prevent termite infestation.

Sample Spring / Fall Preventive-Maintenance Check List

This list *does not* include monthly, weekly or daily check lists for common areas.

Recreational building

Furnaces / evaporative coils / condensers
These components should be serviced twice a year. A maintenance contract with a reputable licensed heating/air-conditioning firm is recommended.

Circulation pump
Annual lubrication is required.

Pool
Standard maintenance programs for start-up and closing of annual pool season. Delegating this task to a certified, licensed pool contractor may be advisable.

Pool acrylic deck surfaces
Examine acrylic deck surfaces and repair cracks or deterioration. A full resealing should be performed every 8 to 10 years.

Tennis court
Standard maintenance programs for start-up and closing of annual tennis season. Delegating this task to a certified, licensed contractor may be advisable.

Irrigation system
Standard maintenance programs with a certified, licensed pool contractor may be advisable.

Asphalt inspection
All asphalt areas should be examined at least annually. Any cracks exceeding ¼ inch should be repaired with a rubberized sealant compound. Irrigation run-off can accelerate degradation, and should be prevented/diverted.

Asphalt seal coat
It is important that this procedure always be undertaken within 6 months of any overlay or resurfacing, and performed thereafter on a 3- to 5-year cycle (typically a warranty requirement).

Concrete block walls
Monitor for cracks at least annually.

Concrete flatwork (sidewalks, concrete driveways)
While this is often a lifetime component, review each spring and fall for cracks and areas where concrete may be pushed up by nearby tree roots. Repair any elevated concrete.

Major tree trimming / removal
Annual tree trimming (operating budget item) should be instituted to minimize the need for major tree topping, which may be detrimental to both the growth and stability of the trees.

Major Structural Renovation Expenses Reserve Cost Comparison

Detached, Single-Family Home

In same neighborhood as Stacked Flat Condominium Association and same time of construction

Brief data for this property example

Year built	1978
Quality level of original construction	Average
Maintenance level since construction	Average
Have any major systems (plumbing, wiring, HVAC) been replaced since construction in 1962?	No
Cost range for reserve study for a single-family home	$1,500 to $3,000

Insight

What are the major repair and replacement costs for a single-family home?

Most home owners know that major repair and replacement costs for a single-family home represent large future outlays of cash, but few have taken the time to create a Reserve Study for a single-family home.

In the list at the right, are projected major repair and replacement costs for a single family home, in the same neighborhood, constructed at the same time as the Reserve Study for the sample Association property in this section.

This list is presented to readers merely as food for thought, and not for the purposes of a direct comparison of costs between a single-family home and a condominium.

Home owner costs that are not included in the list at right, are the additional day-to-day operating expenses for a single-family home such as removal of leaves from roof gutters, lawn care, snow removal, exterior painting, and other routine minor home repairs.

DISCLAIMER—Life expectancy of component parts will vary based on many factors, such as:
- Quality level of original components
- Local climate conditions
- Interim preventive maintenance if applicable

DISCLAIMER—Actual renovation costs can vary widely based on many factors, such as:
- Local availability of skilled labor
- Quality of component parts used
- Current worldwide demand for raw materials

Major Structural Renovation Expenses Reserve Cost Comparison

Detached, Single-Family Home

Component	Approximate quantity	Useful life of component (years)	Remaining useful life of component (years)	Current average replacement cost	Future average replacement cost
Exterior building elements					
Garage door	1	15 to 25	19	$1,200	$2,307
Gutters and downspouts	230 linear ft	15 to 20	11	$2,185	$3,190
Roof, asphalt shingles	22 squares	15 to 20	11	$7,480	$10,921
Walls, aluminum siding and soffits	2,300 sq ft	to 35	10	$12,075	$17,033
Windows and doors, replacement	580 squares	to 45	20	$20,300	$40,393
Building services elements					
Split system, heating and cooling	1	15 to 20	2	$6,000	$6,427
Water heater	1	12 to 15	3	$900	$1,307
Property site elements					
Concrete driveway, sidewalk and patio, partial replacements	250 sq ft	to 65	15	$2,375	$3,979

Who Does What?

Executive Summary of volunteer and paid positions to operate the property

Owners to volunteer to serve on the Board of Directors

- President
- Treasurer
- Secretary
- At-large board members

Off-site property management firm

If no outside Property Management firm is hired, the property is referred to as "self-managed" by volunteers within the association.

Key staff positions often provided by an off-site Property Management firm may include:

- Community manager
- Customer service coordinator
- Maintenance coordinator
- Bookkeeper

Full-time on-site manager and staff

Often, at larger developments and more upscale developments, a full-time site manager and staff are hired.

Paid part-time outside vendors

Financial and mechanical planning services

- Reserve specialist and staff

Mechanical planning services

- Consulting mechanical engineer

Financial and tax-filing services

- Certified public accountant and staff
- Banking services

Legal services

- Attorney and staff
- Usually has experience as a real estate attorney, as well as community association experience

Insurance services

- Insurance agent and staff

Trade and crafts persons

- Roofing crew
- Plumbing crew
- Electrical crew
- "Handyman" for routine day-to-day repairs
- Painting crew
- Concrete and masonry crew (for sidewalk, foundation and masonry repairs)
- Asphalt and paving crew

HVAC (heating, ventilation and air conditioning)

- Boiler / chiller maintenance and repair crew

Grounds services

- Lawn care crew
- Arborist crew for large tree trimming
- Snow removal crew
- Pest control
- Cleaning / janitorial services
- Trash removal services

Warning!

All vendors must submit annual proof of insurance form(s)

All vendors should be fully insured and submit the annual proof of insurance forms for your records. This insurance includes workers comp, liability and whatever is mandated by laws in your state.

Example C:
Mid-Rise

Four-to-eight stories, includes elevator.

Maintenance and Financial Planning Documentation

Financial PRO and CON overview of this housing type example

PRO

Convenient urban location

As with other condominium properties, the owner is not burdened with external maintenance chores. If an owner prefers an urban environment, mid-rises are often in near-downtown locations.

Security

Even if there is no doorman or full-time security staff, as in a condo tower, there is often a lobby door security system in place.

On-site manager or off-site portfolio manager

Due to the size of the association and the complexity of a multistory building, there is often either a full-time manager or an off-site portfolio manager.

A "room with a view"

For some owners, the scenic urban view is what first sold them on their unit.

CON

Mid-rise can cost more than a smaller condo

Due to the urban location and expenses in a multistory building, the mid-rise unit can often cost more than, say, a two-story, garden-style condo in the suburbs.

Noisy neighbors can still be an issue

In multifamily housing, you live with neighbors above, below and/or on both sides of you. This density can create noise issues to resolve.

Brief data for this property example

Number of buildings in the complex	1
Total number of housing units in the complex	78
Year(s) built	2000–2002
Quality level of original construction	Above average
Maintenance level since construction	Above average
Cost range for reserve study	$3,000 to $6,000+
Cost range for reserve study update	$2,250 to $4,500+
Current reserve account balance	**$157,901**
Recommended reserve account balance	**$210,535**

In this example:

Current monthly fee per sample unit $541*

Based on reserve study *and* operating budget analysis

Current monthly fee *underfunding* per sample unit $25

(This is the accumulating deficit per unit, per month, for this sample budget year.)

A Reserve Study, based on the specific components at your Association, is critical for determining an adequate monthly fee.

* In Condominium Associations with units of different sizes, it is customary to base the monthly fee on a cost-per-square-foot per condominium.

DISCLAIMER — Each property is unique. Therefore, each property budget is unique, based on local conditions and local laws. Do not use these budget figures from this specific yet theoretical example for your own property.

Monthly fee includes:

Exterior element maintenance
- Exterior walls (building envelope)
- Roof
- Balconies and railings

Amenities and interior element maintenance
- Parking garage
- Elevator cab interiors
- Hallway painting and carpeting

Building mechanical systems
- Exterior and Common area insurance (You still need to have homeowner's insurance for interior and contents.)

Building mechanical systems
- Elevator equipment
- Fire alarm system
- Boilers and chillers
- Domestic hot water boilers
- Pumps, HVAC (heating, ventilation and A/C)

Administrative services
- Part-time off-site manager and administrative support
- Maintenance staff (routine maintenance)
- Outside contractors for specialized services

Financial reserve expense
- Systematic savings for large capital expenses such as maintenance of building envelope, roof, garage area repairs, chillers, boilers and more

---

Actual reserves on hand vs. reserves called for in Reserve Study

Consider raising reserve levels in order to have cash on hand for anticipated repairs and replacements.

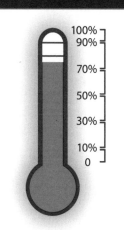

Financial Reserves

75% funded

Sample Annual Budget

Fiscal Year — January 1 through December 31

Income	current year	% of budget	$ per month
Monthly assessments	$529,971	88.9%	$566.21
Special assessments	0	0.0%	0.00
Commercial space rent	58,970	9.9%	63.00
Investment income	6,924	1.2%	7.40
Total income	**$595,865**	**100.0%**	**$636.61**

Operating Expenses (ongoing expenses that occur each year)

Mgmt and Admin Expense	current year	% of budget	$ per month
Management fee	$49,753	8.0%	$53.15
Accounting fees	2,786	0.4%	2.98
Legal and other professional fees	10,029	1.6%	10.71
Office and administration	7,243	1.2%	7.74
Insurance	55,288	8.9%	59.07
Security	8,831	1.4%	9.43
Doubtful account expense	21,199	3.4%	22.65
Total mgmt and admin expense	**$155,129**	**25.0%**	**$165.74**

Repairs and Maint Expense	current year	% of budget	$ per month
Cleaning and janitorial	$57,281	9.2%	$61.20
Trash removal contracts	34,827	5.6%	37.21
General maintenance	22,382	3.6%	23.91
Building repairs	14,207	2.3%	15.18
Elevator contracts	16,748	2.7%	17.89
Plumbing repairs	10,056	1.6%	10.74
Maintenance supplies	7,371	1.2%	7.88
Lawn maintenance	11,700	1.9%	12.50
Irrigation system repairs	2,020	0.3%	2.16
Plant and tree replacement	3,482	0.6%	3.72
Exercise room	3,343	0.5%	3.57
Garage and parking	16,391	2.6%	17.51
Snow removal	14,555	2.3%	15.55
Total repair and maint expense	**$214,363**	**34.6%**	**229.02**

Sample Annual Budget

Fiscal Year — January 1 through December 31

Operating Expenses (cont.)

Utility Expense	current year	% of budget	$ per month
Electricity	$76,217	12.3%	$81.43
Water and sewer	63,514	10.2%	67.86
Natural gas	34,342	5.5%	36.69
Total utilities expense	**$174,073**	**28.1%**	**$185.98**
Total operating expenses	**$543,565**	**87.7%**	**$580.73**

Reserve Expense Allocations (The amounts listed below are added to each year, into interest-bearing accounts, in preparation for high-cost, anticipated major repairs or replacements.)

	current year	% of budget	$ per month
Interior building elements	$6,799	1.1%	7.26
Exterior building elements	24,947	4.0%	26.65
Bldg services elements	13,127	2.1%	14.02
Garage elements	7,427	1.2%	7.93
Total reserve expense allocations	**$52,300**	**8.4%**	**55.88**
Reserves not funded	**$23,835**	**3.8%**	**$25.46**
Total operating exp. & reserve alloc.	**$619,700**	**100.0%**	**$662.07**

**Actual annual budget will have shortfall
due to reserves not being fully funded**

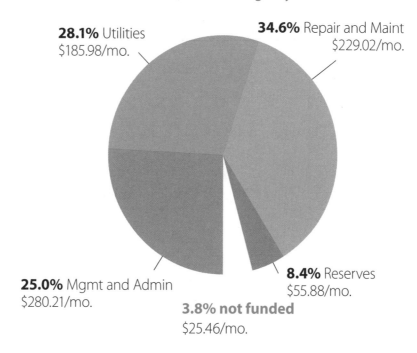

28.1% Utilities
$185.98/mo.

34.6% Repair and Maint
$229.02/mo.

25.0% Mgmt and Admin
$280.21/mo.

8.4% Reserves
$55.88/mo.

3.8% not funded
$25.46/mo.

Sample Monthly Income Statement

Month Ending July 31, 2010

Income	Monthly Actual	Monthly Budget	YTD Actual	YTD Budget	YTD Variance	Annual Budget
Monthly assessments	$42,198	$44,164	$295,386	$309,150	-$13,764	$529,971
Special assessments	0	0	0	0	0	0
Commercial space rent	4,668	4,914	32,679	34,399	-1,720	58,970
Investment income	519	577	4,408	4,039	369	6,924
Total income	**$47,386**	**$49,655**	**$332,473**	**$347,588**	**-$15,115**	**$595,865**

Operating Expenses (ongoing expenses that occur each year)

Management and Admin						
Management fee	$4,063	$4,146	$29,603	$29,023	$580	$49,753
Accounting fees	232	232	1,706	1,625	81	2,786
Legal and other prof fees	794	836	5,499	5,850	-351	10,029
Office and admin	549	604	3,929	4,225	-296	7,243
Insurance	4,699	4,607	32,574	32,251	323	55,288
Security	706	736	4,997	5,151	-155	8,831
Doubtful account expense	1,696	1,767	11,129	12,366	-1,237	21,199
Total mgmt and admin exp	**$12,740**	**$12,927**	**$89,438**	**$90,492**	**-$1,054**	**$155,129**

Repair and Maintenance						
Cleaning and janitorial	$4,821	$4,773	$34,082	$33,414	$668	$57,281
Trash removal contracts	3,076	2,902	21,332	20,316	1,016	34,827
General maintenance	1,716	1,865	12,273	13,056	-783	22,382
Building repairs	1,077	1,184	7,707	8,287	-590	14,207
Elevator contracts	1,424	1,396	9,867	9,770	98	16,748
Plumbing repairs	804	838	5,690	5,866	-176	10,056
Maintenance supplies	559	614	3,870	4,300	-430	7,371
Lawn maintenance	1,248	975	8,190	6,825	1,365	11,700
Irrigation system repairs	167	168	1,143	1,178	-35	2,020
Plant and tree replacement	273	290	1,828	2,031	-203	3,482
Exercise room	262	279	2,028	1,950	78	3,343
Garage and parking	1,284	1,366	9,944	9,561	382	16,391
Snow removal	1,140	1,213	8,830	8,490	340	14,555
Total repair and maint exp	**$17,851**	**$12,927**	**$126,784**	**$125,045**	**$1,739**	**$214,363**

Sample Monthly Income Statement

Month Ending July 31, 2010

Operating Expenses (cont.)	Monthly Actual	Monthly Budget	YTD Actual	YTD Budget	YTD Variance	Annual Budget
Utility Expense						
Electricity	$6,415	$6,351	$45,349	$44,460	$889	$76,217
Water and sewer	5,610	5,293	38,902	37,050	1,852	63,514
Natural gas	2,633	2,862	18,831	20,033	-1,202	34,342
Total utility expense	**$14,658**	**$14,506**	**$103,082**	**$101,543**	**$1,540**	**$174,073**
Total operating expenses	**$45,250**	**$45,297**	**$319,305**	**$317,080**	**$2,225**	**$543,565**

Reserve Expense Allocations (The amounts listed below are added to each year, into interest-bearing accounts, in preparation for high-cost, anticipated major repairs or replacements.)

	Monthly Actual	Monthly Budget	YTD Actual	YTD Budget	YTD Variance	Annual Budget
Interior bldg elements	$555	$567	$4,045	$3,966	$79	$6,799
Exterior bldg elements	2,079	2,079	15,280	14,552	728	24,947
Bldg services elements	995	1,094	7,198	7,657	-459	13,127
Garage elements	631	619	4,029	4,332	-303	7,427
Total reserve expense alloc.	**$4,261**	**$4,358**	**$30,553**	**$30,508**	**$44**	**$52,300**
Total operating expense & reserve allocations	**$49,511**	**$49,655**	**$349,857**	**$347,588**	**$2,269**	**$595,865**
Net income (loss)	**-$2,125**	**$0**	**-$17,384**	**$0**	**-$17,384**	**$0**

Insight

What you learn from an income statement:

In a business, the income statement shows the profit or loss for the month (or the year, if an annual statement).

The income statement sometimes is known as the profit and loss statement.

In a Community Association, this summary shows how actual spending is progressing, compared with the original estimated budget for the year.

Keep in mind, the annual budget is a best guess and a guideline for what will happen during the year.

Actual reserves on hand vs. reserves called for in Reserve Study

Often, monthly assessment fees are too low to meet financial reserve requirements.

Sample Monthly Balance Sheet

Month Ending July 31, 2010

Assets	
Cash in checking (operating checking)	$42,008
Cash in reserve money market account	63,280
Cash in certificates of deposit — reserves	142,000
Assessments receivable	7,483
Prepaid expenses (insurance, taxes, etc.)	7,502
Total assets	**$262,273**
Liabilities and fund balances	
Prepaid owner assessments	$11,015
Accounts payable — operating	8,335
Accounts payable — reserves	4,280
Total liabilities	**$23,630**
Fund balances (equity)	
Operating fund	$37,643
Reserve fund	201,000
Total fund balances	**$238,643**
Total liabilities and fund balances	**$262,273**

Actual reserves on hand vs. reserves called for in Reserve Study

Often, monthly assessment fees are too low to meet financial reserve requirements.

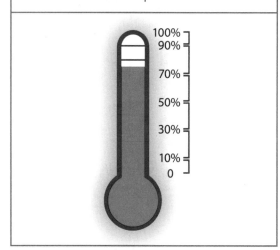

Insight

What you learn from a balance sheet:

The balance sheet is a "snapshot" statement of the assets and liabilities of the Association at a specific date, usually the last day of each month.

Each month, you will see at a glance, the net worth of the Association.

Keep in mind that you must subtract from that total any monthly fees that are late and still owed to the Association.

Sample Monthly Accounts Receivable Report

Month Ending July 31, 2010

Owner Name	Amount	Current	30 Days	60 Days	90 Days
Krassowski	3,421	25	566	566	2,264
Patel	2,855	25	566	566	1,698
Smith	591	25	566	0	0
Kornikova	591	25	566	0	0
Gaddie	25	25	0	0	0
Total Accounts Receivable	**$7,483**		**$2,264**	**$1,132**	**$3,962**

Monthly fee collections are the *lifeblood* for the financial health of your Association and therefore for your property values.

The collection policy of your Association must be clear to owners, along with other information when new owners move in.

Some owners, while pressed hard for credit card debt and mortgage payments, especially during economic recessions, think the monthly Association dues might not be as urgent to pay. But that is an incorrect assumption.

Review the accounts receivable at least monthly. When collections spiral out of control, the maintenance of the Association can suffer.

Have a payment and collections policy.

SAMPLE COLLECTION POLICY
- Monthly payments due by first of month.
- 10 days late - Late letter (or late charge, if permitted by governing documents and local state law).
- 30 days late - More urgently worded late letter.
- 60 days late - Account turned over to a collections attorney, with attorney fees to be paid by the late-paying owner. At the county courthouse, a lien is filed against the property.

COLLECTION LETTERS ARE BEST HANDLED BY COMMUNITY ASSOCIATION LAWYER
- Collections are best handled by a hired outside third party. Often, this is the Community Association lawyer, who will comply with the Federal Fair Debt Collections Act.

DISCLAIMER — Each property is unique. Therefore, each property budget is unique, based on local conditions and local laws. Do not use these budget figures from this specific yet theoretical example for your own property.

Part II | 131

Sample Reserve Study (condensed version)
Mid-Rise

Four-to-eight stories, includes elevator.

Sample Reserve Study (condensed version)

Some thoughts as you review this sample reserve study

 **Insight**

Mid-rise buildings, being multistory, can cost more to build, operate and maintain

While not as expensive to operate as a luxury high-rise condominium tower, there are extra costs associated with a multistory building such as a mid-rise.

Since mid-rises are often in urban settings, with high land values, a multistory building still offers economic efficiencies.

 **Best Scenario**

In the largest U.S. state, contingency reserves are required in Reserve Study calculations

In California, by far the highest-population state in the United States, the Department of Real Estate (DRE) requires that Reserve Study calculations include contingency funding.

Based on DRE experience, higher contingencies are required for units converted from apartment buildings, and for high-rise towers.

Property type	Minimum extra in contingency reserves
All properties	**3% extra**
Conversion from apartment building	**5% extra**
High-rise building (over 70 feet tall)	**10% extra**

 **Warning!**

Sometimes, long-term infrastructure costs are not yet included in the current Reserve Study.

In the few states that mandate a Reserve Study, periodic updates of the Reserve Study, from every 1 to 5 years, are also mandated.

Major infrastructure components, slated to last more than 20 to 30 years, are often not included in the cost of future capital needs. That is because the current estimated useful life of the component extends beyond the 20- to 30-year time range of the current Reserve Study.

Currently, among prominent reserve study practitioners, there is not consensus yet on when to start adding in the replacement cost of longer-life infrastructure components.

One school of thought is that in the periodic reserve study updates, when a major component starts to show signs of premature failure, it is time to include funding plans for that component in the next updated Reserve Study.

Be aware.

Here is the potential danger to consumers and why periodically updated reserve studies are so important to you.

If faulty major components are found – for example, deteriorating plumbing pipes, electrical wiring, foundations, etc. – the infrastructure replacement costs can be very high. If there is only a short time to ramp up funding for those expensive infrastructure components, the special assessment costs for infrastructure repairs can be very high.

Sample Reserve Study (condensed version)

Condition Assessment

The persuasive power of on-site digital photos

Reserve Studies often contain color digital photos of deferred maintenance problem areas. Because deferred maintenance happens slowly, it is easy to walk past gradually worsening problems everyday and not notice. Digital photos help bring the problem into focus with the goal of convincing owners to *act now* to fix the problems.

Repairs to stucco should happen before painting over the stucco. Otherwise, there is a hazard of water intrusion.

Cracked sealant around windows can allow water to enter the wall, which can result in mold growth.

These step cracks in a concrete stairwell should be monitored, because these cracks can be an indicator of a significant settlement problem.

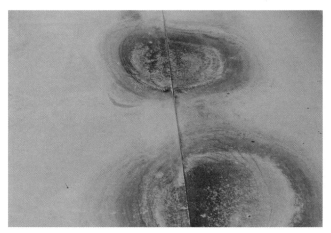

Evidence of water ponding on the roof needs close inspection to ensure that the membrane and joints do not deteriorate, which will result in water leaks into the condominium below.

DISCLAIMER — Do not base your monthly fees or reserves on this specific yet theoretical example. Each property is unique, subject to local conditions and local laws. Budget funds for your Association's custom-created, professional Reserve Study.

Sample Reserve Study (condensed version)

Condition Assessment

Metal railings should be primed and painted, preferably on a regular painting schedule. This way, rust is prevented for as long as possible. Too much rust will require an expensive replacement of the metal railing.

Partial replacements of window sills are necessary as buildings age. Otherwise, crumbling window sills can eventually lead to water-intrusion problems.

Water intrusion has caused significant deterioration of this elevated walkway. Proper maintenance could have avoided the need to replace this walkway.

Crack repairs and the application of an elastomeric coating on the topside of the garage floor will minimize the passage of water through the concrete floor, which can prematurely deteriorate the concrete.

Sample Reserve Study (condensed version)

Executive Summary

Major component parts and estimated remaining useful life of components

Component	Approximate quantity	Useful life of component (years)	Remaining useful life of component (years)	Current average replacement cost	Future average replacement cost
Exterior building elements					
Balconies, capital repairs and waterproof coating applications	78 balconies	8 to 12	6	$62,400	$92,454
Light fixtures, exterior	84	to 15	9	$10,920	$14,883
Paint finishes, balcony doors, ceilings and railings	78 balconies	6 to 8	3	$33,540	$50,211
Roof, flat	180 squares	15 to 20	5	$225,000	$267,229
Sealants, windows and doors, phased replacements	3,500 linear ft	to 20	4	$15,400	$21,300
Walls, masonry, inspection and partial repointing	40,000 sq ft	8 to 10	4	$68,000	$94,052

Sample Reserve Study (condensed version)

Executive Summary

Major component parts and estimated remaining useful life of components (continued)

Component	Approximate quantity	Useful life of component (years)	Remaining useful life of component (years)	Current average replacement cost	Future average replacement cost
Interior building elements					
Floor coverings, carpet hallways	850 sq yards	10 to 15	3	$38,250	$56,729
Life safety system	1	to 30	18	$35,000	$65,012
Light fixtures, hallways	120	to 25	18	$12,600	$23,404
Paint finishes, hallways	29,500 sq ft	8 to 10	3	$29,500	$38,642
Building services elements					
Boilers, building heat	6	20 to 25	10	$81,000	$114,258
Boilers, domestic water	1	12 to 18	2	$13,800	$21,179
Elevators, hydraulic, controls	2	to 35	27	$140,000	$354,419
Elevators, hydraulic, cylinders	2	to 40	30	$100,000	$280,679
Rooftop heating and air conditioning units	2	15 to 20	5	$33,000	$39,194
Garage elements					
Concrete floor, inspection and partial replacements	22,000 sq ft	8 to 12	10	$15,400	$21,723
Paint finishes	36,000 sq ft	15 to 20	6	$27,000	$33,190

DISCLAIMER — Do not base your monthly fees or reserves on this specific yet theoretical example. Each property is unique, subject to local conditions and local laws. Budget funds for your Association's custom-created, professional Reserve Study.

Part II | 137

Sample Reserve Study (condensed version)

Executive Summary

Components that may be **EXCLUDED** from the Reserve Study calculations

 **Insight**

Components that are left out of the custom Reserve Study will vary from community to community, based on Association governing documents and other local existing conditions. Examples are listed in the table below.

Type of excluded component	Definition	Examples
Unit owner responsibility Component exclusion	Based on your association's governing documents, some components are a unit owner responsibility.	Windows, garage doors, unit doors
Long-life Component exclusion	Some long-lasting infrastructure components are not yet included in the most current Reserve Study, because the expected useful life of the component extends beyond the 20- to 30-year range of the Reserve Study.	Plumbing pipes, electrical wiring, foundations
Utility Component exclusion	Some components might be maintained by the local utility company.	Primary electric feeds, telephone cables, gas mains and meters
Maintenance and repair Component exclusion	Some components can have ongoing preventive maintenance and repair. This repair cost is an operating expense and not a capital reserve expense.	Operating expense example: • Annual or semi-annual roof inspection and repair Reserve expense example: • Replacing the whole roof
Below threshold cost Component exclusion	If the reserve component is below a certain dollar amount, it is not included in the Reserve Study.	Some Reserve Studies only include components that cost at least $500 or $1,000 to replace. If the component is less than the threshold amount, it is often counted as an operating expense.
Government funded Component exclusion	If a local government maintains and replaces certain components, then these components are left out of the Reserve Study.	Street paving, sidewalks, storm water management

Sample Reserve Study (condensed version)

Executive Summary

Components **EXCLUDED** from the Townhome / Patio Home example Reserve Study

Unit owner responsibility component exclusions

- Unit windows
- Unit balcony doors
- Heating, ventilating, and air-conditioning (HVAC) equipment that is inside the individual unit

Long-life component exclusions

- Electrical systems
- Foundations
- Pipes, interior building, water and sewer
- Pipes, subsurface utilities

Utility component exclusions

- Primary electric feeds
- Electric transformers
- Cable TV systems and structures
- Telephone cables and structures
- Gas mains and meters

Maintenance and repair component exclusions

- General maintenance to common elements that is paid for from operating expenses
- Doors, metal
- Elevator cab finishes, freight
- Exhaust fans
- Light fixtures, building exterior
- Landscaping

Below-threshold cost-component exclusions

- Expenditures that are less than $4,000. For higher cost of repairs and replacements in a high-rise or mid-rise building, this report uses a $4,000 threshold to include an item as a reserve expense. For a smaller Association of one- and two-story buildings, the cost threshold exclusion may be as low as $500 or $1,000.

Government-funded component exclusions

- Government roadways and parking
- Government sidewalks and curbs
- Government lighting
- Government stormwater management

Sample Reserve Study (condensed version)

Estimated Reserve Fund Expenditures 2008 through 2037

2008
No reserve expenditures planned for this year

$0	Total reserve expenses for year

2009
No reserve expenditures planned for this year

$0	Total reserve expenses for year

2010

$14,783	Building service elements — boilers, domestic water, phased
$14,783	Total reserve expenses for year

2011

$37,186	Exterior building elements — paint finishes, balcony doors, ceilings and railings
$42,408	Interior building elements — floor coverings, carpet, hallways
$32,707	Contingency reserve
$112,301	Total reserve expenses for year

2012

$17,672	Exterior building elements — sealants, windows and doors, phased replacements
$78,032	Exterior building elements — walls, masonry, inspection and partial repointing
$95,704	Total reserve expenses for year

2013

$267,229	Exterior building elements — roof flat
$39,194	Building services elements — rooftop heating and air conditioning units
$306,423	Total reserve expenses for year

2014

$76,706	Exterior building elements — balconies, capital repairs and applications
$33,190	Garage elements — paint finishes
$109,896	Total reserve expenses for year

2015
No reserve expenditures planned for this year

$0	Total reserve expenses for year

2016
No reserve expenditures planned for this year

$0	Total reserve expenses for year

2017

$14,883	Exterior building elements — light fixtures, exterior
$14,883	Total reserve expenses for year

2018

$114,258	Building services elements — boilers, building heat
$21,723	Garage elements — concrete floor, inspection and partial repointing
$135,981	Total reserve expenses for year

2019

$48,967	Exterior building elements — paint finishes, balcony doors, ceilings and railings
$48,967	Total reserve expenses for year

2020

$44,577	Interior building elements — paint finishes, hallways
$44,577	Total reserve expenses for year

2021
No reserve expenditures planned this year

$0	Total reserve expenses for year

Insight

Operating expense versus reserve expenses.

Operating expenses are:

Ongoing, annual expenses, which often arrive as predictable monthly invoices, such as:

- Lawn care services
- Property management and bookkeeping services
- Ordinary, minor repairs
- Insurance, etc.

Reserve expenses are:

Higher-cost, major repairs and replacements, such as:

- Roof replacement
- Foundation repairs
- Siding replacement
- Parking area resurfacing
- Street repaving

Sample Reserve Study (condensed version)

Estimated Reserve Fund Expenditures 2008 through 2037

2022

$24,928	Exterior building elements — sealants, windows and doors, phased replacements
$110,071	Exterior building elements — walls, masonry, inspection and partial repointing
$134,999	Total reserve expenses for year

2023

$23,120	Building services elements — boilers, domestic water, phased
$23,120	Total reserve expenses for year

2024

$108,201	Exterior building elements — balconies, capital repairs and waterproof coating applications
$108,201	Total reserve expenses for year

2025

No reserve expenditures planned for this year

$0	Total reserve expenses for year

2026

$71,049	Interior building elements — floor coverings, Carpet, Hallways
$65,012	Interior building elements — life safety system
$23,404	Interior building elements — light fixtures, hallways
$25,633	Building services elements — boilers, domestic water, phased
$185,098	Total reserve expenses for year

2027

$64,481	Exterior building elements — paint finishes, balcony doors, ceilings and railings
$64,481	Total reserve expenses for year

2028

No reserve expenditures planned for this year

$0	Total reserve expenses for year

2029

$60,753	Interior building elements — paint finishes, hallways
$60,753	Total reserve expenses for year

2030

$32,825	Garage elements — concrete floor, inspection and partial replacements
$32,825	Total reserve expenses for year

2031

$496,376	Exterior building elements — roof, flat
$72,802	Building services elements — rooftop heating and air conditioning units
$569,178	Total reserve expenses for year

2032

$24,934	Exterior building elements — light fixtures, exterior
$155,266	Exterior building elements — walls, masonry, inspection and partial repointing
$61,650	Garage elements — paint finishes
$241,850	Total reserve expenses for year

2033

No reserve expenditures planned for this year

$0	Total reserve expenses for year

2034

$152,628	Exterior building elements — balconies, capital repairs and waterproof coating applications
$152,628	Total reserve expenses for year

2035

$84,909	Exterior building elements — paint finishes, balcony doors, ceilings and railings
$354,419	Building services elements — elevators, hydraulic, controls
$439,328	Total reserve expenses for year

2036

No reserve expenditures planned for this year

$0	Total reserve expenses for year

2037

No reserve expenditures planned for this year

$0	Total reserve expenses for year

30-year TOTAL needed for Reserve Expenses:

$3,176,655

Sample Reserve Study (condensed version)

Estimated Reserve Fund Expenditures by Year

2008 through 2037

Insight

Often, capital expenditures can vary dramatically from year to year, as shown below.

The black line near the bottom of the graph shows the average annual expenditure of money.

As the property ages, it generally costs more to maintain. That is because:

- More building components will reach the end of their useful life and must be replaced.
- Future expenditures are often figured with an estimated inflation rate such as 3% per year.

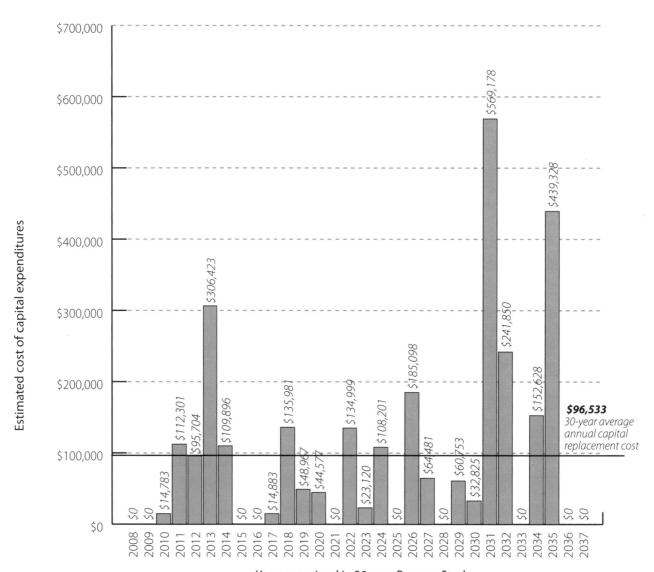

Sample Reserve Study (condensed version)

Estimated Reserve Fund Expenditures by Category

2008 through 2037

30-year total needed for reserve expenses: **$3,176,655**

30-year average annual spending for reserve expenses: **$105,888**

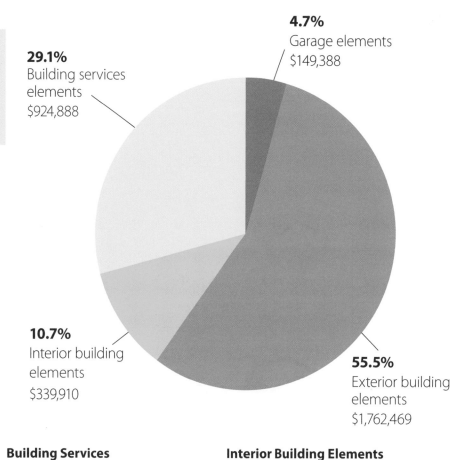

4.7%
Garage elements
$149,388

29.1%
Building services elements
$924,888

55.5%
Exterior building elements
$1,762,469

10.7%
Interior building elements
$339,910

Exterior Building Elements

Paint finishes, balcony doors, ceilings and railings	$235,543
Sealants, windows and doors, phased replacements	42,600
Walls, masonry, inspection and partial repointing	343,369
Roof, flat	763,605
Balconies, capital repairs and waterproof coating applications	337,535
Light fixtures, exterior	39,817
TOTAL	**$1,762,469**

Building Services

Boilers, domestic water phased	$63,536
Rooftop heating and air conditioning units	11,996
Boilers, building heat	114,258
Elevators, hydraulic, controls	354,419
Elevators, hydraulic, cylinders	280,679
TOTAL	**$924,888**

Interior Building Elements

Floor coverings, carpet, hallways	$113,457
Paint finishes, hallways	138,037
Life safety system	65,012
Light fixtures, hallways	23,404
TOTAL	**$339,910**

Garage Elements

Paint finishes	$94,840
Concrete floor, inspection and partial replacement	54,548
TOTAL	**$149,388**

Sample Reserve Study (condensed version)
Three Alternative Funding Plans vs. Component Costs
2008 through 2037

 **Warning!**

Often in a professional Reserve Study, various funding plans are charted. For example, if the monthly maintenance fee starts too low at the beginning of the development and is never raised, there can be dire financial consequences.

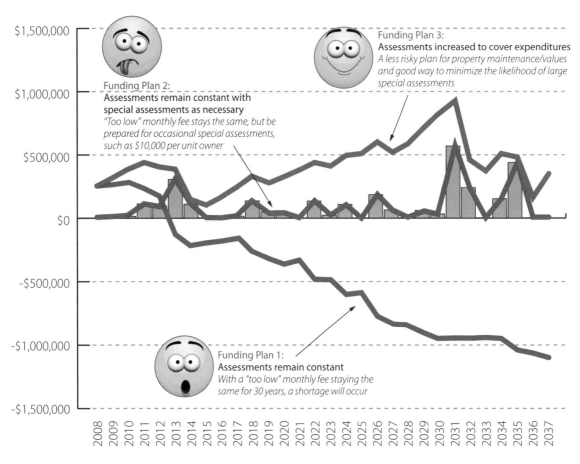

Funding Plan 3:
Assessments increased to cover expenditures
A less risky plan for property maintenance/values and good way to minimize the likelihood of large special assessments

Funding Plan 2:
Assessments remain constant with special assessments as necessary
"Too low" monthly fee stays the same, but be prepared for occasional special assessments, such as $10,000 per unit owner

Funding Plan 1:
Assessments remain constant
With a "too low" monthly fee staying the same for 30 years, a shortage will occur

Years examined in 30-year Reserve Study

Estimated cash needs
Funding Plan 1: Assessments remain constant throughout 30-year projection
Funding Plan 2: Assessments remain constant with special assessments as necessary
Funding Plan 3: Assessments increased to cover expenditures

Sample Reserve Study (condensed version)

Cash-Flow Analysis

2008 through 2037

Just as in a business, having cash available to cover expenses each year is necessary for economic survival. Positive cash flow usually does not happen by accident.

Often in Reserve Studies, there is a cash-flow analysis that projects cash availability with an overlay of:

- Reserve expenditures
- Reserve contributions
- Cash on hand

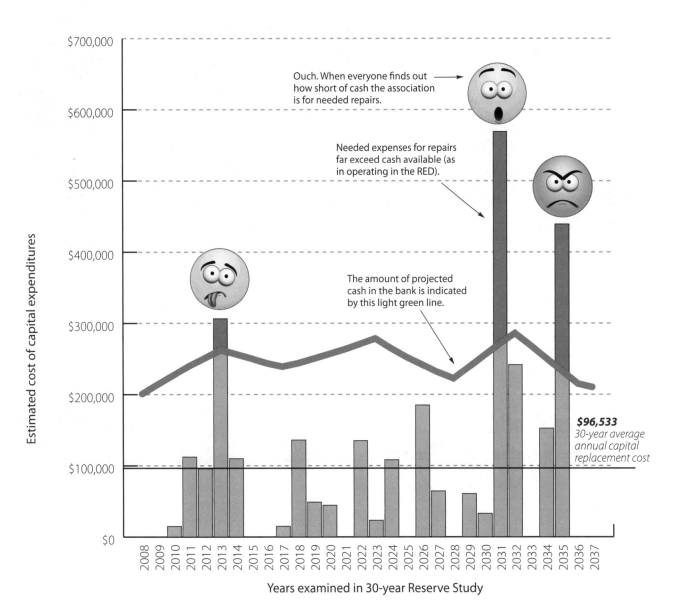

Ouch. When everyone finds out how short of cash the association is for needed repairs.

Needed expenses for repairs far exceed cash available (as in operating in the RED).

The amount of projected cash in the bank is indicated by this light green line.

$96,533
30-year average annual capital replacement cost

Estimated cost of capital expenditures

Years examined in 30-year Reserve Study

Sample Preventive-Maintenance Check List

Executive Summary

Roof membrane
Check for cracks and bubbling of roof membrane.

Roof parapet
Check parapet walls for damage or cracks.

▲ A "low-tech" building visual inspection with binoculars

Building envelope
Use binoculars to check bricks and possible mortar deterioration.

Building envelope
Use binoculars to check window lintels.

Cost-Saving Benefits of a Preventive-Maintenance Program

A preventive-maintenance checklist helps you to manage your property.

By carefully prolonging the life of building components, and systematically monitoring those components seasonally, you can help reduce the frequency of expensive, unanticipated emergency repairs.

Ideas

An engineering consulting firm will often drop scaffolding from the roof, down the side of the building to examine balcony condition, facades and the building envelope. Some building managers perform a preliminary inspection with binoculars.

Sample Seasonal Preventive-Maintenance Check List

This list *does not* include monthly, weekly and daily checklists for your building

	Spring	Summer	Fall	Winter
Roof				
Check cracks and bubbling of roof membrane	X		X	
Check for any signs of ponding	X	X	X	
Check parapet walls for damage or cracks	X	X		
Check cap stone joints for separation or cracks	X		X	
Check flashing for tears or loose parts	X	X	X	X
Check down spouts and splash guards	X	X	X	X
Check gutters, drains	X	X	X	X
Domestic roof tank				
Check hinges and hasp on tank cover door	X	X	X	X
Check floats and alarms	X	X	X	X
Have roof tank cleaned and sanitized		X		
Check tank for any damage over winter	X			
Elevator machine room				
Check machine room for any weather penetration	X		X	
Heating systems				
Have boiler tubes cleaned	X		X	
Have burner overhauled		X		
Have combustion efficiency test done on burner			X	
Clean all Wye Strainers	X			
Clean and repair steam traps		X		
Flush domestic hot water coils	X	X	X	X
Once every 5 years, clean oil tank for #4 & #6 oil				
Check limits and all boiler controls for winter use			X	
Building envelope				
Use binoculars to check:				
• Window lintels, expansion joints	X		X	
• Bricks and possible mortar deterioration	X		X	
Check balcony surfaces & railing for deterioration	X		X	
Check bulk head doors and windows, skylights	X	X		
Clean cooling towers and make ready for use	X			
Check sidewalks for cracks in concrete	X	X	X	X
Check sidewalks for heaving	X			X
Check roof drains for debris & all outdoor lighting	X	X	X	X
Check out door metal for signs of rust		X		

Major Structural Renovation Expenses Reserve Cost Comparison

Detached, Single-Family Home

In same neighborhood as Mid-Rise Condominium Association and same time of construction

Brief data for this property example

Year built	2000
Quality level of original construction	Above average
Maintenance level since construction	Average
Have any major systems (plumbing, wiring, HVAC) been replaced since construction in 2000?	No
Cost range for reserve study for a single-family home	$1,500 to $3,000

Insight

What are the major repair and replacement costs for a single-family home?

Most home owners know that major repair and replacement costs for a single-family home represent large future outlays of cash, but few have taken the time to create a Reserve Study for a single-family home.

In the list at the right, are projected major repair and replacement costs for a single family home, in the same neighborhood, constructed at the same time as the Reserve Study for the sample Association property in this section.

This list is presented to readers merely as food for thought, and not for the purposes of a direct comparison of costs between a single-family home and a condominium.

Home owner costs that are not included in the list at right, are the additional day-to-day operating expenses for a single-family home such as removal of leaves from roof gutters, lawn care, snow removal, exterior painting, and other routine minor home repairs.

DISCLAIMER—Life expectancy of component parts will vary based on many factors, such as:
• Quality level of original components
• Local climate conditions
• Interim preventive maintenance if applicable

DISCLAIMER—Actual renovation costs can vary widely based on many factors, such as:
• Local availability of skilled labor
• Quality of component parts used
• Current worldwide demand for raw materials

DISCLAIMER — Do not base your projected expenses or reserves on this specific yet theoretical example. Each property is unique. Budget funds for your own custom-created, professional Reserve Study.

Major Structural Renovation Expenses Reserve Cost Comparison

Detached, Single-Family Home

Component	Approximate quantity	Useful life of component (years)	Remaining useful life of component (years)	Current average replacement cost	Future average replacement cost
Exterior building elements					
Gutters and downspouts	190 linear ft	15 to 20	11	$1,805	$2,635
Roof, asphalt shingles	15 squares	15 to 20	11	$5,250	$7,665
Walls, masonry, inspections and partial repointing	2,200 sq ft	8 to 12	13	$2,750	$4,301
Windows and doors, replacement	550 sq ft	45 to 55	35	$19,250	$64,172
Building services elements					
Split system, heating and cooling unit	1	15 to 20	10	$6,000	$8,464
Water heater	1	12 to 15	5	$900	$1,069
Property site elements					
Concrete sidewalk, steps and patio, partial replacements	45 sq ft	to 65	15	$428	$716
Railings, metal	16 linear ft	to 40	30	$720	$2,021

Who Does What?

Executive Summary of volunteer and paid positions to operate the property.

Owners to volunteer to serve on the Board of Directors

- President
- Treasurer
- Secretary
- At-large board members

Off-site property management firm

If no outside Property Management firm is hired, the property is referred to as "self-managed" by volunteers within the association.

Key staff positions often provided by an off-site Property Management firm may include:

- Community manager
- Customer service coordinator
- Maintenance coordinator
- Bookkeeper

Full-time on-site manager and staff

Often, at larger developments and more upscale developments, a full-time site manager and staff are hired.

Paid part-time outside vendors

Financial and mechanical planning services

- Reserve specialist and staff

Mechanical planning services

- Consulting mechanical engineer

Financial and tax-filing services

- Certified public accountant and staff
- Banking services

Legal services

- Attorney and staff
- Usually has experience as a real estate attorney, as well as community association experience

Insurance services

- Insurance agent and staff

Trade and crafts persons

- Roofing crew
- Plumbing crew
- Electrical crew
- "Handyman" for routine day-to-day repairs
- Painting crew
- Concrete and masonry crew (for sidewalk, foundation and masonry repairs)
- Asphalt and paving crew

HVAC (heating, ventilation and air conditioning)

- Boiler / chiller maintenance and repair crew

Grounds Services

- Lawn care crew
- Arborist crew for large tree trimming
- Snow removal crew
- Pest control
- Cleaning / janitorial services
- Trash removal services

Warning!

All vendors must submit annual proof of insurance form(s)

All vendors should be fully insured and submit the annual proof of insurance forms for your records. This insurance includes workers comp, liability and whatever is mandated by laws in your state.

Example D: High-Rise

Nine+ stories

Maintenance and Financial Planning Documentation

Financial PRO and CON overview of this housing type example

PRO

Convenience
If an owner has a frequent out-of-town travel schedule, it is convenient to just "close the front door of their unit" and leave on their trip with peace of mind. Adding to the convenience is the in-house staff that are often present at a condominium tower.

Security
An upscale condominium tower often has 24/7 security staff as part of its annual operating budget.

Full-time on-site manager and staff
Many upscale condominium towers budget for a full-time on-site manager as well as full-time, on-site support staff.

A "room with a view"
For some owners, their scenic view from their "home in the sky" is what first sold them on their unit.

CON

Towers are often the highest-cost condominium type to operate and maintain
Towers are expensive to build, insure, staff and maintain. If residents have ample income, these extra expenses are not an issue.

Noisy neighbors can still be an issue
Despite the feeling of luxury and convenience, people are still living very close to neighbors above, below and on both sides of them. This density can create noise issues to resolve.

Brief data for this property example

Number of buildings in the complex	1
Total number of housing units in the complex	128
Year(s) built	1988–1990
Quality level of original construction	Above average
Maintenance level since construction	Excellent
Cost range for Reserve Study	$4,500 to $7,500+
Cost range for Reserve Study update	$3,400 to $5,600+
Current reserve account balance	**$552,263**
Recommended reserve account balance	**$756,525**

In this example:

Current monthly fee per sample unit $1,003*

Based on reserve study *and* operating budget analysis

Current monthly fee *underfunding* per sample unit $24

(This is the accumulating deficit per unit, per month, for this sample budget year.)

A Reserve Study, based on the specific components at your Association, is critical for determining an adequate monthly fee.

* In Condominium Associations with units of different sizes, it is customary to base the monthly fee on a cost-per-square-foot per condominium.

DISCLAIMER — Each property is unique. Therefore, each property budget is unique, based on local conditions and local laws. Do not use these budget figures from this specific yet theoretical example for your own property.

Monthly fee includes:
Exterior element maintenance
- Exterior walls (building envelope)
- Roof
- Balconies and railings
- Driveways and sidewalks

Amenities and interior element maintenance
- Parking garage
- Swimming pools
- Elevator cab interiors
- Hallway painting and carpeting
- Fitness center and meeting room

Building mechanical systems
- Elevator equipment
- Fire alarm system
- Boilers and chillers
- Domestic hot water boilers
- Pumps, HVAC (heating, ventilation and A/C)

Administrative services
- Full time, on site manager and administrative support staff
- Maintenance staff (routine maintenance)
- Security staff
- Outside contractors for specialized services

Financial reserve expense
- Systematic savings for large capital expenses such as maintenance of building envelope, roof, garage area repairs, chillers, boilers and more

---

Actual reserves on hand vs. reserves called for in Reserve Study

Consider raising reserve levels in order to have cash on hand for anticipated repairs and replacements.

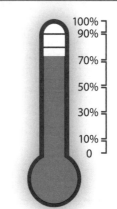

Financial Reserves

73% funded

Sample Annual Budget

Fiscal Year — January 1 through December 31

Income	current year	% of budget	$ per month
Monthly assessments	$1,578,221	90.7%	$1,027.49
Special assessments	0	0.0%	0.00
Commercial space rent	153,978	8.8%	100.25
Investment income	8,614	0.5%	5.61
Total income	**$1,740,813**	**100.0%**	**$1,133.34**

Operating Expenses (ongoing expenses that occur each year)

Mgmt and Admin Expense			
Pay for on-site management staff	$125,061	7.1%	$81.42
Off-site property manager fees	51,892	2.9%	33.78
Social security and medicare	17,256	1.0%	11.23
Office and administration	26,520	1.5%	17.27
Special events	14,677	0.8%	9.56
Accounting fees	1,730	0.1%	1.13
Legal and other professional fees	9,686	0.5%	6.31
Insurance	148,757	8.4%	96.85
Doubtful account expense	34,817	2.0%	22.67
Total mgmt and admin expense	**$430,396**	**24.3%**	**$280.21**

Repairs and Maintenance Expense			
Maintenance labor expense	$116,067	6.5%	$75.56
HVAC repairs and supplies	77,902	4.4%	50.72
Elec / plumbing / carpentry	25,730	1.5%	16.75
Glass repairs / light bulbs	18,508	1.0%	12.05
Cleaning service contract	56,268	3.2%	36.63
Paint and misc supplies	5,189	0.3%	3.38
Parking area repairs	11,409	0.6%	7.43
Roof repairs	10,199	0.6%	6.64
Trash removal	11,997	0.7%	7.81
Metal maintenance	7,379	0.4%	4.80
Window washing	45,232	2.6%	29.45
Total repairs and maintenance expense	**$385,880**	**21.8%**	**$251.22**

Utility Expense			
Electricity	$225,695	12.7%	$146.94
Steam	136,995	7.7%	89.19
Water and sewer	29,426	1.7%	19.16
Gas	2,076	0.1%	1.35
Total utilities expense	**$394,192**	**22.2%**	**$256.64**

Sample Annual Budget

Fiscal Year — January 1 through December 31

Operating Expenses (cont.)

Contract Services	current year	% of budget	$ per month
Elevator service contract	$34,186	1.9%	$22.26
Landscaping	18,584	1.0%	12.10
Pest control	2,283	0.1%	1.49
Security contract	232,545	13.1%	151.40
Fire contract	25,707	1.5%	16.74
Concierge	46,495	2.6%	30.27
Snow removal	11,831	0.7%	7.70
Water treatment	9,714	0.5%	6.32
Total contract services	**$381,345**	**21.5%**	**$248.27**
Total operating expenses	**$1,591,813**	**91.4%**	**$1,036.34**

Reserve Expense Allocations (The amounts listed below are added to each year, into interest-bearing accounts, in preparation for high-cost, anticipated major repairs or replacements.)

	current year	% of budget	$ per month
Interior building elements	$19,445	1.1%	$12.66
Exterior building elements	71,030	4.0%	46.24
Bldg services elements	37,365	2.1%	24.33
Garage elements	21,160	1.2%	13.78
Total reserve expense allocations	**$149,000**	**8.4%**	**$97.01**
Reserves not funded	**$31, 836**	**1.8%**	**$20.73**
Total operating exp. & reserve alloc.	**$1,772,649**	**100.0%**	**$1,154.07**

**Actual annual budget will have shortfall
due to reserves not being fully funded**

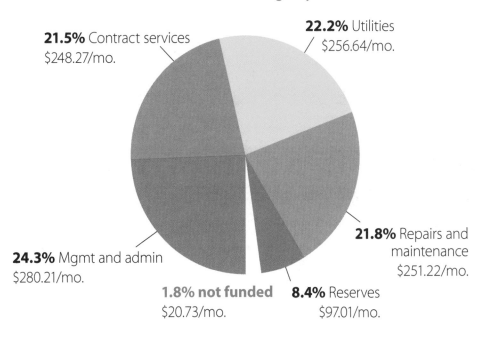

21.5% Contract services
$248.27/mo.

22.2% Utilities
$256.64/mo.

24.3% Mgmt and admin
$280.21/mo.

21.8% Repairs and
maintenance
$251.22/mo.

1.8% not funded
$20.73/mo.

8.4% Reserves
$97.01/mo.

Sample Monthly Income Statement

Month Ending July 31, 2010

Income	Monthly Actual	Monthly Budget	YTD Actual	YTD Budget	YTD Variance	Annual Budget
Monthly assessments	$128,384	$131,518	$898,688	$920,629	-$21,941	$1,578,221
Special assessments	0	0	0	0	0	0
Commercial space rent	12,190	12,832	87,152	89,821	-2,669	153,978
Investment income	646	718	4,408	5,025	-617	8,614
Total income	**$141,220**	**$145,068**	**$990,248**	**$1,015,474**	**-$25,226**	**$1,740,813**

Operating Expenses (ongoing expenses that occur each year)

Management and Admin						
Pay for on-site mgmt staff	$10,318	$10,422	$71,493	$72,952	-$1,459	$125,061
Off-site property manager fee	4,714	4,324	31,784	30,270	1,514	51,892
Social security and medicare	1,366	1,438	10,247	10,066	181	17,256
Office and admin	2,100	2,210	16,862	15,470	1,392	26,520
Special events	1,284	1,223	8,134	8,562	-428	14,677
Accounting fees	147	144	959	1,009	-50	1,730
Legal and other prof fees	880	807	5,226	5,650	-424	9,686
Insurance	11,777	12,396	99,791	86,775	13,016	148,757
Doubtful account expense	2,843	2,901	19,498	20,310	-812	34,817
Total mgmt and admin exp	**$35,427**	**$35,866**	**$263,994**	**$251,064**	**$12,930**	**$430,396**

Repair and Maintenance						
Maintenance labor expense	$9,769	$9,672	$69,060	$67,706	$1,354	$116,067
HVAC repairs and supplies	6,881	6,492	47,715	45,443	2,272	77,902
Elec / plumbing / carpentry	1,973	2,144	14,109	15,009	-901	25,730
Glass repairs / light bulbs	1,404	1,542	10,041	10,796	-756	18,508
Cleaning service contract	4,783	4,689	33,151	32,823	328	56,268
Paint and misc supplies	415	432	2,936	3,027	-91	5,189
Parking area repairs	865	951	5,990	6,655	-666	11,409
Roof repairs	1,088	850	7,139	5,949	1,190	10,199
Trash removal	990	1,000	6,788	6,998	-210	11,997
Metal maintenance	578	615	3,874	4,304	-430	7,379
Window washing	4,071	3,769	27,441	26,385	1,055	45,232
Total repair and maint exp	**$32,816**	**$32,157**	**$228,243**	**$225,097**	**$3,147**	**$385,880**

Insight

What you learn from an income statement:

In a business, the income statement shows the profit or loss for the month (or the year, if an annual statement.)

The income statement sometimes is known as the profit and loss statement.

In a Community Association, this summary shows how actual spending is progressing, compared with the original estimated budget for the year.

Keep in mind, the annual budget is a best guess and a guideline for what will happen during the year.

Sample Monthly Income Statement

Month Ending July 31, 2010

Operating Expenses (cont.)	Monthly Actual	Monthly Budget	YTD Actual	YTD Budget	YTD Variance	Annual Budget
Utility Expense						
Electricity	$18,996	$18,808	$134,289	$131,655	$2,633	$225,695
Steam	12,101	11,416	83,909	79,914	3,996	136,995
Water and sewer	2,256	2,452	16,135	17,165	-1,030	29,426
Gas	157	173	1,126	1,211	-85	2,076
Total utility expense	**$33,511**	**$32,849**	**$235,459**	**$229,945**	**$5,514**	**$394,192**
Contract Services						
Elevator service contract	$2,877	$2,849	$20,341	$19,942	$399	$34,186
Landscaping	1,642	1,549	11,383	10,841	542	18,584
Pest control	175	190	1,199	1,332	-133	2,283
Security contract	17,635	19,379	162,782	135,651	27,130	232,545
Fire contract	2,185	2,142	14,546	14,996	-450	25,707
Concierge	3,720	3,875	24,410	27,122	-2,712	46,495
Snow removal	1,045	986	6,487	6,901	-414	11,831
Water treatment	745	810	5,270	5,667	-397	9,714
Total contract services exp	**$30,023**	**$31,779**	**$246,416**	**$222,451**	**$23,965**	**$381,345**
Total operating expenses	**$131,936**	**$132,651**	**$957,325**	**$928,558**	**$28,768**	**$1,591,813**

Reserve Expense Allocations (The amounts listed below are added to each year, into interest-bearing accounts, in preparation for high-cost, anticipated major repairs or replacements.)

	Monthly Actual	Monthly Budget	YTD Actual	YTD Budget	YTD Variance	Annual Budget
Interior bldg elements	$1,588	$1,620	$11,570	$11,343	$227	$19,445
Exterior bldg elements	5,919	5,919	43,506	41,434	2,072	71,030
Bldg services elements	2,834	3,114	20,488	21,796	-1,308	37,365
Garage elements	1,799	1,763	11,479	12,343	-864	21,160
Total reserve expense alloc.	**$12,139**	**$12,417**	**$87,043**	**$86,917**	**$127**	**$149,000**
Total operating expense & reserve allocations	**$144,075**	**$145,068**	**$1,044,369**	**$1,015,474**	**$28,895**	**$1,740,813**
Net income (loss)	**-$2,855**	**$0**	**-$54,121**	**$0**	**-$54,121**	**$0**

Actual reserves on hand vs. reserves called for in Reserve Study

Often, monthly assessment fees are too low to meet financial reserve requirements.

NECESSARY FINANCIAL RESERVES

E   F

100%
90%
70%
50%
30%
10%
0

Sample Monthly Balance Sheet

Month Ending July 31, 2010

Assets	
Cash in checking (operating checking)	$27,832
Cash in reserve money market account	131,000
Cash in certificates of deposit — reserves	300,000
Assessments receivable	27,075
Prepaid expenses (insurance, taxes, etc.)	5,250
Total assets	**$491,157**
Liabilities and fund balances	
Prepaid owner assessments	$12,675
Accounts payable — operating	8,335
Accounts payable — reserves	1,000
Total Liabilities	**$22,010**
Fund balances (equity)	
Operating fund	$39,147
Reserve fund	430,000
Total fund balances	**$469,147**
Total liabilities and fund balances	**$491,157**

Actual reserves on hand vs. reserves called for in Reserve Study

Often, monthly assessment fees are too low to meet financial reserve requirements.

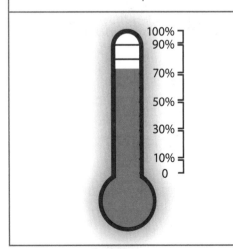

Insight

What you learn from a balance sheet:

The balance sheet is a "snapshot" statement of the assets and liabilities of the Association at a specific date, usually the last day of each month.

Each month, you will see at a glance, the net worth of the Association.

Keep in mind that you must subtract from that total any monthly fees that are late and still owed to the Association.

Sample Monthly Accounts Receivable Report

Month Ending July 31, 2010

Owner Name	Amount	Current	30 Days	60 Days	90 Days
Miller	4,262	50	1,053	1,053	2,106
McGinnis	3,209	50	1,053	1,053	1,053
Giovanazzi	2,156	50	1,053	1,053	0
Schulthies	2,156	50	1,053	1,053	0
Flores	2,156	50	1,053	1,053	0
Smith	1,103	50	1,053	0	0
Costas	1,103	50	1,053	0	0
Holien	1,103	50	1,053	0	0
Pollett	1,103	50	1,053	0	0
Kindt	1,103	50	1,053	0	0
Hunter	1.103	50	1,053	0	0
Ryan	1,103	50	1,053	0	0
Page 2 – not shown	5,415	150	3,159	2,106	0
Totals	**$27,075**	**$750**	**$15,795**	**$7,371**	**$3,159**

Warning!

Monthly fee collections are the *lifeblood* for the financial health of your Association and therefore for your property values.

The collection policy of your Association must be clear to owners, along with other information when new owners move in.

Some owners, while pressed hard for credit card debt and mortgage payments, especially during economic recessions, think the monthly Association dues might not be as urgent to pay. But that is an incorrect assumption.

Review the accounts receivable at least monthly. When collections spiral out of control, the maintenance of the Association can suffer.

Best Scenario

Have a payment and collections policy.

SAMPLE COLLECTION POLICY

- Monthly payments due by first of month.
- 10 days late - Late letter (or late charge, if permitted by governing documents and local state law).
- 30 days late - More urgently worded late letter.
- 60 days late - Account turned over to a collections attorney, with attorney fees to be paid by the late-paying owner. At the county courthouse, a lien is filed against the property.

COLLECTION LETTERS ARE BEST HANDLED BY COMMUNITY ASSOCIATION LAWYER

- Collections are best handled by a hired outside third party. Often, this is the Community Association Lawyer, who will comply with the Federal Fair Debt Collections Act.

Sample Reserve Study (condensed version)
High-Rise

Nine+ stories

Sample Reserve Study (condensed version)

Some thoughts as you review this sample Reserve Study

Insight

High-rise towers are often the highest-cost condominium type to build, operate and maintain.

Towers are expensive to plan, build, insure, staff, maintain and renovate.

For example, even getting water to units, pumped up floor after floor, happens only because of expensive capital equipment. That extra equipment must be maintained, but will also wear out and must eventually be replaced.

As long as residents have ample income, the higher costs associated with a high-rise are not an issue.

Best Scenario

In the largest U.S. state, contingency reserves are required in Reserve Study calculations

In California, by far the highest-population state in the United States, the Department of Real Estate (DRE) requires that Reserve Study calculations include contingency funding.

Based on DRE experience, higher contingencies are required for units converted from apartment buildings and for high-rise towers.

Property type	Minimum extra in contingency reserves
All properties	**3% extra**
Conversion from apartment building	**5% extra**
High-rise building (over 70 feet tall)	**10% extra**

Warning!

Sometimes, long-term infrastructure costs are not yet included in the current Reserve Study.

In the few states that mandate a Reserve Study, periodic updates of the Reserve Study, from every 1 to 5 years, are also mandated.

Major infrastructure components, slated to last more than 20 to 30 years, are often not included in the cost of future capital needs. That is because the current estimated useful life of the component extends beyond the 20- to 30-year time range of the current Reserve Study.

Currently, among prominent Reserve Study practitioners, there is not consensus yet on when to start adding in the replacement cost of longer-life infrastructure components.

One school of thought is that in the periodic reserve study updates, when a major component starts to show signs of premature failure, it is time to include funding plans for that component in the next updated Reserve Study.

Be aware.

Here is the potential danger to consumers and why periodically updated Reserve Studies are so important to you.

If faulty major components are found – for example, deteriorating plumbing pipes, electrical wiring, foundations, etc. – the infrastructure replacement costs can be very high. If there is only a short time to ramp up funding for those expensive infrastructure components, the special assessment costs for infrastructure repairs can be very high.

Sample Reserve Study (condensed version)

Condition Assessment

✓ **Best Scenario**

The persuasive power of on-site digital photos

Reserve Studies often contain color digital photos of deferred maintenance problem areas. Because deferred maintenance happens slowly, it is easy to walk past gradually worsening problems everyday and not notice. Digital photos help bring the problem into focus with the goal of convincing owners to *act now* to fix the problems.

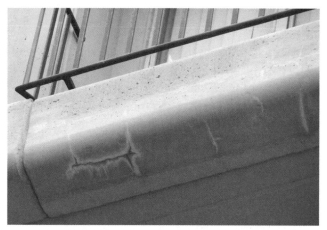

Balcony restoration and maintenance is a frequent line item in budgets. It is important to have ongoing repairs of reinforced concrete and a waterproof coating application to prevent the acceleration of balcony deterioration.

Periodic inspection and repairs of concrete façade cracks will prevent more costly repairs. The owners in the association also face costly litigation when façade pieces fall off, injuring pedestrians below.

Stains on hallway carpeting can indicate water seepage problems. This requires not only investigation of the source of the stain, but also the expense of carpet clearing and/or carpet replacement.

Corrosion of HVAC (heating ventilation and air conditioning) equipment is an indication that repairs are necessary.

Sample Reserve Study (condensed version)
Condition Assessment

Loose flashing and rooftop parapet wall cracks lead to roof leaks, which in turn, leak water into condominium units below. Regular periodic inspection and repair of the roof are necessary to minimize damage.

Evidence of water ponding on the roof needs close inspection to ensure that the membrane and joints do not deteriorate, which will result in water leaks into the condominium units below.

A well-maintained elastomeric coating will minimize deterioration of the concrete and the underlying reinforcing steel, such as the damage shown in the garage area photo above.

Ongoing proper maintenance of pool deck cracks, such as the caulked cracks pictured above, help to prevent water from entering the condominiums below the roof deck.

Sample Reserve Study (condensed version)

Executive Summary

Major component parts and estimated remaining useful life of components

Component	Approximate quantity	Useful life of component (years)	Remaining useful life of component (years)	Current average replacement cost	Future average replacement cost
Exterior building elements					
Door, front entrance	1	to 35	17	$65,000	$116,654
Railing, metal	3,600 linear ft	to 35	17	$180,000	$323,042
Roof, modified bitumen	120 squares	15 to 20	0	$300,000	$428,624
Walls, concrete, inspection and restoration	105,000 sq ft	8 to 12	2	$498,750	$670,799
Interior building elements					
Exercise room, exercise equipment	1	5 to 10	2	$15,000	$20,840
Hallways, floor coverage, carpet	800 sq yards	to 8	3	$56,000	$83,835
Hallways, light fixtures	80	to 25	19	$20,000	$38,450
Hallways, paint finishes	21,000 sq ft	to 8	3	$31,500	$47,158
Lobby, renovation, complete	1	to 25	15	$140,000	$234,549
Stairwells, paint finishes	2	12 to 18	10	$22,000	$31,033

Sample Reserve Study (condensed version)

Executive Summary

Major component parts and estimated remaining useful life of components (continued)

Component	Approximate quantity	Useful life of component (years)	Remaining useful life of component (years)	Current average replacement cost	Future average replacement cost
Building service elements					
Air handling units	2	to 35	9	$40,000	$54,516
Boilers, building heat, capital repairs	2	10 to 15	9	$36,000	$49,064
Boilers, building heat, replacement	2	to 60	17	$184,000	$330,220
Chiller, capital repairs	1	to 10	2	$20,000	$21,425
Chiller, replacement	1	25 to 35	12	$100,000	$151,107
Cooling tower	1	25 to 35	12	$60,000	$90,664
Elevators, controls, hoists and motors	2	to 40	22	$300,000	$639,453
Heat exchanger, domestic hot water	1	to 25	7	$14,000	$17,812
Life safety system	1	to 25	7	$75,000	$95,421
Pumps, domestic water, phased replacements	2	20 to 25	4	$21,800	$25,016
Pumps, HVAC	2	to 20	2	$24,000	$38,433
Pump, fire	1	to 50	30	$40,000	$112,272
Security system, upgrade	1	12 to 15	10	$31,000	$43,729
Trash compactor	1	to 20	2	$8,300	$8,891
Garage elements					
Concrete, inspections and capital repairs	25,600 sq ft	10 to 15	6	$55,040	$84,947
Concrete, traffic membrane applications	25,600 sq ft	10 to 15	6	$115,200	$177,797
Paint finishes	1	to 15	12	$28,000	$42,310
Unit heaters	10	to 25	7	$26,000	$33,079

Sample Reserve Study (condensed version)

Executive Summary

Components that may be **EXCLUDED** from the Reserve Study calculations

 **Insight**

Components that are left out of the custom Reserve Study will vary from community to community, based on Association governing documents and other local existing conditions. Examples are listed in the table below.

Type of excluded component	Definition	Examples
Unit owner responsibility Component exclusion	Based on your association's governing documents, some components are a unit owner responsibility.	Windows, garage doors, unit doors
Long-life Component exclusion	Some long-lasting infrastructure components are not yet included in the most current Reserve Study, because the expected useful life of the component extends beyond the 20- to 30-year range of the Reserve Study.	Plumbing pipes, electrical wiring, foundations
Utility Component exclusion	Some components might be maintained by the local utility company.	Primary electric feeds, telephone cables, gas mains and meters
Maintenance and repair Component exclusion	Some components can have ongoing preventive maintenance and repair. This repair cost is an operating expense and not a capital reserve expense.	Operating expense example: • Annual or semi-annual roof inspection and repair Reserve expense example: • Replacing the whole roof
Below threshold cost Component exclusion	If the reserve component is below a certain dollar amount, it is not included in the Reserve Study.	Some Reserve Studies only include components that cost at least $500 or $1,000 to replace. If the component is less than the threshold amount, it is often counted as an operating expense.
Government funded Component exclusion	If a local government maintains and replaces certain components, then these components are left out of the Reserve Study.	Street paving, sidewalks, storm water management

Sample Reserve Study (condensed version)

Executive Summary

Components **EXCLUDED** from the High-Rise example Reserve Study

Unit owner responsibility component exclusions

- Unit windows
- Unit balcony doors
- Heating, ventilating, and air-conditioning (HVAC) equipment that is inside the individual unit

Long-life component exclusions

- Electrical systems
- Foundations
- Pipes, interior building, water and sewer
- Pipes, subsurface utilities

Utility component exclusions

- Primary electric feeds
- Electric transformers
- Cable TV systems and structures
- Telephone cables and structures
- Gas mains and meters

Maintenance and repair component exclusions

- General maintenance to common elements that is paid for from operating expenses
- Doors, metal
- Elevator cab finishes, freight
- Exhaust fans
- Light fixtures, building exterior
- Landscaping

Below threshold cost component exclusions

- Expenditures that are less than $4,000. For higher cost of repairs and replacements in a high-rise or mid-rise building, this report uses a $4,000 threshold to include an item as a reserve expense. For a smaller Association of one- and two-story buildings, the cost threshold exclusion may be as low as $500 or $1,000.

Government funded component exclusions

- Government roadways and parking
- Government sidewalks and curbs
- Government lighting
- Government stormwater management

Sample Reserve Study (condensed version)

Estimated Reserve Fund Expenditures 2008 through 2037

2008

$300,000	Exterior building elements — roof, modified bitumen
$300,000	Total reserve expenses for year

2009

No reserve expenditures planned for this year

$0	Total reserve expenses for year

2010

$534,273	Exterior building elements — walls, concrete, inspection and restoration
$16,068	Interior building elements — exercise room, exercise equipment
$21,425	Building services elements — chiller, capital repairs
$25,709	Building services elements — pumps, HVAC
$35,581	Building services elements — trash compactor
$606,366	Total reserve expenses for year

2011

$62,088	Interior building elements — hallways, floor coverings, carpet
$34,925	Interior building elements — hallways, paint finishes
$97,013	Total reserve expenses for year

2012

$25,016 domestic	Building services elements — pumps, water, phased replacements
$25,016	Total reserve expenses for year

2013

No reserve expenditures planned for this year

$0	Total reserve expenses for year

2014

$67,658	Garage elements — concrete, inspections and capital repairs
$141,610	Garage elements — concrete, traffic membrane applications
$209,268	Total reserve expenses for year

Insight

Operating expense versus reserve expenses.

Operating expenses are:

Ongoing, annual expenses, which often arrive as predictable monthly invoices, such as:

- Lawn care services
- Property management and bookkeeping services
- Ordinary, minor repairs
- Insurance, etc.

Reserve expenses are:

Higher-cost, major repairs and replacements, such as:

- Roof replacement
- Foundation repairs
- Siding replacement
- Parking area resurfacing
- Street repaving

Sample Reserve Study (condensed version)

Estimated Reserve Fund Expenditures 2008 through 2037

2034

$1,219,922	Exterior building elements walls — concrete, inspection and restoration
$53,322	Building services elements — pumps, domestic water, phased replacements
$1,273,244	Total reserve expenses for year

2035

$141,768	Interior building elements — hallways, floor coverings, carpet
$79,744	Interior building elements — hallways, paint finishes
$70,884	Garage elements — paint finishes
$292,396	Total reserve expenses for year

2036

No reserve expenditures planned for this year

$0	Total reserve expenses for year

2037

No reserve expenditures planned for this year

$0	Total reserve expenses for year

30-year TOTAL needed for Reserve Expenses:

$8,093,896

Sample Reserve Study (condensed version)

Estimated Reserve Fund Expenditures by Year

2008 through 2037

Insight

Often, capital expenditures can vary dramatically from year to year, as shown below.

The black line near the bottom of the graph shows the average annual expenditure of money.

As the property ages, it generally costs more to maintain. That is because:

- More building components will reach the end of their useful life and must be replaced.
- Future expenditures are often figured with an estimated inflation rate such as 3% per year.

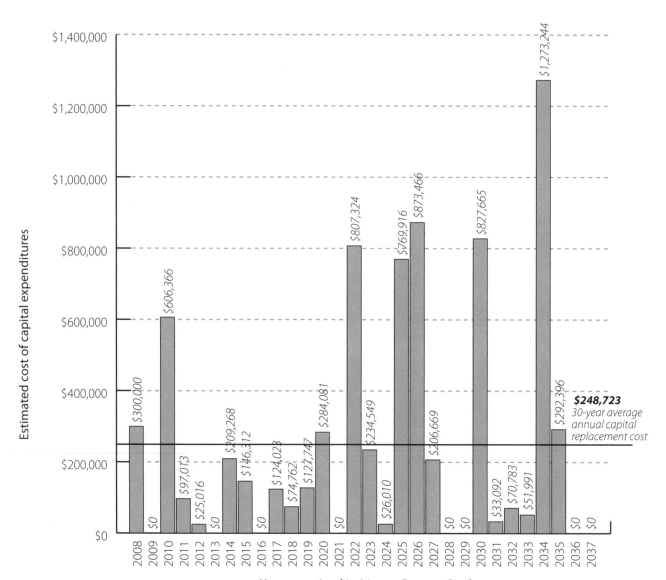

Years examined in 30-year Reserve Study

Sample Reserve Study (condensed version)

Estimated Reserve Fund Expenditures by Category

2008 through 2037

30-year total needed for reserve expenses: **$8,093,896**

30-year average annual spending for reserve expenses: **$269,797**

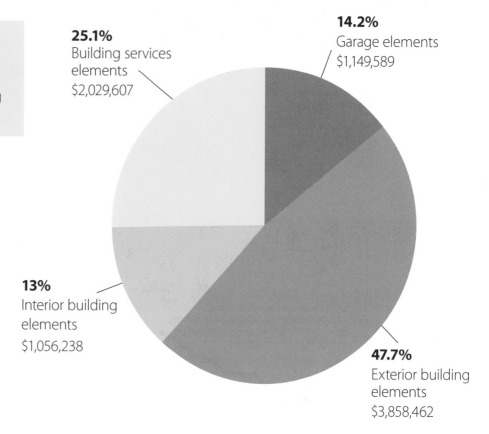

25.1%
Building services elements
$2,029,607

14.2%
Garage elements
$1,149,589

13%
Interior building elements
$1,056,238

47.7%
Exterior building elements
$3,858,462

Exterior Building Elements

Roof modified bitumen	$857,247
Walls, concrete, inspection and restoration	2,567,519
Door, front entrance	116,654
Railings, metal	323,042
TOTAL	**$3,858,462**

Interior Building Elements

Exercise room, exercise equipment	$137,715
Hallways, floor coverings, carpets	393,274
Hallways, paint finishes	221,217
Hallways, fixtures	38,450
Stairwells, paint finishes	31,033
Lobby renovation	234,549
TOTAL	**$1,056,238**

Building Services Elements

Chiller, capital repairs	$64,055
Chiller, replacement	151,107
Pumps, HVAC	76,865
Trash compactor	26,583
Pumps, domestic water phased replacements	78,338
Heat exchanger, domestic hot water	17,812
Life safety system	95,421
Air handling units	54,516
Boilers, building heat, capital repairs	125,798
Boilers, building heat, replacement	330,220
Security system, upgrade	114,512
Cooling tower	90,664
Elevator controls, hoists and motors	639,453
Stairwells, paint finishes	51,991
Pumps, fire	112,272
TOTAL	**$2,029,607**

Garage Elements

Concrete, inspections and capital repairs	$324,380
Concrete, traffic membrane applications	678,936
Unit heaters	33,079
Paint finishes	113,194
TOTAL	**$1,149,589**

Sample Reserve Study (condensed version)

Three Alternative Funding Plans vs. Component Costs

2008 through 2037

Warning!

Often in a professional Reserve Study, various funding plans are charted. For example, if the monthly maintenance fee starts too low at the beginning of the development and is never raised, there can be dire financial consequences.

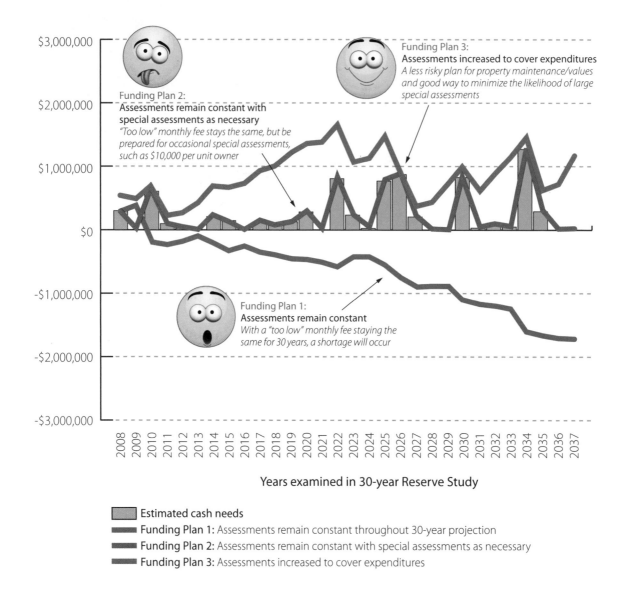

Funding Plan 2:
Assessments remain constant with special assessments as necessary
"Too low" monthly fee stays the same, but be prepared for occasional special assessments, such as $10,000 per unit owner

Funding Plan 3:
Assessments increased to cover expenditures
A less risky plan for property maintenance/values and good way to minimize the likelihood of large special assessments

Funding Plan 1:
Assessments remain constant
With a "too low" monthly fee staying the same for 30 years, a shortage will occur

Years examined in 30-year Reserve Study

■ Estimated cash needs
▬ Funding Plan 1: Assessments remain constant throughout 30-year projection
▬ Funding Plan 2: Assessments remain constant with special assessments as necessary
▬ Funding Plan 3: Assessments increased to cover expenditures

Sample Reserve Study (condensed version)

Cash-Flow Analysis

2008 through 2037

Insight

Just as in a business, having cash available to cover expenses each year is necessary for economic survival. Positive cash flow usually does not happen by accident.

Often in Reserve Studies, there is a cash-flow analysis that projects cash availability with an overlay of:

- Reserve expenditures
- Reserve contributions
- Cash on hand

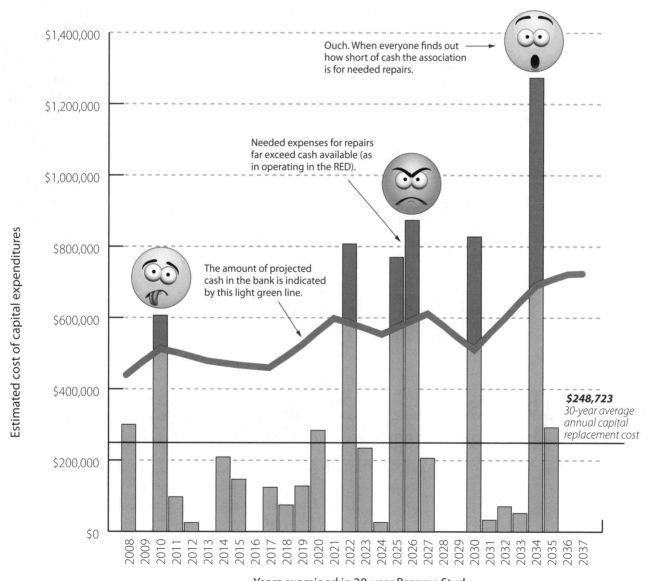

Ouch. When everyone finds out how short of cash the association is for needed repairs.

Needed expenses for repairs far exceed cash available (as in operating in the RED).

The amount of projected cash in the bank is indicated by this light green line.

$248,723
30-year average annual capital replacement cost

Estimated cost of capital expenditures

Years examined in 30-year Reserve Study

Sample Preventive-Maintenance Check List
Executive Summary

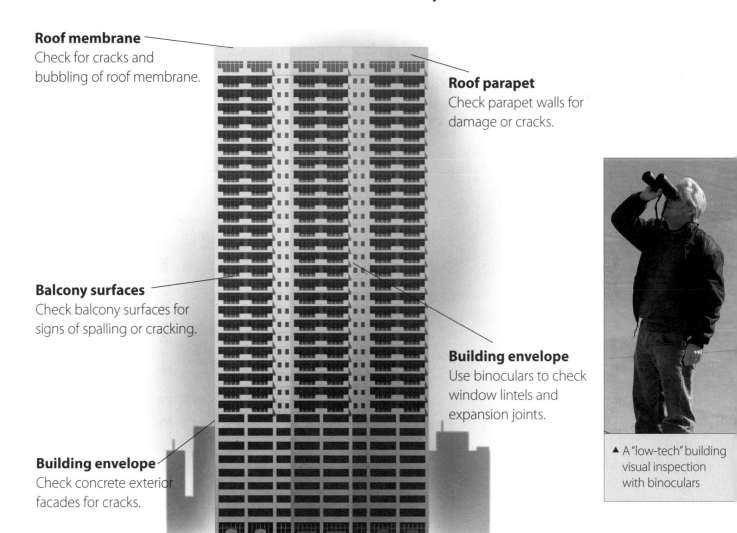

Roof membrane
Check for cracks and bubbling of roof membrane.

Roof parapet
Check parapet walls for damage or cracks.

Balcony surfaces
Check balcony surfaces for signs of spalling or cracking.

Building envelope
Use binoculars to check window lintels and expansion joints.

Building envelope
Check concrete exterior facades for cracks.

▲ A "low-tech" building visual inspection with binoculars

Cost-Saving Benefits of a Preventive-Maintenance Program

A preventive-maintenance checklist helps you to manage your property.

By carefully prolonging the life of building components, and systematically monitoring those components seasonally, you can help reduce the frequency of expensive, unanticipated emergency repairs.

Ideas

An engineering consulting firm will often drop scaffolding from the roof, down the side of the building to examine balcony condition, facades and the building envelope. Some building managers perform a preliminary inspection with binoculars.

Sample Seasonal Preventive-Maintenance Check List

This list *does not* include monthly, weekly and daily checklists for your building

	Spring	Summer	Fall	Winter
Roof				
Check cracks and bubbling of roof membrane	X		X	
Check for any signs of ponding	X	X	X	
Check parapet walls for damage or cracks	X	X		
Check cap stone joints for separation or cracks	X		X	
Check flashing for tears or loose parts	X	X	X	X
Check down spouts and splash guards	X	X	X	X
Check gutters, drains	X	X	X	X
Domestic roof tank				
Check hinges and hasp on tank cover door	X	X	X	X
Check floats and alarms	X	X	X	X
Have roof tank cleaned and sanitized		X		
Check tank for any damage over winter	X			
Elevator machine room				
Check machine room for any weather penetration	X		X	
Heating systems				
Have boiler tubes cleaned	X		X	
Have burner overhauled		X		
Have combustion efficiency test done on burner			X	
Clean all Wye Strainers	X			
Clean and repair steam traps		X		
Flush domestic hot water coils	X	X	X	X
Once every 5 years, clean oil tank for #4 & #6 oil				
Check limits and all boiler controls for winter use			X	
Building envelope				
Use binoculars to check: • Window lintels, expansion joints • Bricks and possible mortar deterioration	X X		X X	
Check balcony surfaces & railing for deterioration	X		X	
Check bulk head doors and windows, skylights	X	X		
Clean cooling towers and make ready for use	X			
Check sidewalks for cracks in concrete	X	X	X	X
Check sidewalks for heaving	X			X
Check roof drains for debris & all outdoor lighting	X	X	X	X
Check out door metal for signs of rust		X		

Major Structural Renovation Expenses Reserve Cost Comparison

Detached, Single-Family Home

In same neighborhood as High-Rise Condominium Association and same time of construction

Brief data for this property example

Year built	1910
Quality level of original construction	Above average
Maintenance level since construction	Above average
Have any major systems (plumbing, wiring, HVAC) been replaced since construction in 1910?	Central air conditioning first installed in 1966
Cost range for reserve study for a single-family home	$1,500 to $3,000

Insight

What are the major repair and replacement costs for a single-family home?

Most home owners know that major repair and replacement costs for a single-family home represent large future outlays of cash, but few have taken the time to create a Reserve Study for a single-family home.

In the list at the right, are projected major repair and replacement costs for a single family home, in the same neighborhood as the Reserve Study for the sample Association property in this section.

Because a new single family home in the center of a high-population urban area can be rare, the single family home Reserve Study comparison used here is an urban townhome, originally constructed in 1910.

This list is presented to readers merely as food for thought, and not for the purposes of a direct comparison of costs between a single-family home and a condominium.

Home owner costs that are not included in the list at right, are the additional day-to-day operating expenses for a single-family home such as removal of leaves from roof gutters, lawn care, snow removal, exterior painting, and other routine minor home repairs.

DISCLAIMER—Life expectancy of component parts will vary based on many factors, such as:
• Quality level of original components
• Local climate conditions
• Interim preventive maintenance if applicable

DISCLAIMER—Actual renovation costs can vary widely based on many factors, such as:
• Local availability of skilled labor
• Quality of component parts used
• Current worldwide demand for raw materials

DISCLAIMER — Do not base your projected expenses or reserves on this specific yet theoretical example. Each property is unique. Budget funds for your own custom-created, professional Reserve Study.

Major Structural Renovation Expenses Reserve Cost Comparison

Detached, Single-Family Home

Component	Approximate quantity	Useful life of component (years)	Remaining useful life of component (years)	Current average replacement cost	Future average replacement cost
Exterior building elements					
Dormers, rebuild	2	to 40	10	$5,000	$7,053
Gutters and downspouts	170 linear ft	15 to 20	10	$1,870	$2,638
Roof, asphalt shingles	15 squares	15 to 20	10	$6,750	$9,522
Walls, masonry, inspections and partial repointing	3,100 sq ft	8 to 12	4	$7,750	$12,008
Windows and doors, replacement	780 sq ft	45 to 55	11	$27,300	$39,857
Building services elements					
Electrical system, upgrade	1	to 75+	1	$15,000	$15,525
Piping, partial replacements	1	to 75+	1	$9,000	$9,315
Split system, heating and cooling unit	1	15 to 20	13	$7,500	$11,730
Water heater	1	12 to 15	5	$1,200	$1,827
Property site elements					
Concrete sidewalk, steps and patio, partial replacements	70 sq ft	to 65	8	$665	$1,056
Railings, metal	16 linear ft	to 40	30	$720	$2,021

Who Does What?

Executive Summary of volunteer and paid positions to operate the property.

Owners to volunteer to serve on the Board of Directors

- President
- Treasurer
- Secretary
- At-large board members

Off-site property management firm

If no outside Property Management firm is hired, the property is referred to as "self-managed" by volunteers within the association.

Key staff positions often provided by an off-site Property Management firm may include:

- Community manager
- Customer service coordinator
- Maintenance coordinator
- Bookkeeper

Full-time on-site manager and staff

Often, at larger developments and more upscale developments, a full-time site manager and staff are hired.

Paid part-time outside vendors

Financial and mechanical planning services

- Reserve specialist and staff

Mechanical planning services

- Consulting mechanical engineer

Financial and tax-filing services

- Certified public accountant and staff
- Banking services

Legal services

- Attorney and staff
- Usually has experience as a real estate attorney, as well as community association experience

Insurance services

- Insurance agent and staff

Trade and crafts persons

- Roofing crew
- Plumbing crew
- Electrical crew
- "Handyman" for routine day-to-day repairs
- Painting crew
- Concrete and masonry crew (for sidewalk, foundation and masonry repairs)
- Asphalt and paving crew

HVAC (heating, ventilation and air conditioning)

- Boiler / chiller maintenance and repair crew

Grounds Services

- Lawn care crew
- Arborist crew for large tree trimming
- Snow removal crew
- Pest control
- Cleaning / janitorial services
- Trash removal services

Warning!

All vendors must submit annual proof of insurance form(s)

All vendors should be fully insured and submit the annual proof of insurance forms for your records. This insurance includes workers comp, liability and whatever is mandated by laws in your state.

Example E:
Home Owner Association

Detached, single-family homes

Maintenance and Financial Planning Documentation

Financial PRO and CON overview of this housing type example

PRO

Affordability, *but with qualifications*

Often, there can be lower monthly fees in a Home Owner Association of detached, single-family homes, compared with other community associations that have greater shared infrastructure expenses and more services offered, such as apartment-style condominiums.

Affordable amenities through shared costs

Through pooled resources, some larger home owner associations of detached, single-family homes may offer amenities, such as a clubhouse / recreational building, pool, tennis courts, and professionally maintained common areas.

Rule enforcement

Some owners prefer a neighborhood where a locally based group of owners (the board of directors, in cooperation with a paid manager) maintains the aesthetic and architectural standard of the community and other rule enforcement.

No shared walls may reduce neighbor noise

As a detached, single-family home, there are no shared walls, as in a townhome or apartment-style condominium. Therefore, there can be reduced likelihood of noise intrusion from neighbors.

CON

Exterior maintenance is your responsibility

Usually, you will solely bear the burden of planning, pricing and supervising your roof replacements, foundation repairs, exterior painting, siding replacement, etc. As with other housing types, interior maintenance is your responsibility as well.

Higher cost of housing

With its own lot, this detached, single-family home may cost more than a similar or smaller condominium unit in the same neighborhood.

Brief data for this property example

Number of detached, single-family homes in this development	400
Year(s) built	1970-1974
Other major buildings/ facilities in the complex	• Clubhouse / recreational building • 2 pools, paddleball court • Small basketball court, small park • Landscaped street frontage
Quality level of original construction	Average
Maintenance level since construction	Average
Cost range for reserve study	$2,500 to $4,000
Cost range for reserve study update with site visit	$1,250 to $2,500
Cost range for reserve study update without site visit	$600 to $1,200
Current reserve account balance	**$216,891**
Recommended reserve account balance	**$328,983**

In this example:

Current monthly fee per lot $44*

Based on reserve study *and* operating budget analysis

Current monthly fee *underfunding* per lot $5

(This is the accumulating deficit per home, per month, for this sample budget year.)

A Reserve Study, based on the specific components at your Association, is critical for determining an adequate monthly fee.

* In Home Owner Associations of detached, single-family homes, the fee is often a fixed rate per lot.

DISCLAIMER — Each property is unique. Therefore, each property budget is unique, based on local conditions and local laws. Do not use these budget figures from this specific yet theoretical example for your own property.

Monthly fee includes:

Pool
- Ongoing pool maintenance including pool heater & filter systems, deck surfaces and pool furniture

Clubhouse / recreational building
- Ongoing maintenance, plus reserves for renovations such as roofing, flooring, HVAC systems, painting and playground equipment

Landscape and paving
- Asphalt seal-coating and asphalt replacement, pavers, landscape upgrades, irrigation time clocks and wooden arbor maintenance

Exterior lighting
- Lighting for streets and recreational areas

Administrative services
- Off-site property management service to plan and budget, take resident phone calls, get bids from vendors, coordinate all community services, bookkeeping and monthly invoice payments, and internal communication newsletters

Financial reserve expense
- Systematic savings for large capital expenses such as the pool, recreational building and other common elements

Actual reserves on hand vs. reserves called for in Reserve Study

Consider raising reserve levels in order to have cash on hand for anticipated repairs and replacements.

NECESSARY FINANCIAL RESERVES

E   F

100%
90%
70%
50%
30%
10%
0

Financial Reserves

66% funded

Sample Annual Budget

Fiscal Year — January 1 through December 31

Income	current year	% of budget	$ per month
Monthly assessments	$236,548	96.9%	$49.28
Facility rental / concessions	6,000	2.5%	1.25
Interest income	50	0.0%	0.01
Other income	1,500	0.6%	0.31
Total income	**$244,098**	**100.0%**	**$50.85**

Operating Expenses (ongoing expenses that occur each year)

Clubhouse and Amenities Expense	current year	% of budget	$ per month
Building maintenance	$7,200	2.8%	$1.50
Pool maintenance	8,400	3.3%	1.75
Pool supplies	3,200	1.2%	0.67
Lifeguard (contract, summer)	8,200	3.2%	1.71
Clubhouse / rec area repairs	6,000	2.3%	1.25
Cleaning / janitorial	9,300	3.6%	1.94
Pest control	3,000	1.2%	0.63
Water / sewer common areas	12,000	4.7%	2.50
Gas — pool heat	6,000	2.3%	1.25
Electricity	3,200	1.2%	0.67
Rental expenses	3,000	1.2%	0.63
Security	8,400	3.3%	1.75
Total buildings expense	**$77,900**	**30.4%**	**$16.23**

Grounds Expense	current year	% of budget	$ per month
Groundskeeping salaries	$28,800	11.2%	$6.00
Payroll taxes / workers' comp	4,900	1.9%	1.02
Tree pruning	3,000	1.2%	0.63
Arborist / consultant	300	0.1%	0.06
Plant / tree replacement	1,200	0.5%	0.25
Irrigation repairs	1,000	0.4%	0.21
Total grounds expense	**$39,200**	**15.3%**	**$8.17**

Sample Annual Budget

Fiscal Year — January 1 through December 31

Operating Expenses (cont.)

Insurance & Administration	current year	% of budget	$ per month
Common area insurance	$12,000	4.7%	$2.50
Management contract	39,940	15.6%	8.32
Office / postage / printing	3,800	1.5%	0.79
Local taxes and fees	1,200	0.5%	0.25
Legal	4,000	1.6%	0.83
Accounting / other professional	3,750	1.5%	0.78
Doubtful account expense	10,000	3.9%	2.08
Total insurance & administration	**$74,690**	**29.1%**	**$15.56**
Total operating expense	**$191,790**	**74.9%**	**$39.96**

Reserve Expense Allocations (The amounts listed below are added to each year, into interest-bearing accounts, in preparation for high-cost, anticipated major repairs or replacements.)

	current year	% of budget	$ per month
Roofs / decks	$1,737	0.7%	$0.36
Arbors / other structure	2,679	1.0%	0.56
Painting	1,879	0.7%	0.39
Mechanical	3,337	1.3%	0.70
Plumbing / electrical	1,245	0.5%	0.26
Flooring	701	0.3%	0.15
Landscape / paving	9,570	3.7%	1.99
Pool	25,444	9.9%	5.30
Recreation facilities	4,208	1.6%	0.88
Miscellaneous	288	0.1%	0.06
Contingency reserve	1,211	0.5%	0.25
Total reserve expense allocations	**$52,308**	**20.4%**	**$10.90**
Reserves not funded	$12,204	4.8%	$2.54
Total operating exp. & reserve alloc.	**$256,302**	**100.00%**	**$53.40**

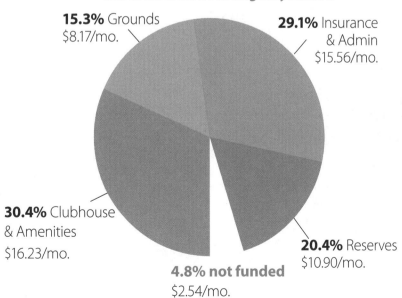

**Annual budget will have shortfall
due to reserves not being fully funded**

15.3% Grounds $8.17/mo.

29.1% Insurance & Admin $15.56/mo.

30.4% Clubhouse & Amenities $16.23/mo.

20.4% Reserves $10.90/mo.

4.8% not funded $2.54/mo.

Sample Monthly Income Statement

Month Ending July 31, 2009

Income	Monthly Actual	Monthly Budget	YTD Actual	YTD Budget	YTD Variance	Annual Budget
Monthly assessments	$17,520	$17,520	$122,640	$122,640	$0	$210,240
Special assessments	900	417	3,150	2,917	233	5,000
Interest income	3	4	22	29	-7	50
Other income	140	100	780	700	80	1,200
Total income	**$18,563**	**$18,041**	**$126,592**	**$126,286**	**$306**	**$216,490**

Operating Expenses (ongoing expenses that occur each year)

Clubhouse and Amenities Expense						
Building maintenance	$550	$575	$3,910	$4,025	-$115	$6,900
Pool maintenance	725	700	5,075	4,900	175	8,400
Pool supplies	225	250	1,850	1,750	100	3,000
Lifeguard (contract, summer)	2,000	667	4,000	4,667	-667	8,000
Clubhouse / rec area	250	500	2,800	3,500	-700	6,000
Cleaning / janitorial	800	750	5,400	5,250	150	9,000
Pest control	300	250	2,100	1,750	350	3,000
Water / sewer common areas	1,110	917	7,110	6,417	693	11,000
Gas — pool heat	300	600	2,750	4,200	-1,450	7,200
Electricity	240	267	1,775	1,867	-192	3,200
Rental expenses	300	208	1,850	1,458	392	2,500
Security	700	350	4,900	2,450	2,450	4,200
Total buildings expense	**$7,500**	**$6,033**	**$43,520**	**$213,197**	**$1,287**	**$72,400**
Grounds Expense						
Groundskeeping salaries	$2,200	$2,333	$16,000	$16,333	-$333	$28,000
Payroll taxes / workers' comp	375	397	2,720	2,777	-57	4,760
Tree pruning	0	250	3,500	1,750	1,750	3,000
Arborist / consultant	0	25	0	175	-175	300
Plant / tree replacement	150	83	800	583	217	1,000
Irrigation repairs	80	42	540	292	248	500
Total grounds expense	**$2,805**	**$3,130**	**$23,560**	**$21,910**	**$1,650**	**$37,560**

Insight

What you learn from an income statement:

In a business, the income statement shows the profit or loss for the month (or the year, if an annual statement.)

The income statement sometimes is known as the profit and loss statement.

In a Community Association, this summary shows how actual spending is progressing, compared with the original estimated budget for the year.

Keep in mind, the annual budget is a best guess and a guideline for what will happen during the year.

Sample Monthly Income Statement

Month Ending July 31, 2009

Insurance & Administration	Monthly Actual	Monthly Budget	YTD Actual	YTD Budget	YTD Variance	Annual Budget
Bldg / common area ins	$950	$1,000	$6,900	$7,000	-$100	$12,000
Management contract	3,200	3,200	22,400	22,400	0	38,400
Office / postage / printing	265	303	1,950	2,118	-168	3,630
Loan repayment	0	0	0	0	0	0
Interest expense	0	0	0	0	0	0
Local taxes and fees	0	125	500	875	-375	1,500
Legal	650	292	2,250	2,042	208	3,500
Acctg / other professional	0	292	1,800	2,042	-242	3,500
Doubtful acct expense	500	167	4,500	1,167	3,333	2,000
Total insurance & admin.	**$5,565**	**$5,378**	**$40,300**	**$37,643**	**$2,658**	**$64,530**
Total operating expenses	**$15,870**	**$14,541**	**$107,380**	**$101,786**	**$15,594**	**$174,490**

Reserve Expense Allocations (The amounts listed below are added to each year, into interest-bearing accounts, in preparation for high-cost, anticipated major repairs or replacements.)

	Monthly Actual	Monthly Budget	YTD Actual	YTD Budget	YTD Variance	Annual Budget
Roofs / decks	$116	$116	$813	$813	$0	$1,394
Arbors / other structure	179	179	1,255	1,255	0	2,151
Painting	126	126	880	880	0	1,508
Mechanical	223	223	1,563	1,563	0	2,680
Plumbing / electrical	83	83	583	583	0	999
Flooring	47	47	328	328	0	563
Landscape / paving	640	640	4,482	4,482	0	7,684
Pool	1,703	1,703	11,918	11,918	0	20,430
Recreation facilities	282	282	1,971	1,971	0	3,379
Miscellaneous	19	19	135	135	0	231
Contingency reserve	82	82	572	572	0	980
Total reserve expense alloc.	**$3,500**	**$3,500**	**$24,500**	**$24,500**	**$0**	**$42,000**
Total operating expense & reserve allocations	**$19,370**	**$18,041**	**$131,880**	**$126,286**	**$5,594**	**$216,490**
Net income (loss)	**-$807**	**$0**	**-$5,288**	**$0**	**-$5,288**	**$0**

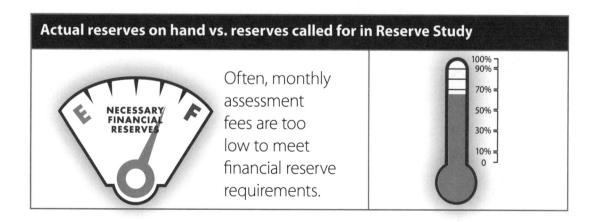

Actual reserves on hand vs. reserves called for in Reserve Study

NECESSARY FINANCIAL RESERVES

Often, monthly assessment fees are too low to meet financial reserve requirements.

Sample Monthly Balance Sheet

Month Ending July 31, 2009

Assets	
Cash in checking (operating checking)	$9,150
Cash in reserve money market account	16,891
Cash in certificates of deposit — reserves	200,000
Assessments receivable	11,847
Prepaid expenses (insurance, taxes, etc.)	1,225
Total assets	**$239,113**
Liabilities and fund balances	
Prepaid owner assessments	$1,620
Accounts payable — operating	3,050
Accounts payable — reserves	0
Total liabilities	**$4,670**
Fund balances (equity)	
Operating fund	$17,552
Reserve fund	216,891
Total fund balances	**$234,443**
Total liabilities and fund balances	**$239,113**

Actual reserves on hand vs. reserves called for in Reserve Study

Often, monthly assessment fees are too low to meet financial reserve requirements.

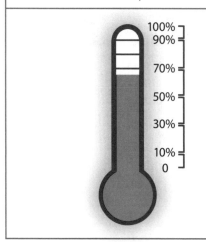

Insight

What you learn from a balance Sheet:

The balance sheet is a "snapshot" statement of the assets and liabilities of the Association at a specific date, usually the last day of each month.

Each month, you will see at a glance, the net worth of the Association.

Keep in mind that you must subtract from that total any monthly fees that are late and still owed to the Association.

Sample Monthly Accounts Receivable Report

Month Ending July 31, 2009

Owner Name/Address	Amount	Current	30 Days	60 Days	90 Days
David & Karen Miller — 3524 Windsor Road	44		44		
Ronald & Angela Solomon — 2511 Crestview Road	88			88	
John & Charlotte Franklin — 3011 E. San Miguel Drive	1,056				1,056
Sean & Sandy Carrico — 2102 A. Amherst Way	88			88	
Roberto & Stephanie Rameriz — 2207 Glenoaks Court	44			44	
James Morse — 1504 San Pablo Place	44		44		
Ben & Belinda Fuentes — 3525 San Gabriel Court	44		44		
Alex & Cheryl Pearlman — 3303 San Miguel Circle	44		44		
Susan Harrison — 2503 Alameda Place	44			44	
Kirk & Beverly Jackson — 2213 Vista Place	88			88	
Calvin & Brenda Kerrick — 2015 Bellevue Place	396				396
Mark McKenna & James Ricketts — 2535 San Miguel Circle	44		44		
(Pages 2–4 of Receivable Report not shown)	$9,823		$1,356	$836	$7,587
Total Accounts Receivable	**$11,847**		**$1,620**	**$1,188**	**$9,039**

Warning!

Monthly fee collections are the *lifeblood* for the financial health of your Association and therefore for your property values.

The collection policy of your Association must be clear to owners, along with other information when new owners move in.

Some owners, while pressed hard for credit card debt and mortgage payments, especially during economic recessions, think the monthly Association dues might not be as urgent to pay. But that is an incorrect assumption.

Review the accounts receivable at least monthly. When collections spiral out of control, the maintenance of the Association can suffer.

Best Scenario

Have a payment and collections policy.

SAMPLE COLLECTION POLICY
- Monthly payments due by first of month.
- 10 days late - Late letter (or late charge, if permitted by governing documents and local state law).
- 30 days late - More urgently worded late letter.
- 60 days late - Account turned over to a collections attorney, with attorney fees to be paid by the late-paying owner. At the county courthouse, a lien is filed against the property.

COLLECTION LETTERS ARE BEST HANDLED BY COMMUNITY ASSOCIATION LAWYER
- Collections are best handled by a hired, outside third party. Often, this is the Community Association Lawyer, who will comply with the Federal Fair Debt Collections Act.

DISCLAIMER — Each property is unique. Therefore, each property budget is unique, based on local conditions and local laws. Do not use these budget figures from this specific yet theoretical example for your own property.

 Part II | 189

Sample Reserve Study (condensed version)
Home Owner Association

Detached, single-family homes

Sample Reserve Study (condensed version)

Some thoughts as you review this sample Reserve Study

 **Best Scenario**

Contingency reserves are extra reserves

A Reserve Study provides a best guess for what may happen in the future at a property. However, it is seldom possible to anticipate every expense/replacement that will be incurred.

Therefore, for example, the California Department of Real Estate (DRE) recommends extra reserve amounts based on their experience with property maintenance costs.

Property type	Minimum extra in contingency reserves
All properties	**3% extra**
Conversion from apartment building	**5% extra**
High-rise building (over 70 feet tall)	**10% extra**

 **Warning!**

Sometimes, long-term infrastructure costs are not yet included in the current Reserve Study.

In the few states that mandate a Reserve Study, periodic updates of the Reserve Study, from every 1 to 5 years, are also mandated.

Major infrastructure components, slated to last more than 20 to 30 years, are often not included in the cost of future capital needs. That is because the current estimated useful life of the component extends beyond the 20- to 30-year time range of the current Reserve Study.

Currently, among prominent Reserve Study practitioners, there is not consensus yet on when to start adding in the replacement cost of longer-life infrastructure components.

One school of thought is that in the periodic Reserve Study updates, when a major component starts to show signs of premature failure, it is time to include funding plans for that component in the next updated Reserve Study.

Be aware.

Here is the potential danger to consumers and why periodically updated Reserve Studies are so important to you

If faulty major components are found – for example, deteriorating plumbing pipes, electrical wiring, foundations, etc. – the infrastructure replacement costs can be very high. If there is only a short time to ramp up funding for those expensive infrastructure components, the special assessment costs for infrastructure repairs can be very high.

Sample Reserve Study (condensed version)
Condition Assessment

Best Scenario

The persuasive power of on-site digital photos

Reserve Studies often contain color digital photos of deferred-maintenance problem areas. Since deferred maintenance happens slowly, it is easy to walk past gradually worsening problems everyday and not notice. Digital photos help bring the problem into focus with the goal of convincing owners to *act now* to fix the problems.

Roof rain gutters will often deteriorate from the inside first. Non-functioning gutters can accelerate roof and siding deterioration and lead to wood rot and termite infestation.

Without proper horticultural maintenance, plants can outgrow their containers, necessitating replacement of the planters as well as the plants. These Mexican-type tiles, when not sealed, may quickly take on a rustic look, which is actually desired by many.

Deteriorating wooden doorjamb will result in failure of the door frame structure, also leading to additional wood rot and termite infestation.

Rusting tube steel fencing shows a lack of regular repainting. Deterioration will often happen from the inside out. Cost to repaint is approximately .75 to 1.50 per sq. ft., but to replace is approximately $6 to $10 per sq. ft.

DISCLAIMER — Do not base your monthly fees or reserves on this specific yet theoretical example. Each property is unique, subject to local conditions and local laws. Budget funds for your Association's custom-created, professional Reserve Study.

Sample Reserve Study (condensed version)
Condition Assessment

Deteriorating flat roof may allow for moisture intrusion into areas beneath roof, which increases the likelihood of wood rot and termite infestation.

A simple seal coat/slurry applied on a 3- to 5-year cycle can cost as low as .08 to .15 cents per square foot, which protects the underlying asphalt. If pavement becomes too deteriorated, to completely replace the asphalt costs two to three times the simpler scrape and overlay process.

Pool furniture in considered as a component in total, versus individual pieces. The deteriorated furniture is primarily an aesthetic issue; however, if it deteriorates to the point of potential failure of the strapping, there are liability issues.

A basement-level garage with a failed waterproofing system can eventually result in structural damage due to rusting of rebar and subsequent failure of concrete block.

Sample Reserve Study (condensed version)

Executive Summary

Major component parts and estimated remaining useful life of components

Component	Approximate quantity	Useful life of component (years)	Remaining useful life of component (years)	Replacement costs for 30 years with inflation factor of 2.85% annually
Pool				
Plaster — pool	3,900 sq. ft	10	2	$86,299
Coping / tile	620 6" tile	20	12	$22,830
Boiler — replace	1 @ 1,010,000 btu	24	0	$59,836
Boiler — overhaul	1 @ 1,020,000 btu	24	12	$11,276
Pool decks — resurface	7,150 sq. ft	15	15	$43,582
Pool decks — replace	7,150 sq. ft	N/A	N/A	$85,000
Pool decks — coating	7,150 sq. ft	3	3	$125,660
Furniture — replace	approx. 85 pieces	15	11	$60,667
Furniture — refurbish	approx. 85 pieces	5	1	$39,357
Landscape / paving				
Asphalt seal coat	14,350 sq. ft & striping	5	0	$25,430
Asphalt replacement	14,350 sq. ft	25	4	$193,819
Wrought iron	260 lin. ft. @ 25%	25	15	$17,525
Pavers	unknown	30	27	$11,525
Irrigation time clocks	1@ 9 stations 1@ 4 stations	10	5	$5,629
Landscape upgrades	over 3 years	N/A	3	$10,001

Sample Reserve Study (condensed version)

Executive Summary

Major component parts and estimated remaining useful life of components (continued)

Component	Approximate quantity	Useful life of component (years)	Remaining useful life of component (years)	Replacement costs for 30 years with inflation factor of 2.85% annually
Clubhouse / rec building				
Furnishings	miscellaneous	15	12	$35,355
Remodel — restrooms	2 restrooms	30	15	$17,145
Remodel — kitchens	1 kitchen	20	17	$24,179
Play structures	1 structure	20	9	$44,313
Roof / decks				
Cap sheet roof — rec bldg	1,900 sq. ft	12	5	$29,867
Clay tile roof	2,600 sq. ft	35	23	$31,000
Structural				
Foundations / structural frame	3 buildings	30+*	30+*	0
Wood arbors — west	1 arbor	20	0	$28,228
Wood arbors — east	2 arbors	20	17	$36,266
Paint				
Wood surfaces	5,000 sq. ft	4	2	$95,302
Interior flatwork	8,300 sq. ft	8	5	$66,624
Mechanical				
Furnaces	2 @ 100,000 btu	20	8	$27,233
Evaporative coils (5 tons)	2 @ 5 tons	24	12	$10,086
Condensers (5 tons)	2 @ 5 tons	12	0	$40,132
Electrical				
Exterior lighting — common	5 fixtures	20	0	$10,326
Flooring				
Tile — rec building	2,400 sq. ft	30	27	$46,105
Tile — restrooms	500 sq. ft	30	15	$6,858

*Please refer to Warning icon on page 191.

Sample Reserve Study (condensed version)

Executive Summary

Components that may be **EXCLUDED** from the Reserve Study calculations

 **Insight**

Components that are left out of the custom Reserve Study will vary from community to community, based on Association governing documents and other local existing conditions. Examples are listed in the table below.

Type of excluded component	Definition	Examples
Unit owner responsibility Component exclusion	Based on your association's governing documents, some components are a unit owner responsibility.	Windows, garage doors, unit doors
Long-life Component exclusion	Some long-lasting infrastructure components are not yet included in the most current Reserve Study, because the expected useful life of the component extends beyond the 20- to 30-year range of the Reserve Study.	Plumbing pipes, electrical wiring, foundations
Utility Component exclusion	Some components might be maintained by the local utility company.	Primary electric feeds, telephone cables, gas mains and meters
Maintenance and repair Component exclusion	Some components can have ongoing preventive maintenance and repair. This repair cost is an operating expense and not a capital reserve expense.	Operating expense example: • Annual or semi-annual roof inspection and repair Reserve expense example: • Replacing the whole roof
Below threshold cost Component exclusion	If the reserve component is below a certain dollar amount, it is not included in the Reserve Study.	Some Reserve Studies only include components that cost at least $500 or $1,000 to replace. If the component is less than the threshold amount, it is often counted as an operating expense.
Government funded Component exclusion	If a local government maintains and replaces certain components, then these components are left out of the Reserve Study.	Street paving, sidewalks, storm water management

DISCLAIMER — Do not base your monthly fees or reserves on this specific yet theoretical example. Each property is unique, subject to local conditions and local laws. Budget funds for your Association's custom-created, professional Reserve Study.

Sample Reserve Study (condensed version)

Executive Summary

Components **EXCLUDED** from the Home Owner Association example Reserve Study

Unit owner responsibility component exclusions

- Complete interior and exterior of detached, single-family home

Long-life component exclusions

- Foundations / structural frame
- Concrete block walls
- Concrete flatwork

Utility component exclusions

- Primary electric feeds
- Electric transformers
- Cable TV systems and structures
- Telephone cables and structures
- Gas mains and meters

Maintenance and repair component exclusions

- Cleaning of asphalt pavement
- Crack sealing of asphalt pavement
- Painting of curbs
- Striping and numbering of parking spaces

Below-threshold cost-component exclusions

- Reserve expenditures that are less than $300 are not included.

Government funded component exclusions

- Government roadways and parking
- Government sidewalks and curbs
- Government lighting
- Government stormwater management

Sample Reserve Study (condensed version)

Estimated Reserve Fund Expenditures 2008 through 2037

2008

$10,250	Structure — wood arbors — west
$2,950	Paint — exterior flatwork
$1,800	Mechanical — evaporative coil (1.5 tons)
$9,200	Mechanical — condensers (5 tons)
$1,650	Mechanical — condenser (1.5 tons)
$1,100	Plumbing — water heaters
$3,750	Electrical — exterior lighting — common
$20,200	Pool — boiler — replace
$3,900	Pool — filters
$1,500	Pool — motors
$1,500	Pool — pumps
$900	Pool — chlorinators
$85,000	Pool — pool decks — replace
$2,900	Landscape / paving — asphalt seal coat
$3,333	Landscape / paving — landscape upgrades
$3,600	Recreation facilities — impact attenuation surface
$7,677	Contingency reserve
$161,210	Total reserve expenses for year

2009

$2,108	Roof — cap sheet (flat) roof — pool equipment
$7,251	Pool — furniture refurbish
$2,571	Pool — diving board / lifeguard station
$3,333	Landscape / paving — landscape upgrades
$763	Contingency reserve
$16,026	Total reserve expenses for year

2010

$11,107	Paint — wood surfaces
$2,538	Paint — ironwork
$28,031	Pool — plaster — pool
$3,334	Landscape / paving — landscape upgrades
$3,861	Recreation facility — office equipment
$2,444	Contingency reserve
$51,315	Total reserve expenses for year

2011

$762	Structure — utility doors
$9,737	Pool — pool decks — coating
$525	Contingency reserve
$11,024	Total reserve expenses for year

2012

$64,223	Landscape / paving — asphalt replacement
$3,211	Contingency reserve
$67,434	Total reserve expenses for year

2013

$6,846	Roof — cap sheet (flat) roof — rec building
$6,675	Paint — interior flatwork
$3,337	Pool — plaster — wading pool
$3,279	Pool — coping / joint
$1,726	Pool — motors
$3,337	Landscape / paving — asphalt seal coat
$1,380	Landscape / paving — irrigation time clocks
$3,682	Recreation facilities — picnic tables
$1,513	Contingency reserve
$31,755	Total reserve expenses for year

 Insight

Operating expense versus reserve expenses.

Operating expenses are:
Ongoing, annual expenses, which often arrive as predictable monthly invoices, such as:

- Lawn care services
- Property management and bookkeeping services
- Ordinary, minor repairs
- Insurance, etc.

Reserve expenses are:
Higher-cost, major repairs and replacements, such as:

- Roof replacement
- Foundation repairs
- Siding replacement
- Parking area resurfacing
- Street repaving

Sample Reserve Study (condensed version)

Estimated Reserve Fund Expenditures 2008 through 2037

2014

$3,491	Structure — structural pest control
$3,491	Paint — exterior flatwork
$12,427	Paint — wood surfaces
$4,261	Plumbing — drinking fountains
$2,130	Electrical — exterior lighting — buildings
$10,592	Pool — pool decks — coating
$8,344	Pool — furniture — refurbish
$1,183	Recreation facilities — gas barbecue
$2,130	Miscellaneous — directory boards
$1,598	Miscellaneous — signs
$2,482	Contingency reserve
$52,129	Total reserve expenses for year

2015

$2,920	Paint — ironwork
$3,348	Recreation facilities — television set
$313	Contingency reserve
$6,581	Total reserve expenses for year

2016

$9,890	Mechanical — furnaces
$1,127	Pool — chlorinators
$438	Recreation facilities — game table
$625	Miscellaneous — monument
$604	Contingency reserve
$12,684	Total reserve expenses for year

2017

$11,523	Pool — pool decks — coating
$16,094	Recreation facilities — play structures
$1,381	Contingency reserve
$28,998	Total reserve expenses for year

2018

$13,904	Paint — wood surfaces
$1,455	Plumbing — water heaters
$5,163	Pool — filters
$1,986	Pool — motors
$3,840	Landscape / paving — asphalt seal coat
$4,767	Recreation facilities — impact attenuation surface
$1,556	Contingency reserve
$32,671	Total reserve expenses for year

2019

$24,038	Pool — furniture replacement
$1,202	Contingency reserve
$25,240	Total reserve expenses for year

2020

$3,012	Structure — coated metal benches
$4,130	Paint — exterior flatwork
$3,360	Paint — ironwork
$10,086	Mechanical — evaporative coils (5 tons)
$12,885	Mechanical — condensers (5 tons)
$2,312	Mechanical — condensers (1.5 tons)
$37,118	Pool — plaster — pool
$22,830	Pool — coping / tile
$11,276	Pool — boiler — overhaul
$12,536	Pool — pool decks — coating
$14,009	Recreation facilities — furnishings
$6,678	Contingency reserve
$140,232	Total reserve expenses for year

2021

$2,952	Roof — cap sheet (flat) roof — pool equipment
$8,357	Paint — interior flatwork
$4,105	Pool — coping joint
$771	Contingency reserve
$16,185	Total reserve expenses for year

2022

$15,557	Paint — exterior flatwork
$1,259	Recreation facilities — bike / skateboard racks
$841	Contingency reserve
$17,657	Total reserve expenses for year

Sample Reserve Study (condensed version)

Estimated Reserve Fund Expenditures 2008 through 2037

2023

$6,858	Flooring — tile — rec bldg
$4,418	Pool — plaster —wading pool
$2,286	Pools — motors
$2,286	Pools — pumps
$43,482	Pool — pool decks — resurface
$13,638	Pool — pool decks — coating
$4,418	Landscape / paving — asphalt seal coat
$17,525	Landscape / paving — wrought iron
$1,828	Landscape / paving — irrigation time clocks
$17,145	Recreation facilities — remodel — restrooms
$4,876	Recreation facilities — picnic tables
$5,943	Contingency reserve
$124,803	Total reserve expenses for year

2024

$1,411	Pool — chlorinators
$11,048	Pool — furniture — refurbish
$1,568	Recreation facilities — gas barbecue
$701	Contingency reserve
$14,728	Total reserve expenses for year

2025

$9,589	Roof — cap sheet (flat) roof — rec bldg
$36,266	Structure — wood arbors — east
$3,866	Paint — ironwork
$1,049	Electrical — emergency exit lights
$5,885	Recreation facilities — office equipment
$4,434	Recreation facilities — television set
$24,179	Recreation facilities — remodel — kitchen
$4,263	Contingency reserve
$89,531	Total reserve expenses for year

2026

$4,888	Paint — exterior flatwork
$17,407	Paint — wood surfaces
$5,969	Plumbing — drinking fountains
$14,836	Pool — pool decks — coating
$580	Recreation facilities — game table
$2,984	Miscellaneous — directory boards
$827	Miscellaneous — monument
$2,375	Contingency reserve
$49,866	Total Reserve expenses for year

2027

No reserve expenditures planned for this year

$0	Total reserve expenses for year

2028

$17,978	Structure — wood arbors — west
$1,926	Plumbing — water heaters
$6,576	Electrical — exterior lighting — common areas
$6,837	Pool — filters
$2,631	Pool — motors
$5,084	Landscape / paving — asphalt seal coat
$6,314	Recreation facilities — impact attenuation surface
$2,367	Contingency reserve
$49,713	Total reserve expenses for year

2029

$5,317	Structure — structural pest control
$10,463	Paint — interior flatwork
$3,246	Electrical — exterior lighting — buildings
$5,139	Pool — coping joint
$16,141	Pool — pool decks — coating
$12,714	Pool — furniture — refurbish
$2,436	Miscellaneous — signs
$2,773	Contingency reserve
$58,229	Total reserve expenses for year

2030

$19,476	Paint — wood surfaces
$4,448	Paint — ironwork
$49,151	Pool — plaster — pool
$3,654	Contingency reserve
$76,729	Total reserve expenses for year

2031

$31,000	Roof — clay tile roof
$1,336	Structure — utility doors
$1,617	Contingency reserve
$33,953	Total reserve expenses for year

DISCLAIMER — Do not base your monthly fees or reserves on this specific yet theoretical example. Each property is unique, subject to local conditions and local laws. Budget funds for your Association's custom-created, professional Reserve Study.

Sample Reserve Study (condensed version)

Estimated Reserve Fund Expenditures 2008 through 2037

2032

$5,784	Paint — exterior flatwork
$3,531	Mechanical — evaporative coil (1.5 tons)
$18,047	Mechanical — condensers (5 tons)
$3,240	Mechanical — condenser (1.5 tons)
$39,636	Pool — boiler — replace
$1,766	Pool — chlorinators
$17,560	Pool — pool decks — coating
$4,478	Contingency reserve
$94,042	Total reserve expenses for year

2033

$4,132	Roof — cap sheet (flat) roof — pool equipment
$5,851	Pool — plaster — wading pool
$3,028	Pool — motors
$5,851	Landscape / paving — asphalt seal coat
$2,421	Landscape / paving — irrigation time clocks
$6,457	Recreation facilities — picnic tables
$1,387	Contingency reserve
$29,127	Total reserve expenses for year

2034

$21,791	Paint — wood surfaces
$36,629	Pool — furniture — replace
$2,077	Recreation facilities — gas barbecue
$3,025	Contingency reserve
$63,522	Total reserve expenses for year

2035

$5,119	Paint — ironwork
$46,105	Flooring — tile — rec bldg
$19,103	Pool — pool decks — coating
$11,525	Landscape / paving — pavers
$21,346	Recreation facilities — furnishings
$5,871	Recreation facilities — television set
$5,453	Contingency reserve
$114,522	Total reserve expenses for year

2036

$17,343	Mechanical — furnaces
$768	Recreation facilities — game table
$1,096	Miscellaneous — monument
$960	Contingency reserve
$20,167	Total reserve expenses for year

2037

$13,432	Roof — cap sheet (flat) roof — rec bldg
$13,098	Paint — interior flatwork
$6,433	Pool — coping joint
$129,596	Landscape / paving — asphalt replacement
$28,219	Recreation facilities — play structures
$1,918	Recreation facilities — bike / skateboard racks
$9,635	Contingency reserve
$202,331	Total reserve expenses for year

30-year TOTAL needed for Reserve Expenses:
$1,692,424

Sample Reserve Study (condensed version)

Estimated Reserve Fund Expenditures by Year

2008 through 2037

Insight

Often, capital expenditures can vary dramatically from year to year, as shown below.

The black line near the bottom of the graph shows the average annual expenditure of money.

As the property ages, it generally costs more to maintain. That is because:

- More building components will reach the end of their useful life and must be replaced.
- Future expenditures are often figured with an estimated inflation rate such as 3% per year.

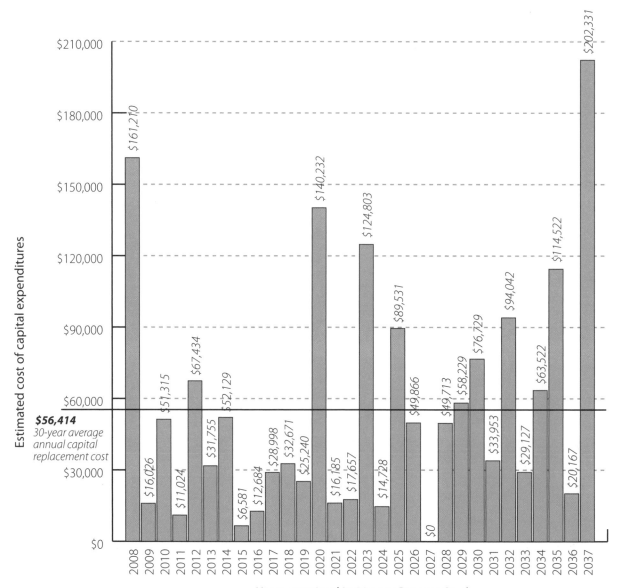

$56,414
30-year average annual capital replacement cost

Years examined in 30-year Reserve Study

Sample Reserve Study (condensed version)

Estimated Reserve Fund Expenditures by Category

2008 through 2037

30-year total needed for reserve expenses: **$1,692,424**

30-year average annual spending for reserve expenses: **$56,414**

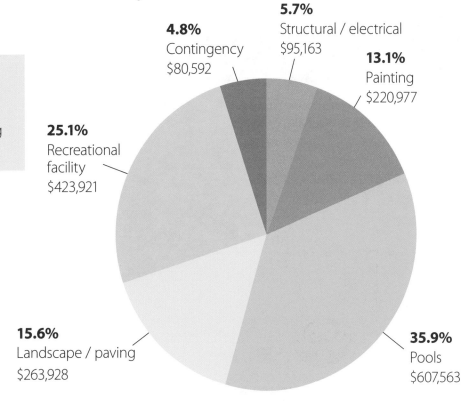

4.8%
Contingency
$80,592

5.7%
Structural / electrical
$95,163

13.1%
Painting
$220,977

25.1%
Recreational
facility
$423,921

35.9%
Pools
$607,563

15.6%
Landscape / paving
$263,928

Landscape / Paving

Asphalt seal coat	$25,430
Landscape upgrade	10,000
Asphalt replacement	193,819
Irrigation time clocks	5,629
Wrought iron	17,545
Pavers	11,525
TOTAL	**$263,928**

Structural / Electrical

Wood arbors — west	$28,228
Wood arbors — east	36,266
Utility doors	2,098
Structural pest control	8,808
Coated metal benches	3,012
Exterior lighting	16,751
TOTAL	**$95,163**

Painting

Exterior flatwork	$36,800
Wood surfaces	95,302
Ironwork	22,251
Interior flatwork	66,624
TOTAL	**$220,991**

Pools

Pool boilers, repair, replace	$71,112
Mechanical systems	38,047
Decks — replace	85,000
Pool decks — coating	125,666
Pool decks — resurface	43,482
Furniture — refurbish	39,357
Furniture — replacement	60,667
Diving board / guard station	2,571
Plaster — pool	86,269
Plaster — wading pool	13,606
Coping / joint	18,956
Coping / tile	22,830
TOTAL	**$607,563**

Recreational Facilities

Impact attenuation surface	$14,681
Office equipment	9,746
Picnic tables	15,015
Leisure elements	9,791
Television sets	13,653
Play structures	44,313
Furnishings	35,355
Remodel restrooms	17,145
Remodel kitchen	24,179
Roofs	70,059
Mechanical HVAC	89,984
Flooring — tile	52,963
Plumbing	14,711
Misc. storage	11,696
TOTAL	**$423,921**

Contingency

TOTAL	**$80,592**

Sample Reserve Study (condensed version)
Three Alternative Funding Plans vs. Component Costs
2008 through 2037

Warning!

Often in a professional Reserve Study, various funding plans are charted. For example, if the monthly maintenance fee starts too low at the beginning of the development and is never raised, there can be dire financial consequences.

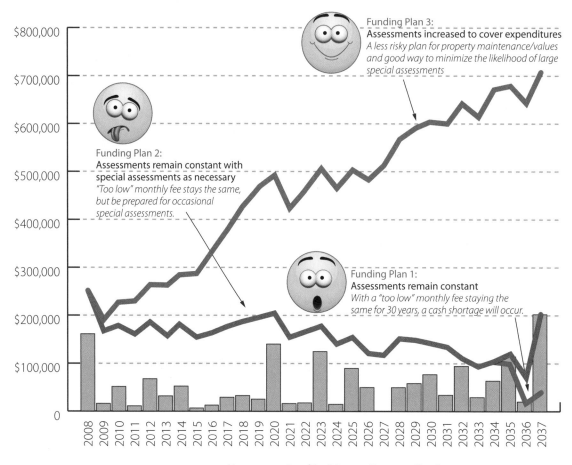

Funding Plan 3:
Assessments increased to cover expenditures
A less risky plan for property maintenance/values and good way to minimize the likelihood of large special assessments

Funding Plan 2:
Assessments remain constant with special assessments as necessary
"Too low" monthly fee stays the same, but be prepared for occasional special assessments.

Funding Plan 1:
Assessments remain constant
With a "too low" monthly fee staying the same for 30 years, a cash shortage will occur.

Years examined in 30-year Reserve Study

Estimated cash needs
Funding Plan 1: Assessments remain constant throughout 30-year projection
Funding Plan 2: Assessments remain constant with special assessments as necessary
Funding Plan 3: Assessments increased to cover expenditures

Sample Reserve Study (condensed version)

Cash-Flow Analysis

2008 through 2037

Insight

Just as in a business, having cash available to cover expenses each year is necessary for economic survival. Positive cash flow usually does not happen by accident.

Often in Reserve Studies, there is a cash-flow analysis that projects cash availability with an overlay of:

- Reserve expenditures
- Reserve contributions
- Cash on hand

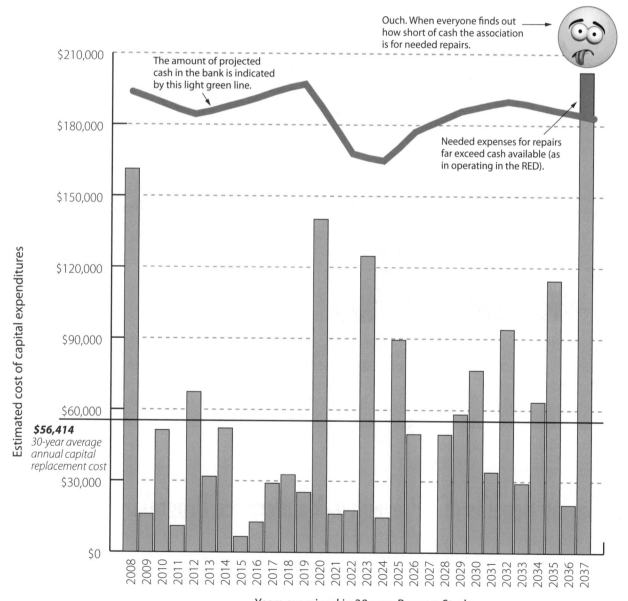

Ouch. When everyone finds out how short of cash the association is for needed repairs.

The amount of projected cash in the bank is indicated by this light green line.

Needed expenses for repairs far exceed cash available (as in operating in the RED).

$210,000

$180,000

$150,000

$120,000

$90,000

$60,000

$56,414
30-year average annual capital replacement cost

$30,000

$0

Estimated cost of capital expenditures

2008 2009 2010 2011 2012 2013 2014 2015 2016 2017 2018 2019 2020 2021 2022 2023 2024 2025 2026 2027 2028 2029 2030 2031 2032 2033 2034 2035 2036 2037

Years examined in 30-year Reserve Study

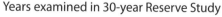

Sample Preventive-Maintenance Check List
Executive Summary

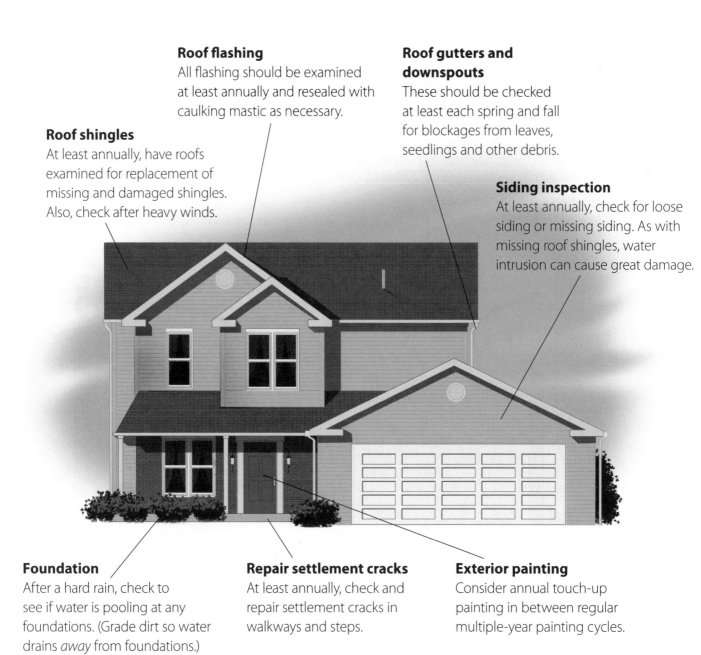

Roof flashing
All flashing should be examined at least annually and resealed with caulking mastic as necessary.

Roof gutters and downspouts
These should be checked at least each spring and fall for blockages from leaves, seedlings and other debris.

Roof shingles
At least annually, have roofs examined for replacement of missing and damaged shingles. Also, check after heavy winds.

Siding inspection
At least annually, check for loose siding or missing siding. As with missing roof shingles, water intrusion can cause great damage.

Foundation
After a hard rain, check to see if water is pooling at any foundations. (Grade dirt so water drains *away* from foundations.)

Repair settlement cracks
At least annually, check and repair settlement cracks in walkways and steps.

Exterior painting
Consider annual touch-up painting in between regular multiple-year painting cycles.

Cost-Saving Benefits of a Preventive-Maintenance Program

A preventive-maintenance checklist helps you to manage your property.

By carefully prolonging the life of building components, and systematically monitoring those components at least each spring and fall, you can help reduce the frequency of expensive, unanticipated emergency repairs.

DISCLAIMER — Each property is unique. Therefore, each property Preventive Maintenance Check List is unique, based on local conditions and local laws. Do not use this example list for your own property.

Sample Preventive-Maintenance Check List

Property Map (Overview of Property)

Ideas

Clearer communication with vendors by providing:

1. Map of property
2. Digital photos of problem areas

If you do not have a map of your property,

1. Check for a copy of the plat, on file at the county courthouse.
2. Go to *www.googlearth*, key in your address, pull up a satellite view of the property, and trace over it for accurate sizing.

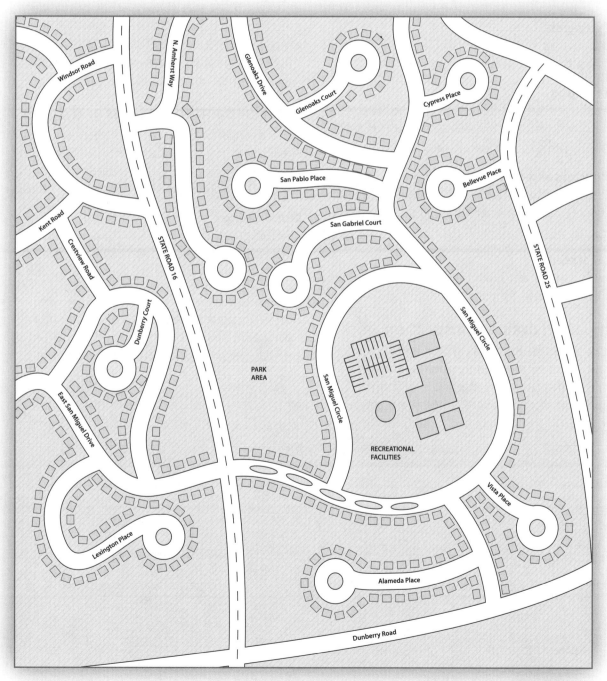

Sample Preventive-Maintenance Check List

This list applies only to the common elements of the Home Owner Association, such as the recreational building, pool, some limited paving areas and other amenities. This list *does not* include monthly, weekly and daily checklists for your property.

Recreational building roof inspection

A maintenance contract with a licensed, insured roofing contractor is strongly recommended. Inspections should be performed every spring. Some Associations will choose to inspect in the fall as well.

Roof shingles

Check for missing and damaged shingles, especially after windy weather and prior to the rainy season.

Roof flashing

Roof flashing occurs where one roofing section joins another roofing section, chimney, attic exhaust fan vent, etc. This is a prime area for leaks to occur.

Roof gutters and downspouts

Spring seedlings and fall leaves can clog roof gutters and downspouts. A clogged downspout can cause water to back up the drainage system.

Gutter screens

Even with gutter screen protection, fine debris should be removed from inside the roof gutter every 4 to 5 years.

Foundation drainage inspection

Drainage should be directed away from the structure. All grading at foundations should slope away from the structure, so that rainwater is directed away from the structure. Check for pooling at the foundations after a hard rain.

Recreational building pest control

Follow local codes. In California, for example, state statutes recommend annual inspections be performed to discover any infestation in its early stages before it comes a serious problem.

A regular on-going maintenance program should be established with a reputable licensed pest control operator. Programs range from monthly spraying for pests to quarterly inspections for termites.

Exterior painted surfaces and doors

Possible annual touch-up painting, in between every 4- to 7-year painting cycle, to extend life of paint job and protect wood surfaces. All peeling paint should be sanded/scraped and bare areas properly primed prior to any finish painting.

Wood siding

Check for cracks and splits in siding. Any protruding nails should be re-driven and sealed. (In this example, siding should be regularly painted at least every 4 years.)

Arbors

Examine for potential decay as part of regular pest-control maintenance program. Re-painting or staining is advocated at 4-year intervals for longevity of this component.

Sample Preventive-Maintenance Check List

This list applies only to the common elements of the Home Owner Association, such as the recreational building, pool, some limited paving areas and other amenities. This list *does not* include monthly, weekly and daily checklists for your property.

Recreational building pools

Standard maintenance programs for start-up and closing of annual pool season. Delegating this task to a certified, licensed pool contractor is strongly advised. The following pool area maintenance procedures are examples of procedures that should occur at a minimum at the start-up and close of the pool season.

Pool deck surfaces

At a minimum, examine pool deck surfaces for cracks and deterioration at the start-up and closing of the annual pool season.

The cementatious pool deck surfaces should be re-sealed every 2 to 3 years to obtain the greatest life expectancy from this component.

Plaster lining of pool

Seasonal inspections are needed as coarseness of the plaster occurs over time. This coarseness is conducive to algae growth and can be injurious to users of the pool.

Pool coping joints

Seasonal maintenance of a well-sealed joint will reduce the potential for cracking and settlement of the pool deck surfaces.

Poolside furniture

Because this furniture is of higher quality, it lends itself toward refurbishment, usually at five year intervals, prior to complete replacement becoming necessary.

Asphalt inspection

All asphalt areas should be examined at least annually. Any cracks exceeding ¼ inch should be repaired with a rubberized sealant compound. Irrigation run-off can accelerate degradation and should be prevented or diverted.

Asphalt seal coat

It is important that the procedure always be undertaken within 6 months of any overlay or resurfacing and performed thereafter on a 3- to 5-year cycle (typically a warranty requirement.)

Recreational building furnaces / evaporative coils / condensers

These components should be serviced twice a year. A maintenance contract with a reputable licensed heating/air-conditioning firm is recommended.

DISCLAIMER — Each property is unique. Therefore, each property Preventive Maintenance Check List is unique, based on local conditions and local laws. Do not use this example list for your own property.

Part II | 209

Who Does What?

Executive Summary of volunteer and paid positions to operate the property.

Owners to volunteer to serve on the Board of Directors

- President
- Treasurer
- Secretary
- At-large board members

Off-site property management firm

If no outside property management firm is hired, the property is referred to as "self-managed" by volunteers within the association.

Key staff positions often provided by an off-site property management firm may include:

- Community manager
- Customer service coordinator
- Maintenance coordinator
- Bookkeeper

Full-time on-site manager and staff

Often, at larger developments and more upscale developments, a full-time site manager and staff are hired.

Paid part-time outside vendors

Financial and mechanical planning services

- Reserve specialist and staff

Mechanical planning services

- Consulting mechanical engineer

Financial and tax-filing services

- Certified public accountant and staff
- Banking services

Legal services

- Attorney and staff
- Usually has experience as a real estate attorney, as well as community association experience

Insurance Services

- Insurance agent and staff

Trade and crafts persons

- Roofing crew
- Plumbing crew
- Electrical crew
- "Handyman" for routine day-to-day repairs
- Painting crew
- Concrete and masonry crew (for sidewalk, foundation and masonry repairs)
- Asphalt and paving crew

Grounds services

- Lawn care crew
- Arborist crew for large tree trimming
- Snow removal crew
- Pest control
- Cleaning / janitorial services
- Trash removal services

Warning!

All vendors must submit annual proof of insurance form(s)

All vendors should be fully insured and submit the annual proof of insurance forms for your records. This insurance includes workers comp, liability and whatever is mandated by laws in your state.

Major Repair and Renovation Project Summaries
Cost estimate ranges and photos

Insight

Home owners are already aware that repair and renovation costs are high in a detached, single-family home.

But in a large Community Association, those same costs can be *staggering* due to the larger size and scope of the projects.

But there is good news for the Community Association that is well managed:

Economy of scale

The economy of scale for major repair and renovation work in a larger Community Association can yield lower cost-per-unit owner repairs than major repairs of a similar nature in a detached, single-family home.

Quality assurance reviews from third-party engineering or construction consultants

In a large Community Association, a paid, outside third-party engineering or construction consultant can be hired to help guarantee quality work. The best of these consultants offer excellent organization and communication skills, as well as their technical ability, in reviewing the work of the contractor who is actually performing the technical work.

Major Repair and Renovation Project Summaries

1. Roofing System Replacements
2. Wood Rot of Siding, Stairwells, etc.
3. Plumbing System Replacements
4. Electrical System Replacements
5. Boiler / Chiller Replacements
6. Concrete Balcony Restorations
7. Lobby and Hallway Renovation

1. Roofing System Replacements

Replacing older, deteriorating roofing

PROBLEMS:
- VISIBLE WATER DAMAGE – Chronic roof leaks cause water damage to unit ceilings, flooring and owner furnishings.
- HIDDEN WATER DAMAGE – The roof leaks can also cause serious hidden structural damage to the building, which can add substantially to repair costs.

CAUSES:

As roofs age, their waterproofing abilities diminish. Years of sun, wind, storms, dirt and debris contribute to normal roof failure. Rooftop mechanical equipment and roof decks can shorten the useful life of a roofing system.

SOLUTIONS:
- When advised by engineering or roofing consultant, completely remove old roofing system and replace new roofing and upgraded insulation.
- Examine drainage design and consider tapering roof insulation.

WHAT IS THE EXPECTED USEFUL LIFE OF THE NEW COMPONENT?:

WARNING – A new roof with a 20-year guarantee cannot be ignored for the next 20 years. Keep in mind that attorneys representing the multi-million dollar roofing corporations have their interests in mind… not yours.

If properly designed and installed, and with at least annual roofing inspection and maintenance, many roofing systems can be serviceable for up to 20 years.

 **Insight**

These sample financial numbers are *not* for your engineering and construction budgeting purposes. The examples are to teach the broad concept that repair and renovation costs at Community Associations can be substantial, and the planning, consensus-building and renovation processes can be slow. Obtain competitive bids for all phases of work to determine current costs in your area.

▲ On this roof parapet, old, dried-out wall flashing splits open to form a funnel for leakage. Conditions like this can lead to both visible water damage to unit ceilings and flooring, as well as hidden structural damage, which can be costly to repair.

▲ In failure mode, organic shingles may curl up as they absorb moisture. This condition is a signal that the roof shingle deterioration process is accelerating, increasing the likelihood of water intrusion and damage.

 DISCLAIMER—Life expectancy of component parts will vary based on many factors, such as:
- Quality level of original components
- Local climate conditions
- Interim preventive maintenance if applicable

 DISCLAIMER—Actual renovation costs can vary widely based on many factors, such as:
- Local availability of skilled labor
- Quality of component parts used
- Current worldwide demand for raw materials
- Local laws and codes in your area

1. Roofing System Replacements

Cost ranges and timelines for two sample projects

**EXAMPLES OF ROUGH PROJECT COST
AND TIME RANGES**

EXAMPLE ONE:
Two-story stacked flats, 24 units in six buildings
Laminated strip or "dimensional" shingles

Phase 1:
Board hires roof consulting/engineering firm to perform evaluation. Services may include:
- Visiting the site for evaluating the roofs
- Examining several attics
- Providing a written report and recommendations with budget estimates to the board
- Developing a scope of work with the board or building committee

**TIME FRAME: 1 month for evaluation report;
1 to 2 months for final specifications and details**
**COST: $1,500 to $2,000 for evaluation report;
$2,000 to $3,000 for specifications and details**

Phase 2:
Roof consultant/engineer assists board with:
- Developing invitation list of licensed, qualified roofing contractors
- Conducting a pre-bid meeting on site with all invited roofers
- Provide standardized construction contract forms

TIME FRAME: 1 month
COST: $1,000 to $1,250

Phase 3:
During roof replacement, board would retain roof consultant/engineer to observe contractor work in progress.
- Conduct pre-construction meeting with contracted roofer
- Review material and substitution submittals from the contractor
- Perform final examination of contractor's work before invoice is paid

TIME FRAME: 6 to 8 weeks
**COST: $4,500 to $5,500 for roof consultant;
$55,000 to $65,000 for roof contractor**

EXAMPLE TWO:
16-story high-rise, 150 units
15,000 square feet of "flat" roof

Phase 1:
Board hires roof consulting/engineering firm to perform evaluation. Services may include:
- Visiting the site for evaluating the roofs (main roof, mechanical penthouses, and entry canopies)
- Removing, examining and patching of a roof construction core cut
- Providing a written report and recommendations with budget estimates to the board
- Developing a scope of work with the board or building committee

**TIME FRAME: 1 month for evaluation report;
1 to 2 months for final specifications and details**
**COST: $1,000 to $1,500 for evaluation report;
$2,500 to $3,500 for specifications and details**

Phase 2:
Roof consultant/engineer assists board with:
- [See bullet point details in Phase 2 at left in Example One]

TIME FRAME: 1 month
COST: $1,000 to $1,250

Phase 3:
During roof replacement, board would retain roof consultant/engineer to observe contractor work in progress.
- [See bullet point details in Phase 3 at left in Example One]

TIME FRAME: 6 to 8 weeks
**COST: $3,500 (part time roof observation) to
$5,500 (full time roof observation for roof
consultant; $120,000 (simple project with few
code requirements) to $220,000 (more difficult
project with strict code requirements) for
roof contractor**

2. Wood Rot of Siding, Stairwells, etc.

Water intrusion quickens deterioration of wooden (and most other) components

PROBLEM:

Wood rot (dry rot) often due to improper installation of roof drain systems, improper flashing and lack of waterproofing of decks. If deterioration continues unstopped, it could result in the property being condemned as unfit for habitation.

CAUSES:

With defective initial construction, drain systems were installed and flashed incorrectly, causing water to drain behind the siding.

SOLUTIONS:

- Remove rotting wood.
- Rebuild roof and roof drain systems.

FUNDING SOURCE(S):

- Project at newer property is partially funded by proceeds from construction defect litigation.
- Project at older property is funded by Association reserve funds and a special assessment.

ADDITIONAL PROBLEMS IF SITUATION IS IGNORED:

- Structural soundness of building at risk
- Condemnation of property
- Property no longer insurable
- Steep drop in property values

WHAT IS THE EXPECTED USEFUL LIFE OF THE NEW COMPONENT?

If new component is properly primed and painted on a regular maintenance schedule, it has an expected useful life of 50+ years.

Insight

These sample financial numbers are *not* for your engineering and construction budgeting purposes. The examples are to teach the broad concept that repair and renovation costs at Community Associations can be substantial, and the planning, consensus building and renovation processes can be slow. Obtain competitive bids for all phases of work to determine current costs in your area.

▲ View of wood rot on balconies and stair framings. Beams were shored up to prevent possible collapse.

▲ View of wood rot behind wood siding, which was caused by improperly installed roof drain systems. This hidden damage had become so severe that imminent collapse was possible.

DISCLAIMER—Life expectancy of component parts will vary based on many factors, such as:
- Quality level of original components
- Local climate conditions
- Interim preventive maintenance if applicable

DISCLAIMER—Actual renovation costs can vary widely based on many factors, such as:
- Local availability of skilled labor
- Quality of component parts used
- Current worldwide demand for raw materials
- Local laws and codes in your area

2. Wood Rot of Siding, Stairwells, etc.

Cost ranges and timelines for two sample projects

**EXAMPLES OF ROUGH PROJECT COST
AND TIME RANGES**

EXAMPLE ONE:
Two-story stacked flats
48 units in six buildings

Phase 1:
Board hires engineering/construction management firm to perform evaluation. Services might include:
- Site visits for evaluation
- Design renovation plans and obtain bids from contractors for repair work
- Assist board with evaluation of repair bids, and make recommendation to board of best bid proposal

TIME FRAME: 3 months
COST: $4,000 to $6,000

Phase 2:
Assist board in educating owners that repair work must be done to save the property.
- In order to pay from current reserves only, without a special assessment, board decides to perform renovation work in smaller phases. This phase will be named "Repair Phase One."

TIME FRAME: 4 months
COST: $6,000 to $9,000

Phase 3:
Construction/renovation
For "Repair Phase One"
- Included in the construction cost listed below, is a project communications coordinator, hired by the construction manager, to communicate with owners and tenants during the project.

This communications coordinator has the labor-intensive task of communication with residents during the renovation, which will include unavoidable tenant inconveniences and disruptions. A successful project communications coordinator will be well organized and have excellent interpersonal skills but not necessarily advanced technical construction knowledge.

TIME FRAME: Approximately 3 months
COST: $200,000 to $300,000

EXAMPLE TWO:
Three-story stacked flats
145 units in 50 buildings

Phase 1:
Board hires engineering/construction management firm to perform evaluation. Services might include:
- Site visits for evaluation
- Design renovation plans and obtain bids from contractors for repair work
- Assist board with evaluation of repair bids, and make recommendation to board of best bid proposal

TIME FRAME: 3 months
COST: $8,000 to $12,000

Phase 2:
Assist board in educating owners that repair work must be done to save the property.
- Engineer conducts walking tour of property, for owners, to answer project questions
- Construction management firm assists board in vote for special assessment to pay for project

TIME FRAME: 4 months
COST: $12,000 to $18,000

Phase 3:
Design/bid phase
- No architectural blueprints could be located for this property, so blueprints for a more precise construction bid had to be re-created from scratch.

TIME FRAME: Approximately 4 months
COST: $20,000 to $30,000

Phase 4:
Construction/renovation
- As with project listed at left, construction management firm hires a communications coordinator for the labor-intensive task of tenant/owner communications during the construction/renovation project.

TIME FRAME: Approximately 12 months
COST: $1.6 million to $2.4 million

3. Plumbing System Replacements

Replacing rusting, galvanized (iron) plumbing pipes

PROBLEM:
Galvanized (iron) plumbing pipes that are rusting through and leaking

CAUSES:
Iron will rust, so this is a natural problem in aging galvanized plumbing pipes

SOLUTION:
Replacing the plumbing pipes

ADDITIONAL PROBLEMS IF SITUATION IS IGNORED:
- Inevitable pipe bursts
- Tap water that is sometimes brown from loose rust and corrosion within pipes
- Loss of building insurability
- Decreased property values

WHAT IS THE EXPECTED USEFUL LIFE OF THE NEW COMPONENT?
- Many galvanized pipes were installed before 1960. Due to rust issues, other pipe materials are often used for renovations.
- Replacement piping systems will have an expected life of 25 to 40 years.

Insight

These sample financial numbers are *not* for your engineering and construction budgeting purposes. The examples are to teach the broad concept that repair and renovation costs at Community Associations can be substantial, and the planning, consensus building and renovation processes can be slow. Obtain competitive bids for all phases of work to determine current costs in your area.

▲ Rusted galvanized pipes can lead to leaks and associated water damage, mold growth and sediment build-up in drinking water.

▲ Deterioration of plumbing system pumps can lead to reduced system pressure, water service outages, as well as leaks and water damage in the basement.

DISCLAIMER—Life expectancy of component parts will vary based on many factors, such as:
- Quality level of original components
- Local climate conditions
- Interim preventive maintenance if applicable

DISCLAIMER—Actual renovation costs can vary widely based on many factors, such as:
- Local availability of skilled labor
- Quality of component parts used
- Current worldwide demand for raw materials
- Local laws and codes in your area

3. Plumbing System Replacements

Cost ranges and timelines for two sample projects

EXAMPLES OF ROUGH PROJECT COST AND TIME RANGES

EXAMPLE ONE:
Two-story stacked flats
24 units in six buildings

Phase 1:
Board hires engineering/construction management firm to perform evaluation. Services might include:
- Site visits for evaluating system including probes to see actual piping conditions
- Written report and recommendations provided to the board with budget projections
- Determine final scope of replacement and develop specifications and project drawings for the work

TIME FRAME: 2 to 4 months for survey report; 3 to 5 months for specifications and drawings
COST: $7,500 to $12,000 for survey report; $20,000 to $30,000 for specifications and drawings

Phase 2:
Engineering/construction manager assists board with the following:
- Competitive bid process for contractor selection
- Filing documents with permitting authorities
- Generation of suitable contract with selected contractor

TIME FRAME: 1 to 2 months
COST: $3,000 to $5,000

Phase 3:
During construction/renovation, the board would retain the engineer/construction manager to oversee the work. Services would include:
- Perform site visits during the course of the work to ensure compliance with project documents
- Provide written reports to the board following each visit
- Review submittals and material substitutions by the contractor
- Review requests for payments
- Sign-off on the project

TIME FRAME: 15 to 20 weeks
COST: $200,000 to $300,000

EXAMPLE TWO:
16-story high-rise
150 units

Phase 1:
Board hires engineering/construction management firm to perform evaluation. Services might include:
- Site visits for evaluating system including probes to see actual piping conditions
- Written report and recommendations provided to the board with budget projections
- Determine final scope of replacement and develop specifications and project drawings for the work

TIME FRAME: 2 to 4 months for survey report; 3 to 5 months for specifications and drawings
COST: $7,500 to $12,000 for survey report; $20,000 to $30,000 for specifications and drawings

Phase 2:
Engineering/construction manager assists board with the following:
- Competitive bid process for contractor selection
- Filing documents with permitting authorities
- Generation of suitable contract with selected contractor

TIME FRAME: 1 to 2 months
COST: $3,000 to $5,000

Phase 3:
During construction/renovation, the board would retain the engineer/construction manager to oversee the work. Services would include:
- Perform site visits during the course of the work to ensure compliance with project documents
- Provide written reports to the board following each visit
- Review submittals and material substitutions by the contractor
- Review requests for payments
- Sign-off on the project

TIME FRAME: 48 to 72 weeks
COST: $1.1 million to $1.5 million

4. Electrical System Replacements

Replacing older, insufficient wiring systems

PROBLEM:

Antiquated wiring is failing. Fuses and circuit breakers trip constantly within units.

CAUSES:

Cloth-insulated wiring deteriorates over time. Also, residents often use more power and appliances today, than what the original electrical system was designed to carry.

SOLUTIONS:

Replace the wiring. Add additional circuits where needed and upgrade the electrical service.

ADDITIONAL PROBLEMS IF SITUATION IS IGNORED:

- Deteriorated wiring can overheat and cause fires.
- Electrical equipment can fail to operate and can cause fires.
- Frequent tripping of circuit breakers or blown fuses can damage equipment.
- Life safety issues if critical building systems fail.

WHAT IS THE EXPECTED USEFUL LIFE OF THE NEW COMPONENT?

Replacement wiring has a service life linked to the life of the protective insulation, which is approximately 30 to 40 years.

▲ Inadequate wiring often causes additional extension cord and power strip use, which can overload wiring, trip breakers and lead to fires.

▲ Antiquated electrical equipment can fail to operate when needed, which leads to damaged equipment, dangerous working conditions and overloaded systems.

 **Insight**

These sample financial numbers are *not* for your engineering and construction budgeting purposes. The examples are to teach the broad concept that repair and renovation costs at Community Associations can be substantial, and the planning, consensus building and renovation processes can be slow. Obtain competitive bids for all phases of work to determine current costs in your area.

 DISCLAIMER—Life expectancy of component parts will vary based on many factors, such as:
- Quality level of original components
- Local climate conditions
- Interim preventive maintenance if applicable

 DISCLAIMER—Actual renovation costs can vary widely based on many factors, such as:
- Local availability of skilled labor
- Quality of component parts used
- Current worldwide demand for raw materials
- Local laws and codes in your area

4. Electrical System Replacements

Cost ranges and timelines for two sample projects

**EXAMPLES OF ROUGH PROJECT COST
AND TIME RANGES**

EXAMPLE ONE:
Two-story stacked flats
24 units in six buildings

Phase 1:
Board hires engineering/construction management firm to perform evaluation. Services might include:
- Site visits for evaluating system
- Written report and recommendations provided to the board with budget projections
- Determine final scope of replacement and develop specifications and project drawings for the work

**TIME FRAME: 1 to 2 months for survey report;
3 to 5 months for specifications and drawings**
COST: $7,500 to $10,000 for survey report;
$15,000 to $25,000 for specifications and drawings

Phase 2:
Engineering/construction manager assists board with the following:
- Competitive bid process for contractor selection
- Filing documents with permitting authorities
- Generation of suitable contract with selected contractor

TIME FRAME: 1 to 2 months
COST: $3,000 to $5,000

Phase 3:
During construction/renovation, the board would retain the engineer/construction manager to oversee the work. Services would include:
- Perform site visits during the course of the work to ensure compliance with project documents
- Provide written reports to the board following each visit
- Review submittals and material substitutions by the contractor
- Review requests for payments
- Sign-off on the project

TIME FRAME: 16 to 24 weeks
COST: $100,000 to $140,000

EXAMPLE TWO:
16-story high-rise
150 units

Phase 1:
Board hires engineering/construction management firm to perform evaluation. Services might include:
- Site visits for evaluating system
- Written report and recommendations provided to the board with budget projections
- Determine final scope of replacement and develop specifications and project drawings for the work

**TIME FRAME: 2 to 4 months for survey report;
3 to 5 months for specifications and drawings**
COST: $7,500 to $12,000 for survey report;
$20,000 to $30,000 for specifications and drawings

Phase 2:
Engineering/construction manager assists board with the following:
- Competitive bid process for contractor selection
- Filing documents with permitting authorities
- Generation of suitable contract with selected contractor

TIME FRAME: 1 to 2 months
COST: $3,000 to $5,000

Phase 3:
During construction/renovation, the board would retain the engineer/construction manager to oversee the work. Services would include:
- Perform site visits during the course of the work to ensure compliance with project documents
- Provide written reports to the board following each visit
- Review submittals and material substitutions by the contractor
- Review requests for payments
- Sign-off on the project

TIME FRAME: 24 to 36 weeks
COST: $600,000 to $800,000

5. Boiler / Chiller Replacements

Boiler replacement and chiller replacement

PROBLEM:

A leaking boiler wastes energy and more fuel is used each season as efficiency decreases. Chiller downtime results in no air conditioning in the summer months.

CAUSES:

Internal and external components in the boiler fail over time due to oxidation and wear, affecting steam/hot water generation and heat exchange. Mineral or sludge deposits can wear away on the internal sections of the chiller.

SOLUTIONS:

Heating plant upgrade and chiller replacement

ADDITIONAL PROBLEMS IF SITUATION IS IGNORED:

- Boiler components may leak further.
- Additional fuel is used because of decreased efficiency.
- Air conditioning system failures if chiller doesn't operate.
- Increased resident discomfort because of insufficient air conditioning.

WHAT IS THE EXPECTED USEFUL LIFE OF THE NEW COMPONENT?

Published data from the American Society of Heating Refrigeration and Air Conditioning Engineers (ASHRAE) indicates that a chiller's useful life can vary from 20 to 25 years and a non-electric boiler can last from 25 to 35 years.

▲ Aging chiller systems with internal failures will increase operating and maintenance costs as well as decrease resident comfort.

▲ Energy and water lost through aging boilers negatively affect system efficiency and resident comfort. This condition causes inadequate heating, less domestic hot water generation and more fuel usage when operating.

Insight

These sample financial numbers are *not* for your engineering and construction budgeting purposes. The examples are to teach the broad concept that repair and renovation costs at Community Associations can be substantial, and the planning, consensus building and renovation processes can be slow. Obtain competitive bids for all phases of work to determine current costs in your area.

DISCLAIMER—Life expectancy of component parts will vary based on many factors, such as:
- Quality level of original components
- Local climate conditions
- Interim preventive maintenance if applicable

DISCLAIMER—Actual renovation costs can vary widely based on many factors, such as:
- Local availability of skilled labor
- Quality of component parts used
- Current worldwide demand for raw materials
- Local laws and codes in your area

5. Boiler / Chiller Replacements

Cost ranges and timelines for two sample projects

**EXAMPLES OF ROUGH PROJECT COST
AND TIME RANGES**

EXAMPLE ONE:
Two-story stacked flats
24 units in six buildings

Phase 1:
Board hires engineering/construction management firm to perform evaluation. Services might include:
- Site visits for evaluating heating plant (distributed versus central) and chiller system
- Written report and recommendations provided to the board with budget projections
- Determine final scope of replacement and develop specifications and project drawings for the work

**TIME FRAME: 1 to 2 months for survey report;
2 to 4 months for specifications and drawings**
**COST: $7,500 to $10,000 for survey report;
$20,000 to $30,000 for specifications and drawings**

Phase 2:
Engineering/construction manager assists board with the following:
- Competitive bid process for contractor selection
- Filing documents with permitting authorities
- Generation of suitable contract with selected contractor

TIME FRAME: 1 to 2 months
COST: $3,000 to $5,000

Phase 3:
During construction/renovation, the board would retain the engineer/construction manager to oversee the work. Services would include:
- Perform site visits during the course of the work to ensure compliance with project documents
- Provide written reports to the board following each visit
- Review submittals and material substitutions by the contractor
- Review requests for payments
- Sign-off on the project

TIME FRAME: 8 to 10 weeks
COST: $200,000 to $300,000 (modular boiler rep.)
$200,000 to $300,000 (chiller replacement)

EXAMPLE TWO:
16-story high-rise
150 units

Phase 1:
Board hires engineering/construction management firm to perform evaluation. Services might include:
- Site visits for evaluating central heating plant and chiller system
- Written report and recommendations provided to the board with budget projections
- Determine final scope of replacement and develop specifications and project drawings for the work

**TIME FRAME: 2 to 4 months for survey report;
3 to 5 months for specifications and drawings**
**COST: $7,500 to $12,000 for survey report;
$20,000 to $30,000 for specifications and drawings**

Phase 2:
Engineering/construction manager assists board with the following:
- Competitive bid process for contractor selection
- Filing documents with permitting authorities
- Generation of suitable contract with selected contractor

TIME FRAME: 1 to 2 months
COST: $3,000 to $5,000

Phase 3:
During construction/renovation, the board would retain the engineer/construction manager to oversee the work. Services would include:
- Perform site visits during the course of the work to ensure compliance with project documents
- Provide written reports to the board following each visit
- Review submittals and material substitutions by the contractor
- Review requests for payments
- Sign-off on the project

TIME FRAME: 12 to 16 weeks
COST: $400,000 to $600,000 (boiler replacement)
$310,000 to $450,000 (chiller replacement)

6. Concrete Balcony Restorations

Concrete balcony repairs are necessary and can be VERY expensive

PROBLEM:
- Concrete cracks on top side of balcony or edges of the slab
- Concrete spalling or delamination of the underside of balcony slab
- Exposed steel reinforcing anywhere
- Corroded handrail post connections

CAUSES:
- Lack of water proofing protection
- Water infiltration leading to corrosion of embedded steel reinforcing
- Freeze/thaw cycles
- Dissimilar materials in contact (e.g. aluminum handrails with concrete)

SOLUTIONS:
Concrete restoration project performed by a qualified concrete restoration contractor
- Minor restoration:
  - Patching of deficient concrete areas
  - Route and seal of cracks
- Major restoration:
  - Structural rebuilding of slabs
  - Repair/replacement of corroded steel embedment

ADDITIONAL PROBLEMS IF SITUATION IS IGNORED:
- Safety hazard to both balcony occupants and anyone near balconies
- Concrete repair costs escalate rapidly when concrete is allowed to continue to deteriorate
- Exposed steel accelerates concrete deterioration
- City-ordered citations against the association
- Loss of building insurability
- Decreased property values

WHAT IS THE LIFE EXPECTANCY OF THE NEW COMPONENT?
- Waterproof membrane recoating every 5 to 7 years
- Previously repaired concrete areas every 7 to 15 years
- Repainting of railings every 5 years

▲ Concrete balcony restoration project costs can vary greatly, especially when the deterioration has progressed to the point of a major restoration. A major concrete restoration, as shown above, includes structural rebuilding of slabs, and repair or replacement of corroded steel embedment.

Protect the concrete surfaces by application of appropriate waterproofing or membrane material.

DISCLAIMER—Life expectancy of component parts will vary based on many factors, such as:
- Quality level of original components
- Local climate conditions
- Interim preventive maintenance if applicable

DISCLAIMER—Actual renovation costs can vary widely based on many factors, such as:
- Local availability of skilled labor
- Quality of component parts used
- Current worldwide demand for raw materials
- Local laws and codes in your area

6. Concrete Balcony Restorations
Cost ranges and timelines for two sample projects

**EXAMPLES OF ROUGH PROJECT COST
AND TIME RANGES**

EXAMPLE ONE:
Three-story stacked flats
48 concrete balconies

Phase 1:
- Board hires engineering firm to perform evaluation
- Engineer performs site visit and material testing
- Engineer develops scope of repair work for competitive bidding and obtaining local construction permits
- Obtain bids for repair work

TIME FRAME: 4 to 6 months
COST: $25,000 to $35,000

Phase 2:
- Engineer and property manager assist board with contractor selection and award construction repair job.
- Property manager communicates with residents about details of job and day-to-day disruptions to expect.
- Contractor obtains permits.

TIME FRAME: 2 to 4 months
COST: $3,000 to $5,000 for engineering assistance

Phase 3:
- Pre-construction meeting with owners, engineer and contractor.
- Contractor submits applicable shop drawings, product data and samples for board and engineer's review.
- Engineer performs regular site visits to observe the work in progress for compliance with contract documents and tabulate quantities of work completed as a basis for payment to the contractor.
- As necessary, engineer may need to re-engineer repair details as may be required by latent conditions, which is common in renovation and restoration work.
- Management and/or engineer review and process contractors certificate of payment, change orders, waivers of lien and develop punch lists for contract close-out.

TIME FRAME: 3 to 8 months
COST: $200,000 to $500,000+

EXAMPLE ONE:
40-story high-rise
228 concrete balconies

Phase 1:
- Board hires engineering firm to perform evaluation
- Engineer performs site visit and material testing
- Engineer develops scope of repair work for competitive bidding and obtaining local construction permits
- Obtain bids for repair work

TIME FRAME: 6 to 10 months
COST: $50,000 to $75,000+

Phase 2:
- Engineer and property manager assist board with contractor selection and award construction repair job.
- Property manager communicates with residents about details of job and day-to-day disruptions to expect.
- Contractor obtains permits.

TIME FRAME: 2 to 4 months
COST: $3,000 to $5,000 for engineering assistance

Phase 3:
- Pre-construction meeting with owners, engineer and contractor.
- Contractor submits applicable shop drawings, product data and samples for board and engineer's review.
- Engineer performs regular site visits to observe the work in progress for compliance with contract documents and tabulate quantities of work. completed as a basis for payment to the contractor
- As necessary, engineer may need to re-engineer repair details as may be required by latent conditions, which is common in renovation and restoration work.
- Management and/or Engineer review and process contractors certificate of payment, change orders, waivers of lien and develop punch lists for contract close-out.

TIME FRAME: 18 to 24 months
COST: $5 million to $6.5 million+

7. Lobby and Hallway Renovation

Beautiful common area decor lifts owners' spirits and might spark interest from potential new buyers

PROBLEM:

Dated, worn out, unattractive public areas

CAUSES:

Excessive wear, improper maintenance, poor performance of product, too long between scheduled refurbishings

SOLUTIONS:

Consider engaging the services of a professional interior designer who can evaluate any salvageable category and recommend replacement and/or upgrading of other categories

ADDITIONAL PROBLEMS IF SITUATION IS IGNORED:

- Continued deterioration of both product and appearance of lobbies and hallways
- Possible health and safety issues due to badly worn or poorly maintained products
- Devaluation of individual unit prices and building desirability

WHAT IS THE LIFE EXPECTANCY OF INTERIOR REFURBISHINGS?

- Unlike many structural renovations, interior refurbishing durability depends upon quality of product, wear and tear and proper maintenance.
- Larger condominium complexes should schedule interior refurbishing on no more than an 8 to 10 year cycle in order to keep public areas looking fresh and up to date.

▲ A view of a well-appointed condominium hallway

Insight

It is valuable to investigate and engage the services of a qualified interior designer for the refurbishing and renovating of public areas of any size condominium complex.

In all phases of refurbishing, the interior designer can work within budget, prevent mistakes, specify appropriate product and establish a professional working relationship with board/committee to prevent individual owner personalities from undue influence of the design process.

DISCLAIMER—Life expectancy of component parts will vary based on many factors, such as:
- Quality level of original components
- Local climate conditions
- Interim preventive maintenance if applicable

DISCLAIMER—Actual renovation costs can vary widely based on many factors, such as:
- Local availability of skilled labor
- Quality of component parts used
- Current worldwide demand for raw materials
- Local laws and codes in your area

7. Lobby and Hallway Renovation

Cost ranges and timelines for two sample projects

EXAMPLES OF ROUGH PROJECT COST AND TIME RANGES

EXAMPLE ONE:
Two-story stacked flats
16 units in four buildings

Phase 1:
Board hires interior design firm to perform evaluation. Services should include:
- Site visits for evaluation of areas to be refurbished, including the following areas – lighting, floor covering (hard surface and/or carpeting), wall covering, painting, furniture, art work and accessories
- Written proposal and recommendations provided to the Board of Directors, with budget projections

TIME FRAME: 1 to 2 months for selection and presentation boards
COST: Some firms may charge an hourly fee (for example, $100 to $150 per hour) or design fee as a percentage of the total cost of the project

Phase 2:
Interior designer works with board or committee selected by board:
- Evaluate product selection and acquire approvals
- Review cost proposals and obtain approvals
- Establish who interior designer is to report to

TIME FRAME: Depends on board ability to agree to design concept. Cost proposals are generally good for 60 days.

Phase 3:
During renovation, with acceptance of design proposal, the interior designer oversees the work. Services would include:
- Ordering, receiving and storing all goods and products proposed by designer
- Performing site visits during the course of the work to ensure work is properly executed
- Reviewing completed renovation and installation with board or board committee for approval and sign-off

TIME FRAME: 8 to 12 weeks
COST: $25,000 to $30,000

EXAMPLE TWO:
5-story mid-rise
40 units

Phase 1:
Board hires interior design firm to perform evaluation. Services should include:
- Site visits for evaluation of areas to be refurbished, including the following areas – lighting, floor covering (hard surface and/or carpeting), wall covering, painting, furniture, art work and accessories
- Written proposal and recommendations provided to the Board of Directors, with budget projections

TIME FRAME: 1 to 2 months for selection and presentation boards
COST: Some firms may charge an hourly fee (for example, $100 to $150 per hour) or design fee as a percentage of the total cost of the project

Phase 2:
Interior designer works with board or committee selected by board:
- Evaluate product selection and acquire approvals
- Review cost proposals and obtain approvals
- Establish who interior designer is to report to

TIME FRAME: Depends on board ability to agree to design concept. Cost proposals are generally good for 60 days.

Phase 3:
During renovation, with acceptance of design proposal, the interior designer oversees the work. Services would include:
- Ordering, receiving and storing all goods and products proposed by designer
- Performing site visits during the course of the work to ensure work is properly executed
- Reviewing completed renovation and installation with board or board committee for approval and sign-off

TIME FRAME: 12 to 18 weeks
COST: $210,000 to $230,000

Why the Growth of Community Associations Is Probably Here to Stay

U.S. trends

Will millions of baby boomers downsize from single-family homes to condos and townhomes?

Approximately 78.2 million U.S. baby boomers, born between 1946 and 1964, have started to enter their retirement years, as the earliest of that generation turned 60 in 2006.

As they age, some may want to downsize to a condominium or townhome, from their too-large, and difficult-to-maintain single-family home.

Steady rise in single-person households

Single-person households have increased from 17% of the U.S. population in 1970 to 26% in 2005.

Single-person households occur more frequently in densely populated urban areas.

Source: U.S. Census Bureau

Worldwide trends

World population is primarily urban starting in 2008.

In 2008, for the first time, half of the world population now lives in urban areas. (More than half the U.S. population became classified as urban dwellers in the 1920 U.S. census.)

By 2050, it is estimated that 70% of the world's population will live in urban areas.

Source: United Nations Population Division Report

Urban living:
Limited land availability and population density

People are drawn to urban living for jobs, access to health care, transportation systems, education, entertainment, nearby police and fire protection, and other enriching community activities.

However, all the people and a limited amount of land sets the stage for dense, "shared-expenses" housing solutions.

Why do consumers choose living in Community Associations?

Convenience —
Delegation of maintenance, repair and other day-to-day details of home ownership are handled collectively.

Affordability —
Especially in lower-cost condominium units, this can be a more affordable form of housing for seniors and singles.

Amenities (like a pool, tennis court and other recreational facilities) can be affordable for a group of owners but out of reach for many individual home owners.

Rule enforcement —
Some home owners perceive that a more uniform set of neighborhood standards exists and is better enforced within an association.

A sense of community —
Living in close proximity with others is desired by some buyers.

The Growth of Community Associations in the U.S.

1970 to present

Residents of Community Associations, in millions

1970	2009
2.1 million	60.1 million

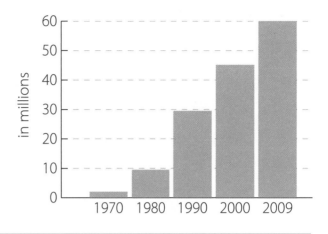

Housing Units, by total and type

1970	2009
701,000	24.4 million

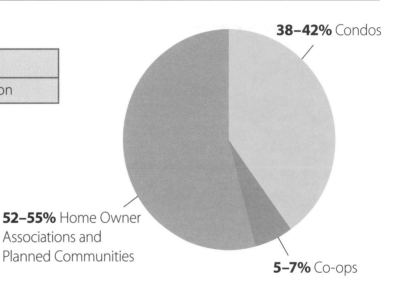

38–42% Condos

52–55% Home Owner Associations and Planned Communities

5–7% Co-ops

Number of Community Associations, in thousands

1970	2009
10,000	305,400

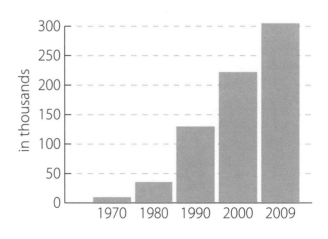

Source: Community Associations Institute

Talking Points for Frequently Asked Questions

What percentage of the budget do we set aside for reserves in order to be safe?

Unfortunately, there is no set percentage to reserve because the conditions of each property are different.

That's why taking the time and money to create a professional Reserve Study, then matching the projected reserve repair and replacement expenses with the association's day-to-day operating budget, is the most accurate way of forecasting the financial needs of the Association.

This question frequently arises from new board members whenever planning for reserves is discussed.

I'll be dead by then anyway. Why should I help pay for a new roof?

- (Be sure to answer with a respectful, even tone.) I understand your concern. You seem so healthy and vigorous. What if you end up living a lot longer than you think you will? Wouldn't it still be good to have a roof over your head that doesn't leak?
- (Be sure to answer with a respectful, even tone.) I understand your concern. But think about this idea. Do you want your heirs to inherit a unit that they will be able to sell? And sell for a good price? That's why we have to pay so much attention to ongoing building maintenance each year.
- In an Association, maintenance and financial readiness are different from what it is for a single- family home. Here, there are shared expenses, and we save for them systematically each year. And for most people, saving systematically each year is easier than coming up with a large, unexpected special assessment.
- If there is a roof with an estimated useful life of 20 years, you are using up about 1/20 of the value of the roof each year. With Association living, we set aside money each year, for that part of the roof that we "use up" each year.
- In states with Reserve Study requirements and disclosure requirements, there is an increasing likelihood that the accumulating Association deficit per unit is easier for new buyers to evaluate. If that potential buyer still has an interest in buying your unit, the deficit per unit is negotiated off the sales price of the unit.

I'll be dead by then anyway. Why should I help pay for a new roof? (continued)

- Especially since the economic crisis of 2008, mortgage lenders, insurers and other financial institutions are looking more closely at the financial strength of an Association before they are willing to allow a loan for a unit within that Association. In other words, funding the reserves is becoming more scrutinized than ever.

If we raise the monthly fees, how can I ever sell my unit?

Two part answer:

The importance of maintaining curb appeal to spark preliminary interest from new buyers

(Be sure to answer with a respectful, even tone.)
I understand your concern. You make a good point that we want to deliver *value* here, so that we are in a good position to continue to attract a steady stream of new buyers in this Association.

Let's look at a buying decision of a new buyer for a minute. What first catches the eye of a potential new buyer? Location? Convenience? Curb appeal?

Especially with curb appeal, there is often some visible element of the property that sparks an interest from a buyer.

If the property initially *looks* good enough, and we have solid documentation to show how our fees translate into a stronger Association, sometimes the buyer will find a way, in his or her mind, to justify the monthly fee.

Are nearby properties – with a low fee – actually underfunded Associations?

That same, better educated buyer may then be able to question and evaluate the monthly fees at nearby competitive properties in a new, more discerning light. That potential new buyer is now thinking about the questions, "Is this fee high enough to operate this Association? Is this fee adequate to fund the reserves?"

Hired Property Management Considerations

A self-managed association

In a self-managed association, owners volunteer to manage the association without assistance from a paid property management firm.

PRO	CON
• Self-management saves money.	• The volunteers can quickly burn out if day-to-day demands are too great. • Volunteers may lack adequate training and not know where to turn for help. • The Association is more vulnerable to financial fraud in collection and disbursement of money, especially if no bonded, outside third party firm is hired as the fiscal agent for the property.

An off-site, part-time, property management firm

With this arrangement, one property management firm handles the management of several Associations.

PRO	CON
• An experienced manager can provide valuable insights to the Board of Directors, based on long-term experience in the field. • In some cases, to increase personal safety, enforcement letters and collections are better handled by an outside third-party firm. The property management firm is better suited to oversee these enforcement duties. • Many day-to-day duties can be delegated to the property manager as well as his/her office support staff.	• A part-time manager can be spread thin, especially if a high-maintenance type of property is in need of extra services. • Support staff at a management firm can be spread thin as well. (Example: one bookkeeper trying to handle the financial affairs for 50+ properties)

A full-time, on-site manager and staff

Often, at larger developments and more upscale developments, a full-time site manager and staff are hired.

PRO	CON
• A full-time, on-site manager and staff can provide a high level of immediate services.	• A full-time manager and staff often cost more than a part-time, off-site manager.

Credentialing and Certifications

Insight

"Property manager" term evolves into "Community Association manager"

The earliest forms of property management involved managing rental property for absentee landlords, with the property manager handling the tenants and property, via delegation from the landlord.

However, among a community of owner-occupants, the Community Association manager has a different role, *advising* and communicating with the Board of Directors and the larger community of owners. The Community Association manager has a different set of skills than an older-style property manager.

State credentialing of Community Association managers is becoming more common

In response to consumer fraud by a small number of dishonest managers and legislative reaction against that fraud, state education requirements and/or licensing of Community Association managers is beginning to occur in a limited number of states, including California, Florida, Virginia and most recently, Illinois.

Two national non-profit organizations offer the most commonly held manager certifications.

Name	Community Associations Institute (CAI)
Web site	www.caionline.org
Local chapters in U.S.	Almost 60

Name	Institute of Real Estate Management (IREM)
Web site	www.irem.org
Local chapters in U.S.	80

What do the property manager credentialing letters stand for?

Manager certifications from the Community Associations Institute (CAI)

PCAM®	Professional Community Association Manager®. The most advanced level of certification offered by CAI.
AMS®	Association Management Specialist®. The second level of certification offered by CAI.
CMCA®	Certified Manager of Community Associations®. The first level of certification offered by CAI.
LSM®	Large-Scale Manager® certification.
AAMC®	Accredited Association Management Company®. This certification applies to the entire firm, not just the individual property manager.

Manager certifications from the Institute of Real Estate Management (IREM)

CPM®	Certified Property Manager®. The most advanced level of certification offered by IREM.
ARM®	Accredited Residential Manager®. The second level of certification offered by IREM.
AMO®	Accredited Management Organization®. This certification applies to the entire firm, not just the individual property manager.

Fees for Property Management Services

Salaries for full-time on-site manager and staff

For various full-time positions, salary surveys and compensation studies are available from the publication divisions of two major non-profit organizations that serve the Community Association industry.

Community Associations Institute
www.caionline.org (go to the Publications link)

Institute of Real Estate Management
www.irem.org (go to the Publications link)

Fees paid to off-site, part-time property management firms

Compared with formal salary survey information for full-time management and staff positions, the fee structure for off-site, part-time managers is less documented and often more variable.

Following are some methodologies for determining fees.

1. Door fee or per-unit fee

Some property management firms charge a flat per-month fee, based on the number of units at the property. Often, for small associations, there is a minimum monthly charge and provisions for additional fees for extra services, based on the annual management contract.

EXAMPLE CHART: $15 per unit per month as base management fee

	10-unit association	**50-unit association**	**200-unit association**
Monthly base fee*	10 units x $15 per unit = $150 per mo. But firm has minimum charge of **$450 per mo.**	50 units x $15 per unit = **$750 per mo.**	200 units x $15 per unit = **$3,000 per mo.**
Annual total base fee*	$450/mo. x 12 mo. = **$5,400 per year**	$750/mo. x 12 mo. = **$9,000 per year**	$3,000/mo. x 12 mo. = **$36,000 per year**

* Other fees may apply, in addition to the base fee. These other fees should be listed in the contract with your property management firm.

Fees for Property Management Services

2. A percentage of total annual budget

A variation of the door fee is to establish a management fee as a percentage of the total budget.

3. Monthly fee determined by list of staff services multiplied by hourly fees per service

Of the fee determination methods discussed here, this pricing scenario takes more time at the beginning to analyze and create, then explain to the board.

This method might also result in a higher fee, especially for smaller associations. Here the problem with a smaller association is that it could take almost as much time to manage as a larger association, but there are fewer owners to help share the cost of management services.

A benefit of this more-detailed initial estimating approach is the clarity and understanding that extra management services are tied to extra costs.

Insight

More thoughts about the door-fee method of determining fees

Often, the pay to the property manager is one-third of the collected door fees. The other two-thirds of the door fees pay for office support staff and overhead expenses of the property management firm.

Especially in lower cost-of-living areas of the country, the $15+ per-month, per-unit management fee has gone unchanged for more than 25 years.

However, in those same, lower-cost-of-living areas of the country, in some mid-rise and high-rise buildings, the monthly management fee may be higher, at $60 to $75+ per unit. High-rise buildings can sometimes require more specialized services and management attention.

Some associations are more time-consuming to manage than others.

If door fees have a history of being unrealistically low in your area of the country, the thoroughness of the property management services can suffer even if you continue to hire different property management firms at that same low rate.

Ultimately, you get what you pay for.

Common Tasks for a Community Manager

Budget planning
- Develop annual budget.
- Review monthly financial statements.

Meeting planning
- Outline the monthly board meeting agenda in advance, especially any materials that require the board members to read and think about in advance of the meeting.
- Prepare for annual or semi-annual owners meeting.

Meeting attendance
- Attend up to five night meetings per year. (See further explanation at the Insight icon on this page.)
- Take meeting minutes (if present at the meeting).

Buildings and grounds planning and administration
- Recruit, hire and supervise cleaning and routine maintenance personnel.
- Liaison with buildings and grounds services providers, such as:
  - Plumber
  - Electrician
  - Roofing contractor
  - Pest control firm
  - Lawn care and snow removal services
  - Arborist services
  - Painting contractors
  - Heating and air conditioning repair staff
  - Paving firms
  - And other vendors

Liaison with other Association service providers, such as:
- Insurance agent
- Legal counsel
- CPA firm
- Reserve Study firm
- Engineering firm
- Local building code inspectors
- Local police department
- Other local government entities
- And other vendors

Administrative tasks
- Approve monthly invoices for payment.
- As a cross-check, a board member may review invoices as well. The monthly payments with documentation are often included in a monthly report for board members.
- Answer e-mails and phone calls from owners that the office administrative assistant has not been able to resolve.

Rule enforcement
- Send enforcement letters.
- Advise the Board of Directors on strategies for solving enforcement issues.

Communications
- Oversee newsletter development.
- Oversee updating of community web site.
- Send letters to owners explaining issues as the issues arise.

Site inspections
- Visit property for non-technical property inspections.

Insight

For an off-site manager, attendance at a limited number of night meetings each year.

Often, for an off-site manager, it is common that the contract specifies attendance at a limited number of night meetings each year.

For example, if the contract specifies attendance at five meetings per year, often a key meeting for the manager to attend is the annual or semi-annual owners meetings. If the Board of Directors meets monthly, the manager may or may not need to attend each of those monthly meetings.

Common Tasks for the Office Support Staff of a Community Manager

Administrative assistant to community manager

- The administrative assistant is often the first person to take phone calls and e-mails from owners.
- Visit property for non-technical property inspections.
- Coordinate mailings to owners.
- Dispatch repair persons for routine repairs.

Accounting and bookkeeping department

- Generate monthly financial reports, such as:
  - Income statement
  - Balance sheet
  - Delinquency report
  - Bank statements for month
- Administrative tasks:
  - Pay monthly invoices.
  - Make bank deposits.
  - Maintain all books and financial records in accordance with generally accepted accounting principles.

Insight

Often, tough decisions rest with the Board of Directors, not the community manager

The community manager is a "generalist" and *advises* the Board of Directors. The community manager and his or her office support staff perform the day-to-day tasks to operate the property.

The Board of Directors, made up of property owners, studies issues affecting the property. The board is often advised not only by the community manager, but in specialized technical issues, the board is also advised by paid, third-party specialists, such as a consulting engineer, reserve specialist, accountant or attorney.

Then, ideally, the Board of Directors provides the courageous leadership to make tough decisions to protect property values, and works in the best interests of all owners.

Best Scenario

The community manager and other vendors can provide "continuity" as board membership changes

Long-term relationships with key vendors can be vitally important for the smooth operation of the association, especially as new board members start to serve.

Two examples are when a community manager has grown to understand the personalities of many owners, or a roofing contractor who has learned the building's ongoing physical problems. The Association benefits when the board has a commitment to maintain long-term, mutually beneficial business relationships.

Should Owner/Volunteers Be Paid?

Generally, it is not a good business strategy to pay owners for services

---

Should owner/volunteers be paid for their work?

With an estimated 300,000+ Community Associations in the United States, there are all sorts of arrangements that have evolved at a grass-roots level.

But owners who get paid for their service work is rare.

While it might be expedient to hire a long-time neighbor, when you know their personality and their high level of commitment to the property, it is a wiser business strategy to write a job description, find and interview qualified candidates, and then hire the outside talent that you need.

Board approved, routine out-of-pocket expenses, usually incurred by a board member, are reimbursed by the Association. Prudent business practices require that receipts accompany the request for reimbursement. Just a few examples of the many items for reimbursement might include approved purchase of cans of paint, refreshments for an annual meeting, newsletter copying or mailing expense, etc.

Insight

Here are some of the problems with payments to owners for services:

1. Other volunteers might understandably want to be paid.

2. It helps to avoid conflicts of interest, and even the *appearance* of conflicts of interest by keeping all association business transactions with third-party service providers. Also, often, the third-party business provider can see some situations in a more detached and businesslike way than someone who lives and owns in the association.

3. Check with your attorney and insurance agent about the laws in your state and city, but sometimes with the first dollar that an owner takes, the status of your legal liability and insurance coverage could change. Some jurisdictions may also require manager licensing.

4. If the quality of the volunteer's commitment or work starts to decline, you have a sticky situation. That owner/employee is still a co-owner and a neighbor. For an outside employee, if performance suffers or relationships become strained, it is easier to terminate an outside vendor and move on.

5. Professional, full-time property managers almost never manage an association where they live. Also, there have been cases where an exceptional volunteer, having gained much experience, enters the property management business. However, they go to work for a nearby association or property management firm, and are not employed by the association where they own a unit and live.

6. Another problem arises if a volunteer gets a small payment – say $100 a month stipend – some other owners may feel that for a small, far-less-than-a-salary payment, the owner/employee now has unlimited obligations of service to them and to the association.

7. Due to most state bar association rules, the attorneys who live in an Association might serve on their board, but those same attorney/owners are not allowed to serve as the official legal counsel for the association where they are owners.

Frequently Asked Questions
When Buying in an Association

Frequently Asked Questions When Buying in an Association
An Overview

 **Insight**

 **Best Scenario**

An Association is a non-profit corporation, often run by *volunteers*, who may or may not have the skills, experience and owner support they need to create and sustain a successful housing corporation.

Buying in a Community Association is like buying a share of stock in a corporation or buying into a partnership. But many consumers buy without knowing or understanding the financial health of that corporation.

If you are looking for an Association to buy into, you may already realize that few Associations are going to get an "A" on every part of their "report card."

But with full disclosure of financial and management information, you can decide how much risk you can tolerate, and which property will be right for you.

Buy carefully. There are risks and the stakes are high.

A good way to gain an understanding of the financial details of an Association is by contracting with an experienced Association financial investigator to review Association documents and then explain the details to you.

An innovative private-sector business in California sells this service. The firm was founded by experienced Home Owner Association specialists in 1998 in San Jose. The firm now offers their services throughout California to buyers, sellers, property management firms, banks and other financial institutions.

The name of the firm is Community Association Datasource. The firm's web site is www.HOAdocumentReview.com

This business model works best in the handful of states where an Association Reserve Study is required by law. In this business model, the specialist examines the Reserve Study, compared to current financial reserves on hand, as well as other Association financial and governing documents.

A profile of services offered by this firm is also listed on page 53, as Idea #3, in the list of nine ideas to improve the financial soundness of Community Associations.

Assessing Association Management and Administrative Strength

Is there a paid management at the association, or is it self-managed by owners who volunteer as administrators?

- Who carries out the day-to-day work of organizing, planning and communicating within the association?
- Is this a self-managed association managed only by owners who volunteer?
- Is there a part-time, off-site property manager?
- Is there a full-time, on-site manager?

What RULES are you going to have to live with, within this association?

Before you buy, understand the rules and policies regarding such hot-button topics as:

- Pet policies
- Parking policies
- Collection policies for monthly & special assessments
- Rental restrictions
- Is this an age-restricted community (often over age 55) If so, what is the policy regarding underage residents, like your grandchildren?
- Are there any grandfather clauses in place, regarding rules?
- What are the rules regarding noise?
- Architectural guidelines, including such topics as:
  - Approved paint colors
  - Patios and fences
  - Permissions for building alterations
- Other rules and policies in the governing documents

If you do not like the rules that you read for association members, save yourself (and your neighbors) the grief, and *don't buy there.*

Who enforces the rules?

- Does a third-party property manager send enforcement letters?
- Is enforcement handled by volunteer owners?
- At what point is an association attorney involved in rule enforcement?
- When is a disturbance an issue for the local police department? (such as a violation of local noise ordinances)

Assessing Association Management and Administrative Strength

Is there a written collections policy?

If there is a collections policy, *who* is responsible for enforcing it?

Sample collection policy

- Monthly assessment fee due by the first of the month
- 10 days late – Late letter (or late charge, if permitted by governing documents and local state law)
- 30 days late – More urgently worded late letter
- 60 days late – Account turned over to a collections attorney, with attorney fees to be paid by the late-paying owner. At the county courthouse, a lien is filed against the property.

Is there a written preventive maintenance check list?

If there a preventive maintenance check list, *who* is responsible for making sure that the list is carried out?

There are sample preventive maintenance check lists for the five example associations in this book.

A preventive maintenance check list helps you manage the physical aspects of your property.

By carefully prolonging the life of building components, and systematically monitoring those components at least each spring and fall, you can help reduce the frequency of expensive, unanticipated emergency repairs.

What is the condition of the curb-appeal elements of the property?

Always maintaining curb appeal – whatever the age of your property – may help to attract new buyers throughout the useful life of the property.

Even though the full exterior painting cycle may be every four to seven years, touch-up painting each spring can be a wise investment.

How is your association faring with:

- Lawn care and grounds maintenance?
- Paving and seal coating?
- Exterior surfaces and painting?
- Hallways, lobbies and common elements?
- Entryways and signage?

Assessing Association Management and Administrative Strength

Is there a pest management program in place?

Is there a termite management program in place?

Regarding pest control, follow local laws and codes.

There should be a pest management program and termite management program in place.

Often, part of the service from the pest control firm is to receive a brief written report about the most recent scheduled inspection. Ask to see a copy of this report.

Many condominium associations choose an exterior- only program, with interior inspection/treatments performed only when requested by the homeowner. Based on governing documents and the specifics of the situation, the interior pest control inspection/treatment is often a homeowner expense.

The most common termite management programs involve either a treatment with conventional liquid termite control product, a baiting program or simply a monitoring program.

What channels of communication exist within the Association?

- If you buy a unit at the property, whom would you call or e-mail if there's a day-to-day problem to solve?
- Is an owner/volunteer handling these communication duties, or is it a paid property manager?
- How are significant board actions explain to the owners?
- How often do letters or newsletters go to owners? Is there a community web site?
- Is there an information kit for new owners? (If so, ask to see the information kit before you buy.)
- How often are general meetings for all owners? (Often, there is a state requirement for at least an annual owners meeting, to comply with local non-profit corporation statutes.)
- How often are board meetings? Can owners attend the meetings, except the portions of the meetings that are deemed executive sessions due to discussion of personnel matters or some legal matters.

DISCLAIMER — Financial and physical property conditions are different within each association. Before you buy, retain qualified counsel to assist you in interpreting & evaluating these local conditions and local laws.

Part II | 241

Assessing Association Financial Strength

Does a third-party review the Association financial statements each year?

Does a certified public accounting firm or bonded bookkeeping service perform some type of review of the Association financial statements each year?

At a CPA firm, varying levels of service are offered to clients, in reviewing the annual financial statements.

Level of Service	Name of Service	Level of Service
Level 1	Audit	The most thorough and labor intensive type of review of the annual Association financial statements
Level 2	Review	Mid-level of service
Level 3	Compilation	Lowest level of service

Due to the time and expense of a full audit, often only the largest Associations would pay for this fullest level of service, in review of the annual financial statements. Some larger Associations may have an audit every third year, and a review in the other two years of the 3-year cycle.

Does a third-party prepare and file the Association's tax return?

It is helpful to hire a firm that already has experience preparing tax returns for Condominium Associations and Home Owner Associations.

Assessing Association Financial Strength

What are the key documents to review to learn about Association financial strength?

- Annual budget
- Latest monthly balance sheet and income statement
- Delinquency report
- Reserve Study (executive summary)
- Transition Study (if association is still under developer control)
- Reserve Study update (if available)
- Engineer's report (if one exists)

How many of the unit owners are delinquent in paying monthly fees, and how many unit owners are in foreclosure?

Mortgage lenders are now looking closely at the numbers of delinquencies and foreclosures within the Association.

A delinquency is when the unit owner is late paying their monthly assessment fee. When the delinquency reaches various monetary thresholds, the delinquency could turn into a foreclosure in order to recover the debt owed by the unit owner.

Delinquencies and foreclosures signal that the Association likely has reduced monthly income that is needed for funding both day-to-day operations and funding the reserves for major repairs and replacements.

Was the Reserve Study performed by an accredited Reserve Study professional, a volunteer owner or someone else?

There are two primary non-profit organizations within the United States that have a designation program for Reserve Study professionals, which are listed below.

Organization name	Community Associations Institute (CAI)
Web site	www.caionline.org
Designation	RS — Reserve Specialist

Organization name	Association of Professional Reserve Analysts (APRA)
Web site	www.apra-usa.com
Designation	PRA — Professional Reserve Analyst

DISCLAIMER — Financial and physical property conditions are different within each association. Before you buy, retain qualified counsel to assist you in interpreting & evaluating these local conditions and local laws.

Assessing Association Financial Strength

From the latest Reserve Study, what is the current reserve account balance compared with the recommended reserve account balance?

In the five sample reserve studies in this book, at the beginning summary for each sample report, you see examples of this key comparative financial data.

When it comes to shining a light on potentially large special assessments, the Reserve Study's current estimation of what the reserves *should be* right now, versus the association's current reserves on hand, is critical financial information for any new buyer.

From Example A: Two-or Three-Story Stacked Flats
Reserves are 38% funded (see pages 60 and 61)

Current reserve account balance	**$150,000**
Recommended reserve account balance	**$392,661**

From Example B: Townhome/Patio Home
Reserves are 47% funded (see pages 92 and 93)

Current reserve account balance	**$1,138,028**
Recommended reserve account balance	**$2,406,639**

From Example C: Mid-Rise
Reserves are 75% funded (see pages 124 and 125)

Current reserve account balance	**$157,901**
Recommended reserve account balance	**$210,535**

From Example D: High-Rise
Reserves are 73% funded (see pages 152 and 153)

Current reserve account balance	**$552,263**
Recommended reserve account balance	**$756,525**

From Example E: Home Owner Association
Reserves are 66% funded (see pages 182 and 183)

Current reserve account balance	**$216,891**
Recommended reserve account balance	**$328,983**

DISCLAIMER — Financial and physical property conditions are different within each association. Before you buy, retain qualified counsel to assist you in interpreting & evaluating these local conditions and local laws.

Assessing Association Financial Strength

What elements were left *out* of the Reserve Study?

To lower the likelihood of financial surprises, review what elements were left *out* of the Reserve Study. Examples of what is sometimes excluded in a Reserve Study are in the five sample Reserve Studies in this book.

The categories of elements left out of a Reserve Study include:

- Unit owner responsibility component exclusions
- Long-life component exclusions
- Utility component exclusions
- Maintenance & repair component exclusions
- Below-threshold cost-component exclusions
- Government-funded component exclusions

How recently was the Reserve Study updated?

Like an annual budget, the Reserve Study is a *guide* to future spending, not an ironclad list that is not subject to review and revision as time passes.

A Reserve Study can become quickly outdated. In California, the Reserve Study must now, by law, be updated each year.

What causes a Reserve Study to become outdated?

- Some components may wear out sooner than expected. Other components may last longer than expected, especially with proper, regular preventive maintenance procedures.
- A change in local laws or building codes in your area.
- Repairs or replacements that may be required by banks, insurance companies or other financial institutions.
- A change in spending priorities by a new Board of Directors.
- Current worldwide demand for raw materials impacts the costs and affordability of the forecasted repairs.
- Local availability of skilled labor.

DISCLAIMER — Financial and physical property conditions are different within each association. Before you buy, retain qualified counsel to assist you in interpreting & evaluating these local conditions and local laws.

Part II | 245

Assessing Association Financial Strength

What major repairs and replacements are due and when, as listed in the Reserve Study?

The Reserve Study will forecast major repairs and replacements for each of the next 20 to 30 years.

If you are living at the property for a shorter time, you may have an interest in seeing the forecast for needed repairs, especially for the next 5 years.

Will there be enough money to pay for those repairs?

Are any special assessments pending? What special assessments have been required in the past?

The past may give you a view of how the board chooses to raise needed revenue. If there are too many special assessments, the board may be relying on special assessments instead of raising the monthly fee.

If an engineer's report is available, ask to review it.

A Reserve Study is a non-invasive building component report and financial forecast. It is different from a consulting engineer's report.

The term "non-invasive" means the reserve specialist will not, for example, open walls to inspect the condition of plumbing pipes and electrical wiring.

Some Associations may also have a consulting engineer's report which comments about such areas as the structural integrity of the building or latent or hidden defects. If such an engineering report exists, ask to see it.

Definition:
Regular assessment fee versus special assessment fee

Term	Definition
Regular assessment fee	The fee, often due monthly at condominiums and town-homes, to cover operating and reserve expenses.
Special assessment fee	The fee when there is a cash shortfall, when the regular assessment fee has not generated sufficient income for repairs or other expenses. The "special assessment" fee is an extra fee to generate more revenue for the association.

DISCLAIMER — Financial and physical property conditions are different within each association. Before you buy, retain qualified counsel to assist you in interpreting & evaluating these local conditions and local laws.

Assessing Association Financial Strength

How much are the regular assessment fees, and when are they due?

While many buyers may be impressed with a low monthly fee, if that fee is not adequate to maintain the property, the future could hold either a special assessment or deferring needed repairs and replacements due to a lack of funds, which could impact property values.

In most condominiums, with higher infrastructure costs, the regular assessment fees are often due monthly. In some Home Owner Associations, with fewer shared expenses than a condominium or townhome association, the fee may be due quarterly or annually.

What does the assessment fee cover?

What does the fee *not* cover?

The seller will likely have a list of items that the monthly fee covers. For items not covered, check your association's governing documents and with your insurance agent, before you buy.

A few examples of frequent owner financial responsibilities in condominium associations:

Common items for personal responsibility	Comments
Insurance coverage "from the walls in"	In condominiums, often you pay for your own insurance coverage "from the walls in". This means that like renters insurance, you would pay to insure the contents of your home, and certain improvements like built-in cabinets.
Water damage to adjacent units	The uninitiated are often surprised at this personal expense, but water damage to adjacent units is a common problem. Often, the owner's personal insurance must cover water damage to their unit and any adjacent unit that is damaged by water. For example, water damage may occur when a bathtub overflows, a sink or toilet leaks, or a dishwasher breaks and floods units below.
Window and door replacements	Major expenses that are often owner expenses are window replacements or outside entry door or garage door replacements. The association may establish an architectural guideline for which type of replacement window or door is permissible to install.
Heating and cooling equipment	If the building does not have a central boiler and chiller system, it is common that an owner is responsible for repair, maintenance and replacement of their own heating and cooling equipment.

Assessing Association Financial Strength

How long has it been since the monthly assessment fee was raised?

Is the monthly assessment fee keeping up with the annual inflation rate?

Unlike a fixed mortgage rate, or a fixed car payment, the monthly assessment fee pays for a range of locally based, labor-intensive services. Just as payroll is often the largest expense at a firm, a large percentage of the monthly assessment fee – when you trace it back – goes to pay local people to perform services for you and your Association.

Home owners at associations should also realize that just as medical costs increase as the human body ages, the costs of building repairs and replacements increase as a building ages.

There is a limit to the human medical cost analogy though. In the long-term useful life of a building, as major components wear out (as shown in the Reserve Study 30-year forecast), there are eras of large capital expenditures, a slight reprieve for a few years, and then the expense of component replacements begins again.

Therefore, even when monthly assessment fees are at the correct amount to fund both day-to-day operating expenses and the big-ticket-item capital reserve expenses, budgets will often increase in most years – at least slightly – to account for annual inflation in the buying of goods and services for the Association.

Social Security checks generally increase slightly each year, so it makes sense that the monthly maintenance fee is going to increase at least slightly each year.

Some Reserve Specialists note that the U.S. Labor Department's Producer Price Index (PPI), which would include the costs of oil-based building materials, may rise faster than the Consumer Price Indexes (CPI).

DISCLAIMER — Financial and physical property conditions are different within each association. Before you buy, retain qualified counsel to assist you in interpreting & evaluating these local conditions and local laws.

Assessing Association Financial Strength

Is there any current or pending litigation against the Association?

Has the Association ever been involved in litigation? When was it, and what was the outcome?

Prolonged litigation can quickly drain the Association's financial reserves.

At a new development, there could be pending litigation against the developer for construction defects. For owners, a problem with this construction-defect litigation is that it is often handled by a law firm on a contingency basis, with the law firm getting 30% or more of the judgment.

And once the contingency fee is subtracted from the settlement, there still may not be enough cash from the settlement to cover the cost of repairing the defects.

If owners are suing the Board of Directors, or suing other owners, this is often the no-win equivalent of a mutually destructive civil war occurring within the association.

Investments of time and energy in alternative dispute resolution – before lawsuits occur – can help protect the financial health of the Association.

The Directors and Officers (D&O) insurance policy, which covers some actions taken by the Board of Directors, can help the Association to lower this financial risk of costly litigation.

DISCLAIMER — Financial and physical property conditions are different within each association. Before you buy, retain qualified counsel to assist you in interpreting & evaluating these local conditions and local laws.

Part II | 249

Assessing Association Financial Strength

Is the Association even insurable?

Some Associations, especially those with aging, poorly maintained buildings, are deemed no longer insurable by commercial insurance firms. Be aware of your risks of buying in this type of Association.

Before buying, consider retaining competent counsel, with knowledge of the insurance business, to help you evaluate an Association's risks and current coverages.

The types of insurance coverages needed by an association will vary, based on local conditions and local laws.

Insuring for various risks at an association is a complex subject. You are advised to retain competent local counsel to help you understand the coverage that is needed, matched against a review of the current insurance certificates the Association possesses.

Your counsel can help you understand and evaluate these and other risks to be covered:

- General liability insurance for the Association, compared with what may be required in the governing documents and local laws.
- Directors and Officers (D&O) Liability insurance for the volunteer board of directors.
- If the property policy is a comprehensive type, using the special coverage form which covers the buildings against all risk of loss with the exception of the named exclusions and limitations rather than a named peril coverage form, this provides for broader and more coverage against property losses.
- The valuation section of the policy should provide replacement cost coverage rather than actual cash value coverage. This provides for the settlement of claims at the cost of replacing damaged materials at current prices with no provision for depreciation of the replacement cost of damaged materials.
- Are annually mandated insurance certificate on file for all Association vendors? These certificates should be required of each vendor annually, showing that the vendor has current coverage in effect for general liability, workers' compensation and business auto, with adequate limits of liability as determined by the governing documents and local laws.

Assessing Association Financial Strength

Is this condominium converted from being an apartment building?

Condominium conversions are a *red flag* for potential financial trouble.

A condominium conversion refers most often to an apartment building that has been converted to condominiums.

Was this development just a "paper conversion"? That means, did the developer just buy an old apartment building, apply a fresh coat of paint, then file legal documents to convert the property to condominium status at the local county courthouse? If so, you still may be stuck with old component parts (roofs, windows, plumbing pipes, wiring) that are near the end of their useful life.

If an older apartment building had a gut renovation of key component parts, such as plumbing, wiring, HVAC and other systems, before conversion to condominiums, there is less financial risk of sudden and expensive key component failure.

What property issues are financial institutions looking at more closely after the financial crisis of 2008?

Mortgage lending and insurance requirements are in a state of negotiation and change right now, headed in the direction of tighter requirements.

For the latest changes in requirements, check with your local counsel. The lending and insurance areas being evaluated include:

- Percentage of reserve fund contributions
- Percentage of delinquencies
- Percentage of owner occupants
- Percentage of units owned by one investor
- In new developments, percentage of units sold to owners
- Developer leases of amenities to the association in a long-term lease

---

Association meeting minutes — A generally uncensored disclosure of current association problems

In addition to the rest of these questions, the Association meeting minutes will often provide a relatively uncensored view of current problems that the Association is dealing with.

Sample Requests for Proposal (RFP)

Detailed planning before major purchases increases efficiency and manageability.

Insight

FOR BEST RESULTS, VOLUME BUYING OF SERVICES IN ASSOCIATIONS BENEFITS FROM CREATION OF A DETAILED REQUEST FOR PROPOSAL (RFP).

Buying services for multiple households in a Community Association is different from buying for just your own household. The stakes are higher – and the deployment of resources is more complex – when the scale of the job is bigger.

Let's look at this "fixing dinner" example, to explain why jobs on a bigger scale require a more thorough planning approach to create solutions with efficiency and manageability.

Dinner preparation for your family at Thanksgiving	Dinner preparation for 150 guests
This is a planning and creation challenge, but it's do-able	This will be more efficient and successful when handled by an experienced caterer.

A FAST WAY TO GET A PRICE

"So how much to take care of the grounds?"

A BETTER WAY TO GET A PRICE

"Please bid on our RFP for lawn care."

© iStockphoto.com / Duncan Walke

1. Summary List of Annual Lawn Care Services

Page 1 of 4

Summary List of Annual Lawn Care Services	Quantity per year	Cost per service	Total
Mowing, weed eating and blowing off all areas when completed	28		
Picking up debris, litter, etc. before mowing	28		
Removing leaves in the fall (This is not leaf mulching with a mower.)	3		
Picking up debris and litter during the winter months every other week, including removing from the property	7		
Hedge trimming and pruning all shrubs and trees less than 15 feet in height	2		
Applying hardwood mulch	1		
Applying cedar mulch	1		
Applying cypress mulch	1		
Maintaining mulched beds during the growing season	2 times per month		
Flipping mulch in the fall	1		
Over-seeding/power seeding areas if necessary	1		
Fertilizing all trees and shrubs	1		
Spraying insecticide on trees and shrubs if necessary	1		
Using pre-emergent for crabgrass	2		
Using insecticide on turf area if necessary	1		
Using fungicide on turf area if necessary	1		
Applying broadleaf weed control	4		
Applying a granular fertilizer at a light rate in early fall	1		
Applying a granular fertilizer at a heavy rate in early winter	1		

Date of proposal _____ Company name _____

Submitted by _____ Contact name _____

Contact phone number _____

DISCLAIMER — Each property is unique. Therefore, each property Request for Proposal (RFP) is unique, based on local conditions and local laws. Do not use this RFP for your own property.

Part II | 253

2. Regular Mowing Maintenance Specifications

2A. Mowing and trimming heights

Mowing and trimming of all turf areas will be completed on a regular basis throughout the growing season. Height of mowing will generally be no less than 3 inches or greater than 4 inches in height. All blades should be kept sharp to give a clean cut, thus reducing the possibilities of promoting disease and fungus issues.

2B. Equipment being utilized

Equipment being utilized on the job should be of proper size for the area being mowed and the operator must be properly trained for the equipment they are utilizing.

2C. Mowing intervals

The lawn area will be mowed approximately every 7 days during the peak growing season. Regular mowing services may be reduced during the summer months due to dry conditions if no irrigation system is being utilized. If an irrigation system is being utilized, the association president will coordinate the watering schedule with the selected contractor to maximize the watering efficiency and the normal day of mowing.

2D. Trimming specifications

Weed-eaters will be used on each mowing visit to maintain a professional appearance on all curbs, edges, tree rings, landscape beds, walks, fences, etc. Weed-eating will be completed in such a manner not to throw the grass into the landscape beds or other undesirable location. Any trimmings that should get into these areas must be removed. After completing the mowing and trimming, all areas including patios, sidewalks, steps, parking areas, streets, etc. will be blown or cleaned off.

2E. Preliminary debris removal

Before mowing, picking up a reasonable amount of debris such as limbs, paper, trash, etc. from the property is expected. This debris should also be removed from the property. This *does not* include a cleanup after a storm. Cleaning up after a storm will be completed as a separate service.

2F. Leaf removal

Provide leaf removal in the fall, and remove the leaves from the property. Leaf mulching is not considered leaf removal. All turf areas, landscape beds, curb lines etc. are expected to be included in this clean-up.

3. Landscaping, Seeding, Fertilizing and Weed Control Specifications

3A. Mulching specifications

Mulching of all existing beds in the spring. The depth of the new mulch added should be a minimum of 2 inches and shall not exceed the recommended depth of mulch for the plants in the beds being mulched. For example: do not apply 4 inches or greater around trees. The timing of the installation of the new mulch will be coordinated with the designated contact or the property manager.

3B. Quote alternative grades of mulch

Provide a quote for dark hardwood mulch, cedar mulch, and cypress mulch.

3C. Assessment of thickness of mulch

If the current mulch layer is too thick or too thin, contact the Association president for approval before making any changes in the scope of the work to be provided.

3D. Mulch bed weeding and maintenance

Mulch beds are to be regularly weeded and maintained during the growing season. Hand weeding as well as herbicide applications may be utilized.

3E. Flip mulch in the fall

Flip or rake the mulch in the fall to refurbish curb appeal and promote water and fertilizer movement though the mulch bed for the winter.

3F. Trim hedges twice during season

Two times during the season, trim all hedges, ornamental plants and trees that are less than 15 feet tall, to maintain a professional appearance. If any plants or trees require additional service, we will consult with the designated contact or the property manager.

3G. Over-seed / power seed

Over-seed / power seed turf areas at the proper time of the year where necessary. This service must be approved by the Association president. If seeding is required, allow proper time before seeding based on your most recent herbicide application.

3H. Winter months property inspection

Provide an every-other-week property inspection during the winter months and remove any litter or debris from the property.

3I. Fertilizing of trees and shrubs

Fertilize all trees and shrubs as required at the proper time of the year based on accepted agronomy standards for a medium maintenance program. Insecticides and fungicides may also be necessary during the season.

3J. Fertilizing turf areas

Fertilizer and weed control for all turf areas to maintain a healthy lawn. A posting sign must be left after each application to notify everyone that an application has been made to the lawn and or landscape areas.

A typical fertilization and weed control program should include the following applications. Timing of these applications is approximate.

1. Late February to mid-March – pre-emergent application for crabgrass and other annual undesirable grasses

2. Mid-March to mid-April – second application of pre-emergent and broadleaf weed control

3. May to July – broadleaf weed control and check for disease, fungus and insect issues

4. August to September – broadleaf weed control and check for insect damage

5. Late September to October – broadleaf weed control and light rate of fertilizer

6. November to December – heavy rate of granular fertilizer

4. Terms and Conditions

Page 4 of 4

4A. Terms

4A-1. Contract will begin March 1, _____ and continue through February _____.

4A-2. All work is to be completed in a timely manner

4A-3. Any modifications to this agreement must be in writing and signed by both parties.

4B. Cancellation

Either party may terminate this agreement with thirty (30) days written notice mailed to the party at the address listed in this contract. During this thirty (30) day period, lawn service will continue at the normal rate agreed upon under this contract. Upon cancellation, the monies due for services provided up to and including the cancellation date will be paid.

4C. Insurance

A certificate of insurance must be provided by the contractor prior to the execution of this contract. A minimum of one million ($1,000,000) dollars general liability and statutory worker's compensation insurance limits must be kept in force during the term of this contract.

4D. Sub-contractors

In the event that any sub-contractors are utilized by the contractor, the sub-contractor(s) must have in force and maintain the same minimum insurance coverage as the contractor secured by the association.

4E. Payment schedule

Payment during the year will be paid in twelve equal installments. Payments will be made by the 20th of each month covered under this contract. Contractor must provide a monthly statement by the first of each month detailing the services provided for that month.

DISCLAIMER — Each property is unique. Therefore, each property Request for Proposal (RFP) is unique, based on local conditions and local laws. Do not use this RFP for your own property.

1. Snow & Ice Management Specifications

Page 1 of 2

1A. Snow-plowing services

Snow-plowing services will be provided for all areas not obstructed by parked vehicles. Three or more adjacent parking spaces not being utilized will also be plowed. Plowing will commence when the snow has reached approximately 2 inches or greater in depth.

1B. Follow-up visits to property

Follow-up visits will continue until the weather conditions subside or at the request of the designated contact or the property manager. During unusually heavy snow events over 8 inches accumulation, plowing services will initially be completed to keep drive lanes, entrances, and exits passable to allow for emergency vehicles to access the property. If conditions exist that the snow cannot be handled effectively by conventional plowing vehicles, additional equipment may be utilized only if prior approval is obtained from the designated contact or the property manager. These arrangements should be considered as part of the snow and ice management plan during contract negotiations.

1C. Ice melt applications

The planned application of ice-melter whether liquid or granular will be established prior to the event. Any ice-melter utilized should be applied at the manufacturer's specified rate of application for that product. The selected ice-melter must also be safe for the type of surface it is being utilized on as well as for the temperature range for which it is expected to be effective.

1D. Sidewalks, balconies and building entrances

Any sidewalks, balconies, entrances to buildings, etc., may require service when the parking areas do not require plowing. Weather conditions will exist that require servicing sidewalks, balconies, entrances to buildings, etc., when there are less than 2 inches of snow. Examples of such weather conditions are freezing rain, sleet, light snow, etc. In that event, the above mentioned areas must receive customary and ordinary effort to maintain a safe environment until the weather has cleared.

2. Terms and Conditions

Page 2 of 2

2A. Equipment Standards

Contractor agrees that the equipment being utilized for this project is in good working condition and safe order according to industry standards of equipment being utilized for similar work. Contractor also agrees that contractor will have the available labor and replacement equipment if necessary due to equipment breakdowns, labor shortages, etc.

2B. Insurance

Contractor agrees to maintain a minimum of $1,000,000.00 in public liability insurance as well as the mandatory workers' compensation insurance for all employees. Any subcontractors utilized by the contractor will also have to enforce these same minimums.

2C. Contractor Liability

Contractor assumes all responsibility for damages to the physical property that are caused by the contractor's gross negligence or intentional misconduct.

2D. Termination of Contract

Contractor's failure to complete the work as specified above may result in the immediate termination of this contract with no notice required.

2E. Continuity of Pricing of Equipment, Labor and Ice-Melting Products

Pricing for equipment, labor and ice-melting products will be initially agreed upon and held constant throughout the scope and duration of this contract regardless of any increases incurred by the contractor after the initial contracting obligation. If for any reason such as supply, distribution, or availability of product beyond the contractors' control, pricing for ice-melter may be changed if said changes are agreed upon by the Association and an addendum set forth in the contract.

2F. Time Period of Contract

The terms of this agreement are good for a period of _____ year (s) beginning on _____ and continuing through _____.

2G. Pricing Schedule

Pricing for plowing, shoveling and deicing will be provided according to the following schedule:

Truck with _____ plow = $_____ per hour - minimum charge $_____
Truck with _____ plow = $_____ per hour - minimum charge $_____
Skid loader with _____ pusher or box plow = $_____ per hour – minimum charge $_____
Hand Labor per hour $_____
Other Equipment and cost/hour _____
_____ _____
_____
_____ _____
_____

Ice-melter per pound $_____
Estimated amount required per application _____
Type of ice-melter being utilized _____
_____
Sodium chloride (salt) per ton $_____
Estimated amount required per application _____

I accept the terms of this proposal on behalf of the _____ Association on this the _____ day of _____, _____.

Title: _____ Name:_____

Print name: _____

Local Resources to Help You

Many local non-profit organizations exist to help neighborhoods and associations. An online search engine inquiry could be a good starting point to help you find groups in your area.

In larger metropolitan areas, some local government offices offer neighborhood leadership training.

Four of the larger regional and national non-profit organizations are listed below:

National Organizations

Community Associations Institute (CAI)
www.caionline.org
225 Reinekers Lane, Suite 300
Alexandria, Virginia 22314
Local chapters in the U.S.: Almost 60
Year founded: 1973

CAI is the primary national non-profit organization serving home owners as well as vendors to Community Associations in the United States.

From its headquarters in Alexandria, Virginia, CAI offers publications for home owners, national seminars and meetings and the coordination of legislative advocacy for Home Owner Associations at a state and national level.

Through its local CAI chapters, home owners are offered educational meetings and seminars in their local area, as well as coordination of local advocacy efforts.

Institute of Real Estate Management (IREM)
www.irem.org
430 North Michigan Avenue
Chicago, Illinois 60611
Local chapters in the U.S.: 80
Year founded: 1933

This organization serves professional property managers, who manage both commercial properties and residential communities. Publications, seminars, meetings and legislative advocacy for the property management industry are coordinated through IREM.

Two major regional organizations:

Council of New York Cooperatives and Condominiums (CNYC)
www.cnyc.coop
250 West 57th Street, Suite 730
New York, New York 10107
Year founded: 1975

CNYC offers educational meetings and seminars for home owners, as well as legislative advocacy for condominium and coop associations.

Executive Council of Homeowners (ECHO)
www.echo-ca.org
1602 The Alameda, Suite 101
San Jose, California 95126
Year founded: 1972

ECHO offers educational meetings and seminars for home owners, publications, as well as legislative advocacy for California-based home owner associations.

Building Community is Always Hard Work

Doing work in organizing your own Association – your own neighborhood – means embracing the grass-roots realities that surround you. You often can sense what you want to achieve for your neighborhood, but you must reach out, brainstorm, compromise and build together.

Some thoughts to encourage the patience, wisdom and occasional courage you will need for this journey

Be kind, for everyone you meet is fighting a hard battle.
—Plato, Greek philosopher, 427 BC - 347 BC

Peace begins with a smile.
We must be constantly forgiving of each other.
—Mother Teresa, Missionary, 1910 – 1997

Have a bias for action.

Ordinary people doing extraordinary things.

Some ideas that might give you hope & energy

- Simplicity
- Community
- Incremental Progress
- Everyday Heroes
- Grace
- The Power of Love

Index

Notes